Penguin Education

Penguin Modern Sociology

General Editor: Tom Burns

Cognitive Sociology
Aaron V. Cicourel

Aaron V. Cicourel

Cognitive Sociology
Language and Meaning in Social Interaction

Penguin Education

Penguin Education
A Division of Penguin Books Ltd,
Harmondsworth, Middlesex, England
Penguin Books Inc, 7110 Ambassador Road,
Baltimore, Md 21207, USA
Penguin Books Australia Ltd,
Ringwood, Victoria, Australia

First published 1973
Copyright © Aaron V. Cicourel, 1972

Made and printed in Great Britain by
Cox & Wyman Ltd,
London, Reading and Fakenham
Set in Monotype Times

Contents

Preface

The collection of papers in this volume span some eight years of work. They are intended to place in one publication several manuscripts that are not easily accessible to sociologists. The volume also indicates changes in my thinking about sociology and its relation to other disciplines. These changes indicate the directions my work has taken over the past six to eight years. No attempt has been made to provide a general collection of my papers that would suggest some kind of continuity over a longer span of academic activity. There are several recent and forthcoming publications not represented in this volume because they are either partially reflected in the papers published, or because they represent transitional materials.

For the past eight years my interests have included a deep preoccupation with how language and meaning are constitutive of the way in which everyday social interaction is assembled and represented. I have tried to use the notion of 'interpretive procedures' to articulate ideas from writers on phenomenology and ethnomethodology with work on language acquisition and use, memory and attention, or the general idea of information processing. Rather than use notions like role theory, I have tried to substitute terms like 'interactional competence' to indicate a broader idea that would help pinpoint the relations between cognitive processes, contextual emergence, and accounting vocabularies. *Social structure remains an accountable illusion of the sociologist's common sense knowledge unless we can reveal a connection between the cognitive processes that contribute to the emergence of contextual activities, and the normative accounting schemes we use for claiming knowledge as laymen and researchers.*

The first chapter re-examines the notions of status and role and was written initially during 1964-5 and presented at an anthropological conference organized by the Institute of International Studies at the University of California, Berkeley. The paper was not published at the time of the conference but slightly revised about three years later at the time I was beginning to draft the paper on 'The Acquisition of Social Structure'. The paper tries to articulate structural conceptions of status and role with the contingencies of everyday social interaction. I hoped to make explicit the role of cognition and context in the study of social structure. Cognitive processes and contextual meaning are central for understanding how normative rules of a general and ideal-typical sort are created or invoked when accounts must be provided for explaining or justifying particular activities or events.

The second chapter deals with problems of language and the acquisition of social structure and was intended to broaden ethnomethodological views that only addressed adult practical reasoning and adult accounts of social structure. I tried to link sociological conceptions of socialization with recent work in linguistics and developmental psycholinguistics as well as research in cognitive anthropology. This paper was a preliminary theoretical statement to provide a basis for research I was then initiating on language socialization in the US, Mexico, and Argentina.

The third chapter seeks to link linguistic and philosophical views of language and meaning with nonverbal features of communication. I tried to contrast a sociological view of generative semantics with linguistic notions of generative grammar or semantics by locating the thrust of the theoretical and methodological issues in the context of interaction rather than in some notion of an innate, context-free grammatical structure and a dictionary conception of meaning. At the time the paper was written I was beginning to examine the problem of nonverbal communication through the study of the manual sign language of the deaf. It seemed clear that we should not conceive of nonverbal communication by utilizing a structural linguistics model. The use of the body as a medium of expression required conceptualization that was independent of oral language communication.

The fourth chapter entitled 'Ethnomethodology' seeks to present my views of what this term might include by explicitly indicating how problems of memory and attention could link with a conception of language that would not be dominated by oral language conceptions of syntax and semantics. My interest in language socialization among hearing and deaf children became the basis for questioning modern linguistic views of language and meaning. My exposure to computer problems in semantic information processing provided another perspective with which to clarify the complexities of cross-modal communication. Computer simulation of natural language forces the researcher to clarify the extent to which everyday language is a mixture of algorithmic 'islands', heuristic strategies, and taken for granted common-sense knowledge that we trade on implicitly when making sense of the programmes we write and execute.

The fifth and final chapter on cross-modal communication explores the problem of how we can describe the relationship of several modalities with our thought processes as an information processing system. How we represent oral and sign languages with oral or manual or written conventions forces us to recognize that tacit context-sensitive information is always presupposed when we seek to describe our experiences with context-free expressions. Our descriptions of social structure, therefore, must always incorporate the ways in which normative accounts presuppose an unstated reliance on thought processes, socially organized memory, selective attention, and several sensory modalities. Rather than viewing the blind or the deaf as social problems, we can reconceptualize our feelings and treatment of such persons by recognizing that they develop special strategies for dealing with their lack of a modality. These special communicational strategies are important for understanding the complex activities of hearing-seeing persons, and recognizing how our reliance on verbal communication distorts and truncates our understanding of everyday interaction.

My current research seeks to extend some of the above notions to the general problem of how persons in different social or cultural groups have sought to develop, represent, and evaluate their communicational strategies. Stated another way, this means how social or cultural groups create something we have called 'language', the way this representational form captures and truncates our experiences, and the way we use language to make claims about knowledge. I think our understanding of social structure as accounts of situated social interaction requires a complex conception of how human groups evolve representational devices for communicating their experiences and their claims to knowledge. The acoustic, pictographic, or iconic representation of group experiences provided initial normative forms. How these iconic representations evolved in some social or cultural groups into more abstract (context-free) forms, and their relation to oral or manual sign language categories remains obscure. What is important here is the way in which normative and situated representational devices were and are now used to stand for experiences and conceptions of everyday social structure. Our future understanding of social structure will depend on our ability to clarify the complex processes which generate different representations, and the extent to which these processes are truncated by the fact that we are highly dependent on normative verbal systems which strive for context-free ('objective') expressions. So long as we continue to reify terms like 'social structure', 'culture', and 'language', we shall miss the contextual and cognitive significance of everyday social organization. The present volume is a rather modest beginning in the direction of exploring the implications of studying social structure as cognitive and contextual processes.

La Jolla, May, 1972

1 Interpretive Procedures and Normative Rules in the Negotiation of Status and Role

Introduction

It is commonplace in sociology for writers to acknowledge the ultimate importance of the interacting situation between two or more actors. The assumed relationship between structure and process, however, is often no more than an expression of faith rather than the integration of social process with social structure (or role theory with institutional theory). The present paper seeks to modify and build upon some recent literature by re-examining the utility and meaning of current conceptions of 'status', 'role', 'norm', and 'social interaction', to suggest a more explicit foundation for integrating social process with the structural or institutionalized features of everyday life.

Goode suggests that 'when the social analyst refers to a social position which is definitely institutionalized (e.g. mother, physician), he is more likely to use the term "status". By contrast, he is more likely to use the term "role" when referring to a social relation which is *less* institutionalized (e.g. peer relations in play groups).' Thus statuses are defined '*as the class of roles which is institutionalized*', and this leads to the suggestion that 'the analysis of social change must treat of the processes by which roles do become institutionalized, that is, become statuses' (1960, p. 249).

In this paper I argue that any reference to the actor's perspective must cover both the researcher's and the actor's attempts to negotiate field work and everyday activities, and not become an abstract label removed from the work necessary for recognizing and organizing socially acceptable behaviour we label the social structures. Thus, the researcher's model of the actor must rest on interpretive procedures common to both the actor's and observer's methods for evaluating and generating appropriate courses of action. Goode's formulation and the many papers on the subject do not clarify the following distinctions:

1. Terms like 'status' and 'role' are convenient for the observer as a kind of intellectual shorthand for describing complex arrangements and activities in social life, but of limited utility for specifying how the actor or observer negotiates everyday behaviour. Such terms seem to provide only a general *orientation* for describing behaviour, and as Goode notes, 'no line of theory

has been developed from the distinction' (1960, p. 246). The usual imagery associates 'status' with wider community relationships like kinship and occupational structure, and the assumption is that more stability is implied than when the term 'role' is used to speak of behavioural expectations.

2. Can we say that individual actors employ such terms in defining social situations for themselves and others? How does the actor in everyday life order and assign meanings to objects and events in his environment? The point is whether the social analyst is using the terms as a convenient shorthand to describe what he thinks is the actor's perspective or whether the actor's vocabulary includes the same terms and meanings, or their equivalents, as those of the observer.

3. When the researcher seeks to analyse written documents, he must decide on the level of abstraction of the materials so as to know the extent to which they are 'coded' by the writer and the extent to which they represent verbatim or edited versions of observed activities, imputations, and implied or explicit inferences by the writer or others. Here the researcher must reconstruct the context of interaction and its 'status-role' components. Such reconstruction is dependent, however, upon some solution to the following points.

4. When interviewing or participating within some group or community, the social analyst must decide on the relevance of the vocabulary he uses for asking questions and the language used by the actor for responding. The empirical question here is how do observer and actor interpret each other's verbal and nonverbal behaviour and the context-restricted setting?

5. When the researcher seeks to establish contacts for field research in his own or some foreign country, how does he acquire, and to what extent does he employ, specifiable notions of 'status' and 'role' in carrying out his field work? What conceptions does he impute to respondents? Does he decide their 'statuses' and 'roles' as a condition to developing strategies of entering, maintaining and terminating (perhaps temporarily) his relationships with informants? Does he employ different conceptions with those who 'run interference' in contacting respondents and informants, as opposed to subjects with whom he conducts actual interviewing or participant observation? Does he (and if 'yes', how does he) distinguish between vocabularies he uses for 'maximum' communication with others of different 'status' in field research, and are such vocabularies different from the language of social research used to communicate theoretical and empirical findings and conclusions to colleagues?

The general question is how do respondents and observer-researchers conduct themselves during social interaction with various types of 'others', and whether or not such conduct is governed by conceptions congruent with terms like 'status' and 'role'. The terms as currently defined do not allow for explicit shifts between the social analyst's concepts of social organization as used in published communication with his colleagues, the social analyst's common sense conceptions used for managing his own affairs, the observer-researcher's tacit working conceptions when engaged in participation and observation in field studies, and the researcher's model of how the actor's common-sense perspective is used for understanding and taking action in some environment of objects.

Anyone engaged in field research will find that the shorthand vocabulary of social science is very similar to the general norms stated in some penal code: they do not correspond to explicit sequences of events and social meanings, but the fit is 'managed' through negotiated socially organized activities of the police, prosecution, witnesses, the judge, and the suspect or defendant (Sudnow, 1965, pp. 255–76 and Cicourel, 1968a). It is not clear that terms like 'status' and 'role' are relevant categories for the actors nor relevant for the observer's understanding of the action scene he seeks to describe.

Status as structure and process

Goode notes that even interaction between strangers involves some minimum normative expectations, and hence some kind of social organization is presumed by participants ignorant of their 'actual' statuses and roles. Thus some set of minimal 'boundary conditions' informs our actors of each other even if their imputations are seen as mistaken during subsequent reflection. The basis for social interaction among strangers therefore, is presumably those properties attached to the most institutionalized activities of everyday life. Thus, 'whether a given relationship can be characterized as a status *is a matter of degree. Statuses are, then, the role relationships which are more fully institutionalized* or which contain a greater number of institutionalized elements' (1960, p. 250).

What emerges is that status relationships are based upon norms (external to immediate interaction) that have a broad consensus by 'third parties' in ego and alter's social networks or some larger community. This suggests that the more spontaneous or intimate the relationship, and hence the interaction, the less 'institutionalized' the behaviour of each. Thus strangers will respond to more impersonal or 'safe' definitions of the situation in interacting with one another. Close friends would be more likely to innovate before each other during social interaction, or they would be less constrained by 'third parties'. In order for individual actors to innovate as 'loners', they would presumably reject the social network of 'third parties' or the community. By way of analogy we can refer to Mead's distinction between the

'I' and the 'me' or 'generalized other', and make the obvious link between the impulsive features of the 'I' or the less institutionalized features of the role. On the other hand we have the reflective, community-at-large, reference group connotation of the 'me' and its links to norms viewed as commonly accepted in some group or community sense, or backed by 'third parties'.[1]

The general problem is that we know very little about how persons establish 'statuses' and 'roles' in everyday social interaction. Initial social encounters are based upon 'appearance factors' and/or general 'background' information. The initial encounter may lead to an acceptance of individuals qua individuals before, or in the process of, exchanging information about membership in 'legitimate' or 'acceptable' status slots. Empirically, we must know how introductions and identifications are accomplished, the ways in which actors employ sequencing rules to order their exchanges, infer and establish relevant 'facts', over the course of interaction (Sacks, 1966a and b; 1967).

The presumed conformity or nonconformity of actors to norms raises the question of how the actor decides what 'norms' are operative or relevant, and how some group or 'community' (or its representatives) decides that actors are 'deviant' and should or should not be punished or sanctioned negatively? The following quotation illustrates one set of difficulties when seeking conceptual clarification and empirical evidence on conformity and deviance:

When the individual's norms and goals are in accord with those of the group, his behaviour will meet approval. However, if the individual finds that his behaviour deviates from the group norms, he has four choices: to conform, to change the norms, to remain a deviant, or to leave the group. Of course, he may also be removed from the group without his consent (Hare, 1964).[2]

1. Kingsley Davis (1948, p. 90) makes essentially the same point: 'How an individual actually performs in a given position, as distinct from how he is supposed to perform, we call his *role*. The role, then, is the manner in which a person actually carries out the requirements of his position. It is the dynamic aspect of status or office and as such is always influenced by factors other than the stipulations of the position itself. This means that from the point of view of the social structure it always contains a certain novelty and unpredictability.' A footnote then appears: 'What Mead calls the "me" is the internally perceived position while the "I" is the actual behaviour in the position.' Davis then quotes from Mead as follows: 'The response to that situation as it appears in his immediate experience is uncertain, and it is that which constitutes the "I".' (Mead, 1934, p. 175).

2. Translating structural notions like a legitimate order of authority into cognitive and behavioural activities at the level of social interaction remains unchartered territory, except for the truncated small groups studies which do not permit an assessment of the relevance of such work if moved to the more complicated stage of everyday life, where persons 'keep score' and worry about consequences under different kinds of pressures. I am suggesting that the qualitative differences between

The statement by Hare provides us with a set of abstract concepts based on small-group research which does not allow for the negotiated and constructed character of interpersonal exchanges in daily life. In a laboratory setting we can easily lay down general and specific rules governing play in some game or simple task. But even here there is negotiation *vis-à-vis* rules or instructions, and this latter environment of objects cannot be tied easily to notions like status, role and norms, employed by actors in less structured or controlled everyday situations (Rosenthal, 1966). Establishing 'norms and goals for the actor', much less for some group or wider community, is not obvious theoretically, nor procedurally clear methodologically. The fit between abstract community and legal categories of deviance and reported or observed behaviour is an exceptionally difficult one to describe with any accuracy, and its empirical status remains only partially clarified, cf. Lemert, 1951; Goffman, 1959; Messinger, Sampson and Towne, 1962; Newman, 1956, pp. 780–90; Becker, 1963; Sudnow, 1965; Cicourel, 1968.

References to conformity and nonconformity are not clear because social scientists have not made explicit what they mean by normative and non-normative conditions, and role and non-role behaviour. Presumably the various statuses one occupies cover a wide range of identifying characteristics and conduct, most of which would be subsumed under 'status' categories like 'male', 'female', 'student', 'father', 'husband', 'mother'. 'Non-role' behaviour might then refer to scratching one's head, picking one's nose, 'some' laughing or crying (assuming there are no imputations about a 'sick' role). But when would walking 'too fast' or laughing 'too loud' or smiling 'too often' or dressing in 'poor taste' be considered as a 'normal' feature of some set of 'statuses' and corresponding 'roles', taken singly or in some combination, as opposed to the generation of imputations that suggest or demand that the actor be viewed as 'sick' or 'criminal', and so forth? The sociologist's model of the actor's competence and performance remains implicit and does not address how the actor perceives and interprets his environment, how certain rules govern exchanges, and how the actor recognizes what is taken to be 'strange', 'familiar', 'acceptable', about someone so as to link these attributes with a preconceived notion of status or role.

Goode suggests alternatives when he states:

If 'role' includes only that part of behaviour which is an *enactment* of status obligations ('idea'), then there is little point in studying role behaviour. In his

---

currently conceived small-group experiments and 'spontaneous' and 'institutionalized' activities in everyday life are not shown to be in correspondence, and that the relation between our formal theoretical concepts about structure and process and the small-group theorist's formulations appear unconvincing.

role behaviour the actor cannot face any moral problem, and there can be no deviation from the norm; else by definition there is no role behaviour. Necessarily, all the important data on roles would then be contained in a description of statuses. The alternative interpretation is also open – that the actor *can* face a moral problem, whether to enact the status demands, (i.e., role behaviour) or not. Then the study of role behaviour versus non-role behaviour would be a study of conformity versus non-conformity. However, this interpretation is not followed by Linton or, to my knowledge, by anyone else (Goode, 1960, p. 247).

The problem is to specify those sectors of the actor's actions which the social scientist wishes to 'explain' or leave untouched by terms like 'status', 'role', and 'norms'. Statements to the effect that 'statuses' are 'roles' which are 'institutionalized' do not indicate how the observer decides that the actors are able to recognize or make evaluations about 'appropriate' status obligations and then act on them in some way, or that the actors engage in procedures which can be interpreted as evaluations of action scenes in ways that are 'more' or 'less' institutionalized.

I want to underline the necessity of linking the strategies of interaction among actors with the structural framework employed by the social analyst. The observer must make abstractions from complex sequences of social interaction. How does he decide the role-status-norm relevance of the exchanges about which he observes or interviews? To what extent must he take the actor's typifications, stock of knowledge at hand, presumed appearance to others, conception of self, strategies of self-presentation, language and the like, into account in deciding the institutionalized character of status relationships, role relationships, and the normatively based expectations employed or imputed?

Some examples may help illustrate the conceptual complexity here. In a large university a new faculty member who arrives to assume his duties has already been told what classes he is to teach and may be shown his office by a secretary who addresses him as 'Mr' or 'Dr'. He may have met the other members of the department during an interview some months earlier. His initial contacts with other members of the department may occur in the hallways or at some party given by the chairman early in the autumn term. He is faced with a number of status dilemmas because of the way his colleagues introduce themselves or the way he introduces himself to them. Do they (or he) use first names, last names, formal titles, or 'Mr', or do they use their full name and refrain from calling him by his name when making or receiving a telephone call? If at the chairman's party he is introduced as 'Mr', is it because of an initial superficial formality or because he has yet to terminate his degree? How does he address the secretary, answer the phone, and sign his mail? The interaction sequences with non-academic personnel, administration officials, colleagues inside and outside of his department, constitute encounters which may be quite fragile for our new instructor. His imputations as to 'what is going on' and how he should explain his relationships within the university may also depend upon age differences, whether he has a regular appointment or temporary one, how his colleagues and others address and speak to him, and how (if married) his wife might react to her elevation (perhaps sudden) to 'faculty status' even though she may have recently completed her undergraduate work. The young instructor will probably encounter the same type of difficulties with his new neighbours. Does he introduce himself as 'Joe', 'Dr', 'Professor' or 'Mr'? What if his wife engages in first name introductions and he with more formal usages? How or when does his occupational status enter the neighbourhood scene?

The ways in which our young instructor 'presents' himself will convey different connotations to different 'others' depending on his physical appearance, clothing, language, and more importantly, how and when his occupational status is revealed, whether after or during the initial encounter. But in what sense are the 'old hands' now looking at our new instructor as someone fulfilling or not fulfilling the 'rights and duties' of his new status? What evidence do they have about his teaching and research or contacts with students? How do they observe his conduct in their presence as 'adequate' or 'inadequate' 'role' behaviour? Who is keeping score, and how?

In his new status as professor, therefore, our colleague must generate 'adequate' performances commensurate with his position through a continued sequence of encounters and exchanges with others, despite having been officially granted his degree. New acquaintances may accept and impute considerable importance to him, but he must somehow 'carry it off', and often without any explicit 'norms' or 'rules' to go by. We obviously do not hand our new instructor a 'script' outlining his 'role' in detail. Use of terms like 'anticipatory socialization' or 'on-the-job training' add little to our understanding of actual encounters, for research on such matters is either missing or weak.

Successive encounters may not 'achieve' the status expected by others, in that those with whom he shares formal status-equality in the institutionalized sense of 'college professor' may invoke extra academic criteria that we loosely call 'personality factors' in everyday life, while others may invoke publication or conversational criteria ('is he bright') in 'granting' or withholding the treatment they give to instructors who 'come on' and 'do well'. The fragility or precariousness of our new colleague's status as seen by him and others cannot be ascertained without reference to the interactional sequences of everyday life where our young instructor must 'bring it off'.

The social analyst who goes to a foreign country (or does research in his own) encounters similar problems. Explaining yourself as a 'professor of sociology' in your own country in order to gain access to a police department for a study of juvenile justice can be a difficult problem. In another country the problem can be compounded by many additional elements (see Ward *et al.*, 1964; and Cicourel, forthcoming). For example, making the necessary field contacts may be the most difficult part of the study. How does the field researcher go about doing it? Can he pass himself off as simply an 'American professor' of anthropology, sociology or political science? Obviously, 'it depends'. Some groups really may not care what his credentials are, but only want to know if he is some equivalent of a 'good guy', a 'nice guy', or a 'right guy', that is, trustworthy in their eyes. For others, his official credentials may be invaluable and some nice letters of introduction with large gold seals affixed even impressive to many. If our researcher is based at a foreign university, problems always revolve around how 'official status' is handled or managed in subsequent interaction with foreign colleagues who work within quite a different university atmosphere, where students are a powerful and vocal group, and most professors earn their living by 'moonlighting'. Dealing with big-city bureaucrats and village functionaries may require quite a different set of strategies for gaining information or further access. Finally, interviews and/or participant observation with informants and subjects at work or at home may require further strategies and/or modifications of earlier procedures. The general problem of how we can establish, maintain and successfully terminate our contacts in field settings cannot be resolved with existing social-science role theory, although there are many works which are very informative about how people manage their presence before others.

Social scientists working in their own country take for granted their own vocabulary and common sense or implicit conceptions of others, places, and things, and also take for granted the vocabulary and implicit conceptions of the people they study. In another country, working in a village or a large city, the social analyst becomes painfully aware of the inadequacy of social science status and role concepts in guiding his own research and the necessity of negotiating his own status and role behaviour *vis-à-vis* informants or respondents. There is no adequate theory of social process by which to guide his establishment of contacts, informants, subjects, and simultaneously inform him of strange patterns of bureaucratic life in foreign areas. Each researcher must decide these matters for himself. There is, therefore, the inevitable problem of sorting out (and perhaps coding) large quantities of information and subsuming such material ambiguously under commonly used and accepted concepts like 'status', 'role', 'norm', 'values'. The grounds for deciding the 'appropriate' recognition and what is an adequate description of different 'statuses', 'roles', and 'norms', are seldom discussed.

Conceptions of status

The notion of status as a structural feature of social order leads to formal definitions and some abstract examples, but seldom points to interactional consequences. References to the literature usually begin with Linton's definition: 'A status, as distinct from the individual who may occupy it, is simply a collection of rights and duties. Since these rights and duties can find expression only through the medium of individuals, it is extremely hard for us to maintain a distinction in our thinking between statuses and the people who hold them and exercise the rights and duties which constitute them' (Linton, 1936, p. 113). Linton's definition presupposes consensus as to the meaning of 'rights and duties', and he does not make the observer's and actor's indicators for recognizing status an integral part of the concept. Even if we could agree on formal positions within the table of organization of some kinship system or firm, the empirical evidence is not plentiful and does not make problematic variations in how individuals perceive and interpret formal statuses. The fact that we must always observe individuals and/or obtain reports about them from others or these same individuals, means that we are always confronted with the problem of knowing how to evaluate what we observe, how we ask questions, and what to infer from the answers.

Kingsley Davis's work is another well-known source on the meaning of 'status'.

A person therefore enters a social situation with an identity already established. His identity refers to his *position*, or *status*, within the social structure applicable to the given situation, and establishes his rights and obligations with reference to others holding positions within the same structure. His position and consequently his identity in the particular situation result from all the other positions he holds in other major social structures, especially in the other structures most closely related to the one he is acting in at the moment.

To aid in establishing the identity of the person, external symbols are frequently utilized. A common indicator, for example, is the style of dress . . . .

In the course of an individual's life very broad positions are first acquired . . . . As he goes through life he acquires more specific positions, and his actual behaviour in the various situations to which these positions apply serves to refine and modify the initially assigned identity . . . .

The normative system lays down the formal rights and obligations in connection with a position. Though it permits a certain amount of legitimate variation within the limits imposed, it also lays down rules to be followed in case the individual oversteps the limits. A right is a legitimate expectation entertained by a person in one position with respect to the behaviour of a person in another position. From the point of view of the other person this claim represents an obligation . . . .

An individual carries his social position around in his head, so to speak, and puts it into action when the appropriate occasion arises. Not only does he carry it in his head but others also carry it in theirs, because social positions are matters of reciprocal expectation and must be publicly and commonly conceived by everyone in the group . . . . The term status would then designate a position in the general institutional system, recognized and supported by the entire society, spontaneously evolved rather than deliberately created, rooted in the folkways and mores. Office, on the other hand, would designate a position in a deliberately created organization, governed by specific and limited rules in a limited group, more generally achieved than ascribed (Davis, 1948, pp. 86–9).

Davis's comments presume information carried 'in the head', some un-stated principles for recognizing when 'appropriate' action is necessary, and suggest the importance of changes over time and situated action. His remarks refer to specific and vague attributes associated with the concept 'status'. On the 'specific' side persons enter situations with readily recognized 'identities' and 'rights and obligations'. Further, actors acknowledge the 'rights and obligations' and are supported by the 'normative system'. Finally, 'statuses' are spontaneously evolved and recognized and supported by the entire society, while 'offices' are more explicitly known in deliberately created organizations. The 'vague' elements include the fact that over time the actor's status may well be refined, broadened, and modified in un-specified ways. The norms governing behaviour may vary with the actor's status and the situations he encounters. Finally, since actors 'carry' social positions around in their 'heads', each interaction scene presumably is a potentially problematic state of affairs. The dialectic between what appears as 'obvious' and structurally or institutionally invariant, and what depends upon the actor's perception and interpretation-implementation of his status or statuses, is stressed as important by Davis, but is not conceptually clear. It is necessary to show how the 'vague' features that unfold and become concretized over the course of interaction, alter, maintain, or distort the 'specific' or 'institutionalized' features of 'status'. The interesting question is how we 'integrate' the apparent discrepancy between the processes necessary to understand the structure, and whether the structure is in fact an invariant set of conditions for 'explaining' or 'knowing' the significance of the processes. Or does the process recreate the structure continuously during the course of interaction? A necessary complex set of properties for understanding status and its behavioural components requires a model of the actor that includes how 'external symbols' and appropriate rules are recognized as relevant to the actor and interpreted by him over the course of interaction. Cognitive procedures (in the head) and a theory of social meaning are presupposed when the terms status and role are used. But our model of the actor refers both to the researcher as observer and actor as participant.

Parson's usage of status refers to role-expectations.

Role-expectations, on the other hand, are the definitions by *both* ego and alter of what behaviour is proper for each in the relationship and in the situation in question . . . . Sanctions are the 'appropriate' behavioural consequences of alter's role-expectations in response to the actual behaviour of ego.

Both role-expectations and sanctions may be institutionalized to a greater or lesser degree. They are institutionalized when they are integrated with or 'express' value-orientations *common* to the members of the collectivity to which both ego and alter belong, which in the limiting case may consist only of ego and alter (Parsons and Shils, 1951, p. 154).

Parsons' position in *The Social System* is similar to that of Linton, though he refers to the 'status-role bundle' (Parsons, 1951).[3] Parsons' formulation includes the actor in some interaction scene, but the observer and actor appear to be locked in the same social arena in unknown ways, and it is difficult to know how the observer or actors perceive 'proper role-expectations', how the observer decides on the 'fit' between ego and alter's perspectives, and what ego, alter and the observer take into account based on the 'institutionalized' features of the interaction. Thus, in focusing upon the interactional context for structural properties of social order, Parsons directs our attention to 'common' value-orientations. But this apparent conceptual 'answer' avoids the crucial questions of what passes as 'common' and how our actors decide on their own or some collectivity's 'common' value-orientations; how consistent are actors in honouring or excepting such orientations if we assume they exist; and how varying degrees of institutionalization would refer to value-orientations 'more' or 'less' common to a group? Explicit cognitive procedures and a theory of meaning are absent from Parsons' formulation.

According to Homans, 'A man's status in a group is a matter of the stimuli his behaviour towards others and others' behaviour towards him –

3. Consider the following quotation: 'On the one hand there is the positional aspect – that of where the actor in question is "located" in the social system relative to other actors. This is what we will call his *status*, which is his place in the relationship system considered as a structure, that is a patterned system of *parts*. On the other hand, there is the processual aspect, that of what the actor does in his relations with others seen in the context of its functional significance for the social system. It is this which we shall call his *role*.' (Parsons, 1951, p. 25.)

including the esteem they give him – present both to the others and to himself, stimuli that may come to make a difference in determining the future behaviour of all concerned' (Homans, 1961, p. 337). The 'stimulus' view presented by Homans is rather general and apparently everything depends upon the actors' interpretation of implicit stimuli. But later Homans clarifies his position as follows:

In their private speculations, some sociologists were once inclined to think of the small informal group as a microcosm of society at large: they felt that the same phenomena appeared in the former as in the latter but on a vastly reduced scale – a scale that, incidentally, made detailed investigation possible . . . . But to say that the two phenomena have points in common is not to say that one is a microcosm of the other, that the one is simply the other writ small. The two are not alike if only because in an informal group a man wins status through his direct exchange with the other members, while he gets status in the larger society by inheritance, wealth, occupation, office, legal authority – in every case by his position in some institutional scheme, often one with a long history behind it (1961, p. 379).

While the stimuli, to use Homans's term, that are available to actors in face-to-face exchanges are usually quite different from stimuli available through indirect means such as the mass-media, a biography, or *Who's Who*, interpretation of the stimuli according to typified conceptions occurs in both cases. It is not clear how the actor utilizes 'external symbols' (including structural information about occupation, age, wealth) when engaged in direct exchanges with others. Nor does Homans clarify how the actor infers 'what is going on' over the course of interaction. A model of the actor that presupposes inductive procedures and a theory of meaning is also evident in Homans, but such notions remain implicit features of his discussion.

Work by Blau contains an elaborate analysis of social process, more realistically rooted in empirical studies, but it also suffers from implicit references to the actor's use of inductive procedures and a theory of meaning when engaged in social exchanges. Blau, like the others cited above, does not disentangle the observer's interpretations (requiring inductive procedures and a theory of meaning) from those of the actor, preferring to tell the reader about social life through the eyes of a detached observer armed with many complex abstract notions that subsume a rather impressive range of activities. Thus, his central notion 'of social exchange directs attention to the emergent properties in interpersonal relations and social interaction. A person for whom another has done a service is expected to express his gratitude and return a service when the occasion arises. Failure to express his appreciation and to reciprocate tends to stamp him as an ungrateful man who does not deserve to be helped' (Blau, 1964, p. 4). Precisely how actors recognize appropriate services and establish rates of exchange, how the observer and actor assess their significance, and decide their 'normal' management, are not explicit features of Blau's framework.

Basic concepts of social interaction that presupposes tacit notions of induction and meaning are not discussed at their own level, but taken for granted as 'obvious' and meaningful. Consider the following:

The internal differentiation of status and the associated distribution of rewards in substructures may be based on standards that are, from the perspective of the encompassing social structure, universalistic or particularistic, although these standards are, by definition, universalistic within the narrower compass of each substructure, that is, they are generally accepted criteria of achievement *within the subgroup*. If internal status in substructures is governed by standards universally accepted as valid throughout the macrostructure, as is typical for criteria of instrumental performance, superior internal status indicates assets that are valued in other collectivities too . . . . If, however, internal status in substructures rests on diverse standards that are particularistic from the perspective of the macrostructure, the higher a person's status is in one collectivity, the less likely are his qualifications to make him acceptable in another with different value standards (1964, p. 297).

Blau's remarks seek to integrate social process with social structure, but he begins and ends with propositions considerably removed from theoretical and empirical clarification of the elements of process as seen by both the actor and social analyst. His theorizing does not specify how actor and researcher learn, recognize, and use standards as universalistic or particularistic, nor the kind of interpretive procedures the actor must possess to carry out social exchanges that enable him to recognize what standards are appropriate for particular social settings.

Goffman's work brings us closer to the kinds of events in everyday life from which social analysts make inferences about process and structure. Goffman's descriptions also convey the idea of a fully informed third party who has intimate knowledge of social exchanges. There are times when the reader feels Goffman has perhaps observed or experienced (from the 'inside') some of our more delicate and/or embarrassing encounters in daily life. While he fails to clarify from whose point of view, and by what procedures, the observer is to infer the details of everyday life social encounters, Goffman gives the reader a very convincing impression of being on the spot and 'knowing' what takes place from the perspective of an 'insider'. Implementing Goffman's perspective is difficult because:

1. Goffman's assumptions about the conditions of social encounters are substantively appealing but lack explicit analytic categories delineating how the actor's perspective differs from that of the observer, and how both can be placed within the same conceptual frame.

2. All of Goffman's descriptive statements are prematurely coded, that is, interpreted by the observer, infused with substance that must be taken for granted, and subsumed under abstract categories without telling the reader how all of this was recognized and accomplished.

Consider the following:

When an individual enters the presence of others, they commonly seek to acquire information about him or to bring into play information about him already possessed. They will be interested in his general socio-economic status, his conception of self, his attitude toward them, his competence, his trustworthiness, etc. (1959, p. 1).

How the actor acquires information (the interpretation of external symbols, the use of language categories) or utilizes information already possessed so as to link the presumed knowledge 'appropriately' to a particular setting, requires explicit reference to inference procedures and a theory of how the actor assigns meaning to objects and events. But Goffman's model of the actor does not reveal how the actor (or observer as actor) negotiates actual scenes, except through the eyes of an ideally situated and perceptive 'third party'. The wider community relevance of the notion of 'status' is provided in the following quotation:

Society is organized on the principle that any individual who possesses certain social characteristics has a moral right to expect that others will value and treat him in a correspondingly appropriate way . . . In consequence, when an individual projects a definition of the situation and thereby makes an implicit or explicit claim to be a person of a particular kind, he automatically exerts a moral demand upon the others, obligating them to value and treat him in the manner that persons of his kind have a right to expect (1959, p. 13).

Goffman's implicit reference to status as process alludes to many possible (but unexplicated) rules the actor might use, provides a vivid glimpse of the action scene itself, and how the interacting participants might treat each other in 'more' or 'less' institutionalized ways. But the idea of projecting a definition of the situation, and hence a claim to being a certain type of person, demands rules that both actor and observer follow in generating behavioural displays, and assigning the meanings with which Goffman endows the action scene.

Role as process

The idea of 'role' as the dynamic aspect of 'status' or the 'less' institutionalized class of statuses implies a problematic or innovational element in behaviour. The problematical elements of 'role' are emphasized by

Goffman and exemplified in his remark that 'Life may not be much of a gamble, but interaction is' (1959, p. 243). A notion like 'status' provides us with an ideal normative label for understanding how both actor and observer subsume initial impressions based on appearances, and verbal identifications and introductions to establish some preliminary basis for mutual evaluation. At the level of interaction actors are constrained by the possible formality of ritualized introductions, whereby the communicants (or some third party) provide verbal material to support or detract from the appearance (Goode, 1960, p. 251). I am suggesting that labels designating a range of features that we call 'status' are used by observer and actor as practical language games for simplifying the task of summarizing a visual field and complex stimuli that are difficult to describe in some precise, detailed way (Wittgenstein, 1953). This means that the labels do not recover the appearances and imputations subsumed by the participant unless imagined details are supplied by an auditor during the course of interaction. Whereas this elaboration by the actor – an elaboration not subject (by him) to verification – serves his practical interests, the scientific observer cannot afford to rely on the same tacit elaboration; his model of the actor must clarify how his observations are necessarily deficient. Films or videotapes can provide access to the original source of observations and the possibility of improving the common sense observer's limitations. We are faced with the problem of deciding the actor's 'logic-in-use' versus his reflections or 'reconstructed logic' after he leaves the scene (see Kaplan, 1964, p. 8). Even though Goffman provides rich 'third party' descriptive accounts of the course of social exchanges, he does not tell us how the social analyst as observer and/or participant translates the 'logic-in-use' of his field work into the 'reconstructed logic' of his theorizing. The works of others cited above have also avoided this problem. Goffman, however, makes more of a frontal attack on the 'notion' of 'role-expectation' and the 'definition of the situation'.

To summarize, then, I assume that when an individual appears before others he will have many motives for trying to control the impression they receive of the situation. This report is concerned with some of the common techniques that persons employ to sustain such impressions and with some of the common contingencies associated with the employment of these techniques. . . . I shall be concerned only with the participant's dramaturgical problems of presenting the activity before others (1959, p. 15).

Goffman's remarks presume that the actor possesses well developed procedures for coping with his environment, procedures employed by the actor when satisfying what the observer (with unstated procedures) loosely labels 'role' behaviour, if it stems from, or is 'oriented by', some set of more formalized imputations and claims about kinship relationships, positions in groups, communities and work organizations. The perceptive remarks by Goffman extend conceptions of role generally found in the literature. The critical feature of role, as stressed by Goffman among others, lies in its construction by the actor over the course of interaction. This construction makes status-emitting stimuli problematic for the actor because of situational constraints.

This notion of construction, despite a lack of conceptual clarity, can be seen in the following quotation from Mead.

The generalized attitude of the percipient has arisen out of cooperative activities of individuals in which the individual by the gesture through which he excites the other has aroused in himself the attitude of the other, and addresses himself in the generalized attitude of the other, and addresses himself in the role of the other. Thus he comes to address himself in the generalized attitude of the group of persons occupied with a common undertaking. The generalization lies in such an organization of all the different cooperative acts as they appear in attitudes of the individual that he finds himself directing his acts by the corresponding acts of the others involved – by what may be called the rules of the game (Mead, 1938, p. 192).

Mead's remarks stress the problematic features of how two participants evoke a kind of cooperative exchange. Turner has stated the constructive elements of role behaviour clearly in the following passages:

Roles 'exist' in varying degrees of concreteness and consistency, while the individual confidently frames his behaviour as if they had unequivocal existence and clarity. The result is that in attempting from time to time to make aspects of the roles explicit he is creating and modifying roles as well as merely bringing them to light; the process is not only role-taking but *role-making*.

The actor is not the occupant of a position for which there is a neat set of rules – a culture or set of norms – but a person who must act in the perspective supplied in part by his relationship to others whose actions reflect roles that he must identify. Since the role of alter can only be inferred rather than directly known by ego, testing inferences about the role of alter is a continuing element in interaction. Hence the tentative character of the individual's own role definition and performance is never wholly suspended (1962, pp. 22–3).

Turner's exposition of role behaviour emphasizes the creative and modifying elements of role-taking and role-making. As noted in the earlier quote from Mead, the participants of an action scene emit stimuli that each must identify as relevant for taking (while perhaps modifying) the role of the other, or making (creating) the role. The role of each participant can only be inferred and never known directly, and the role behaviour displayed is always tentative and being tested over the course of interaction.

But the model of the actor implied here lacks explicit statements about how the actor recognizes relevant stimuli and manages to orient himself (locate the stimuli in a socially meaningful context) to the behavioural displays so that an organized response can be generated which will be recognized as relevant to alter. The actor must be endowed with mechanisms or basic procedures that permit him to identify settings which would lead to 'appropriate' invocation of norms, where *the norms would be surface rules and not basic to how the actor makes inferences about taking or making roles*. The basic or interpretive procedures are like deep structure grammatical rules; they enable the actor to generate appropriate (usually innovative) responses in changing situated settings. The interpretive procedures enable the actor to sustain a *sense of social structure* over the course of changing social settings, while surface rules or norms provide a more general institutional or historical validity to the meaning of the action as it passes, in a reflective sense. To the Meadian dialectic of the 'I' and the 'me' is added the explicit requirement that the actor must be conceived as possessing inductive (interpretive) procedures, procedures designed to function as a base structure for generating and comprehending the behavioural (verbal and non-verbal) displays that can be observed. An implicit basic or interpretive procedure in Mead's theory would be the notion that participants in social exchanges must assume that their use of verbal and nonverbal signs or symbols are the 'same', or this 'sameness' (in an ideal sense) must at least be assumed to hold (Stone, 1962, p. 88).

The social analyst's use of abstract theoretical concepts like role actually masks the inductive or interpretive procedures whereby the actor produces behavioural displays which others and the observer label 'role behaviour'. Without a model of the actor that specifies such procedures or rules, we cannot reveal how behavioural displays are recognized as 'role-taking' or 'role-making'.

The extensive coverage of the research literature by Sarbin employs the following definitions of 'status' (called 'position' by Sarbin) and 'role'.

In other words, a position is a cognitive organization of expectations, a shorthand term for a concept embracing expected actions of persons enacting specified roles. These expectations, organized as they are around roles, may justifiably be called role expectations. Thus, a position is a cognitive organization of role expectations. . . .

A *role* is a patterned sequence of learned *actions* or deeds performed by a person in an interaction situation. The organizing of the individual actions is a product of the perceptual and cognitive behaviour of person A upon observing person B (Sarbin, 1953, p. 225).

Sarbin's remarks stress the learned elements of 'role' in everyday life, and refer to various studies which suggest the ambiguities of 'roles' for different actors. But Sarbin leans on the short-hand concepts of sociologists and anthropologists, taking for granted the 'positions' and 'roles' in society that social scientists treat as 'known' and 'clear', but which do not specify the mechanisms, procedures or rules employed by the actor to recognize and attribute expectations to others. While Sarbin's discussion of 'role' and 'self' takes us beyond the focus of this paper, his remarks on the self changing over time, based upon experience, are important for underlining the significance of actual 'role-enactment' on 'position' over time. But the construction of role behaviour over the course of interaction would stress learning mechanisms that would be selective in scanning the visual field or behavioural displays, rather than simply learning actions which the observer labels patterned sequences or roles. Memory would always be contingent upon procedures or rules that identify or recognize objects and events as socially meaningful.

In summarizing this section I want to stress two problems which preclude our present use of the concept 'role':

1. It is difficult to say what role-taking and role-enactment are all about if it is not explained how the 'statuses' or 'positions' to which they refer come to be recognized from both the actor's and the observer's perspective. The problem may be confounded if 'non-role' behaviour (that is, not following from some recognized 'status') as opposed to 'role' behaviour, is not clarified as a residual category, for such information could be a more important complex attribute in the evaluation by others including the observer of the actor's role behaviour.

2. To what extent does our understanding of conduct, subsumed under the label 'role', depend upon a clear analysis of the perception of 'norms', inasmuch as many writers shift their structural argument about 'status' as institutionalized to the idea of 'role' as a set of implicit 'norms'.

What we have failed to learn since the impact of Mead's work are the 'rules of the game', how many 'games' there are, and how actors and the observer come to treat some sequence of events as a 'game' or legitimate social activity. Presumably the actor's perception and interpretation of an environment of objects is established and continually re-established in unknown specificity and vagueness but according to some set of 'standards', 'rules', or 'norms'. A closer look at the concept 'norm' is the next order of business.

Norms and the problematic character of everyday life

A major difficulty in analytically based accounts of 'role' lies in the 'norms' or 'rules' by which the actor is presumably oriented in perceiving and interpreting an environment of objects. The literature reveals continual reliance on some notion of 'status' to suggest stable meanings about 'position' *vis-à-vis* others in a network of social relationships. There is an implied consensus about the 'rights and obligations' of actors occupying some commonly known and accepted 'status'. The variability attached to 'role' (its innovative or 'less institutionalized' character) appears to stem from the various actors who may come to occupy a given 'status'. The actor's differential perception and interpretation of 'statuses' implies ambiguity for all participants.

The notion of 'norms', including legal norms, is a variable element of social interaction. The common view is to characterize our theoretical conceptions of 'norms' as stable features of society (with acknowledged differences between the mores and folkways), evoking consensus in groups.

Norms are problematic to all interaction scenes because our reflective thoughts, as participants or observers, reify and reconstruct the 'rules of the game'. The analogy which fits here is that of Mead's distinction between the 'I' and the 'me'. Although interaction is always a gamble for all concerned, we have managed to exempt that abstract entity called 'society'. The reflective 'me' of the participants and observers (including the social analyst) imputes meanings and re-interprets perceptions and actions after the social scene unfolds, but it is the 'I' which is 'leading the way' with potentially impulsive, innovative, spontaneous interpretations of the situation. Another way of characterizing the problem is to speak of role-taking as 'logic-in-use' and status as 'reconstructed logic'. The rehearsal elements of role-taking involve 'logic-in-use' because the actor is taking more than 'internalized norms' or stored information into account, for it is the appearance, behaviour and reactions of others in a particular setting that activates normative categories. The 'reconstructed logic' comes into play after the interaction as a way of evaluating 'what happened' and connecting it to others or some wider group or community. The particular action scene the actor must attend requires that he locate emergent (constructed) meanings within the wider context of general rules or policies (Rawls, 1955, pp. 3–32). The general rules or policies are norms whose meaning in emergent (constructed) action scenes must be negotiated by the actor.

Statuses, like general rules or policies, require recognition and interpretation during which interacting participants must elicit and search appearances for relevant information about each other. Role-taking and role-making require that the actor articulate general rules or policies (norms) with an emergent (constructed) action scene in order to find the meaning of one's own behaviour or that of some other.

With our present conceptions of status, role, and norms, we would be hard-pressed to explain role behaviour by simulation techniques. We would fare better consulting theatrical directors. Suppose that the government printing office began publishing manuals, prepared by the US Office of Education, and based upon the 'expert' advice of social scientists, that purport to contain detailed descriptions of all the important 'statuses' of the society, complete with 'role variability' permitted regionally, nationally, and qualified for such categories as 'nuclear family', 'extended family', 'close friends', 'casual friends', 'acquaintances but not friends', 'strangers', 'foreigners', and 'children up to pre-teens'. Presume that the 'norms' or 'rules' governing interaction are described for each 'status' and 'role', and the settings in which variation is permitted. Suppose that another manual outlines 'role-playing procedures' beginning with children who can speak and covering all adult possibilities, including 'old-age'. Assume that grants to adult-education centres and school systems by the government provide an organizational basis for implementing the programme.

The obvious point to our example of writing simulation manuals is that the human organism must possess basic or interpretive procedures that emerge developmentally and continue to provide innovations late in the life cycle. The dramaturgical metaphor of the stage is defective in explaining how actors are capable of imitation and *innovation* with little or no prior rehearsal, just as a child is capable of producing grammatically correct utterances that he has never heard, and of understanding utterances that have never been heard before. Terms like attitudes, values, need dispositions, drives, expectancies, are inadequate because there is no explicit attempt to formulate interpretive procedures which the actor must learn in order to negotiate novel experiences as well as to be able to construct constancy in his environment. The language and meaning acquisition principles which would permit interpretive procedures to emerge must allow for the operation of memory and selection procedures which are consistent with pattern recognition or construction, active (searching for documentary evidence) and passive (taking the environment for granted, until further notice, as 'obvious' or 'clear') hypothesis testing, and must be congruent with the actor's ability to recognize and generate novel and 'identical' or 'similar' behavioural displays (Cicourel, 1970a).

The distinction between interpretive procedures and norms is tied to the difference between consensus or shared agreement and a sense of social structure. Interpretive procedures provide the actor with a developmentally changing sense of social structure that enables him to assign meaning or relevance to an environment of objects. Normative or surface rules enable the actor to link his view of the world to that of others in concerted social action, and to presume that consensus or shared agreement governs interaction. The shared agreement would include consensus about the existence of conflict or differences in normative rules. The following two quotations from Goode and Shibutani reveal the negotiated or constructed character of consensus or shared agreement which exists in normative behaviour:

Perhaps the social structure is under no threat under modern conditions of apparently weak consensus if the conformity to which ego is pressed is merely of a 'general' nature, that is, the norms permit a wide range of rough approximations to the ideal. But whether norms in fact are general is not easy to determine. Which is in fact 'the' norm? You should not lie (only a loose conformity is demanded); or you may not tell lies of the following types in these situations but not in others, and the wrongness of other lies is to be ranked in the following order. The first is a general norm, and of course there will be only a rough conformity with it, but it is not a correct description. The second would be empirically more accurate, but no one has established such a matrix of obligations on empirical evidence (Goode, 1960, pp. 254–5).

In recurrent and well organized situations men are able to act together with relative ease because they share common understandings as to what each person is supposed to do. Cooperation is facilitated when men take the same things for granted. We are willing to wait in line in a grocery store on the assumption that we will be waited on when our turn comes up. We are willing to accept pieces of paper of little intrinsic value in return for our labours on the assumption that money can subsequently be exchanged for the goods and services that we desire. There are thousands of such shared assumptions, and society is possible because of the faith men place in the willingness of others to act on them. Consensus refers to the common assumptions underlying cooperative endeavours (Shibutani, 1961, p. 40).

The quotations from Goode and Shibutani emphasize the necessity of viewing normative behaviour as including variations in the interpretation of general rules, as well as tacit assumptions about how ego and alter will trust their environment in the absence of cumbersome and redundant details about the meaning of 'familiar' activities. Persons will recognize the grocery store queue as a particular instance of a general case and not ask the clerk or other persons standing in line if the 'general rule' holds in 'this grocery store'. The idea of interpretive procedures employed by actors is implicit in how the actor decides a general rule is implied or operative.

The interpretive procedures provide a sense of social order that is fundamental for normative order (consensus or shared agreement) to exist or be negotiated and constructed. The two orders are always in interaction, and it would be absurd to speak of the one without the other. The analytic distinction parallels a similar separation in linguistics between the surface structure utterance (the normative order of consensus statements), and the deep structure (the basic social order or sense of social structure) (Chomsky, 1965). The distinction is necessary and presupposed in a reference to how the actor recognizes social scenes as normatively relevant, and in the differential perception and interpretation of norms and action scenes *vis-à-vis* role behaviour. But unlike the rather static notion of internalized attitudes as dispositions to act in a certain way, the idea of interpretive procedures must specify how the actor negotiates and constructs *possible* action, and evaluates the results of *completed* action. Our model of the actor must specify:

1. How general rules or norms are invoked to justify or evaluate a course of action, and

2. How innovative constructions in context-bound scenes alter general rules or norms, and thus provide the basis for change.

Hence the learning and use of general rules or norms, and their long-term storage, always require interpretive procedures for recognizing the relevance of actual, changing scenes, orienting the actor to possible courses of action, the organization of behavioural displays and their reflective evaluation by the actor.

Terms like 'internalized norms' or attitudes appear inadequate when we recognize how socialization experiences revolve around our use of language and linguistic codifications of personal and group experiences over time. Our perception and interpretation of social reality is continually modified by the acquisition of new and different context-bound lexical items. The educational process is designed to teach us how to think abstractly and utilize language to order our experiences and observations. Linguistic structures enable us to extend our knowledge and subsume a wide spectrum of experiences and observations, but it also filters these activities both as inputs and outputs. For those with less educational experience, the social meanings of the world of everyday life may be represented differently (Bernstein, 1958; 1959; 1960 and 1962). The study of language use is important for understanding how actors routinize or normalize their environments, perceive and interpret them as threatening, disruptive, new or strange.

Structural arrangements provide boundary conditions by using what the actor takes for granted; typified conceptions that make up the actor's stock of knowledge, ecological settings, common linguistic usage and biophysical conditions. The interaction remains structured by such boundary conditions, but is also problematic during the course of action. But the actor's typified orientation to his environment minimizes the problematic possibilities of social encounters: the fundamental importance of common sense ways of perceiving and interpreting the world is the taken-for-granted perspective which reduces surprise, assumes that the world is as it appears today, and that it will be the same tomorrow. The actor constructs his daily existence by a set of tried and proven recipes (Schutz, 1962 and Garfinkel, 1967).

A more refined conceptual frame for understanding norms will have to specify interpretive procedures as a set of invariant properties governing fundamental conditions of all interaction so as to indicate how the actor and observer decide what serves as definitions of 'correct' or 'normal' conduct or thought. The interpretive procedures would suggest the nature of minimal conditions that all interaction presumably would have to satisfy for actor and observer to decide that the interaction is 'normal' or 'proper' and can be continued. The acquisition and use of interpretive procedures over time amounts to a cognitive organization that provides a continual sense of social structure.

Some features of interpretive procedures and their field research relevance

In this final section of the chapter I want to outline some of the elements that the notion of interpretive procedures would possess if terms like status, role, and norm are to retain any usefulness. In presenting my discussion I will lean heavily on the writings of Alfred Schutz because I believe he has made more explicit the ingredients of social interaction also discussed by James, Mead, Baldwin, and others. I find Schutz's writings to be quite compatible with some elements of the linguistic theory known as generative-transformational grammar, and hence will draw upon elements of both in my discussion.

Both Chomsky and Schutz stress the importance of the *intentions* of speaker-hearers. In transformational grammar considerable emphasis is placed upon the speaker-hearer's competence to generate and understand acceptable (grammatically correct) utterances. This competence presumes a deep structure whereby the speaker's intentions are first formulated according to base or phrase structure or rewrite rules. The base structure utterance, therefore, can be viewed as an elaborated (before the fact) version of what is actually spoken (and heard by a hearer). Transformational rules operate on the deep structure so as to delete or rearrange the utterance so that a surface structure comes out as a well-formed or grammatically correct sentence. For present purposes we can say that speakers and hearers possess two common sets of phonological and syntactic rules whereby each is capable (possesses the competence) of generating and comprehending deep and surface structures.

Schutz is concerned with the semantic or meaning component of social interaction. The linguist is not interested in focusing on interaction itself, but his statements can be extended logically to include conditions formulated by Schutz for understanding how social order or social interaction is possible. I consider the following passage from Schutz to be central to the problem of social order, as well as compatible with elements of the formulations of generative-transformational linguists.

More or less naïvely I [referring to the common sense actor's view of things] presuppose the existence of a common scheme of reference for both my own acts and the acts of others. I am interested above all not in the overt behaviour of others, not in their performance of gestures and bodily movements, but in their intentions, and that means in the in-order-to motives for the sake of which, and in the because motives based on which, they [others] act as they do (Schutz, 1964, p. 11).

The notion of a common scheme of reference includes the idea of action that is motivated by a plan of projected behaviour which Schutz calls an 'in-order-to' motive, and the possibility of reflective behaviour whereby some reason is assigned to the past, completed action (called a 'because motive' by Schutz). Many readers may not feel that Schutz has presented material that goes beyond the work of James, Baldwin, Mead, or others, but I believe the extension by Schutz of ideas by these writers can be found in several features making up the 'common scheme of reference' which can be viewed as interpretive procedures capable of being studied empirically. The following features are proposed as basic to all interaction, but not exhaustive, yet a necessary first step in clarifying the fundamental base structure of social interaction.

1. The first procedure refers to a *reciprocity of perspectives* which Schutz divides into two parts. The first part instructs the speaker and hearer to assume their mutual experiences of the interaction scene are the same even if they were to change places. The second part informs each participant to disregard personal differences in how each assigns meaning to everyday activities, thus each can attend the present scene in an identical manner for the practical matter at hand. Schutz uses a question and answer format to further illustrate this procedure. The question-answer sequencing requires a reciprocal rule whereby my question provides a basis (reason) for your answer, while the possibility of a future answer from you provides a basis (reason) for my question. When I ask a question I have intentions (a deep structure) or a more elaborated version in mind than what I actually ask you. My 'pruned' or 'deleted' surface question, therefore, presumes a more elaborated version which I assume you 'fill in', despite receiving only my surface message. Your answer, therefore, is based upon both the elaborated and surface elements of my question, and I in turn 'fill in' your answer so as to construct your elaborated intentions. Both participants, therefore, must presume that each will generate recognizable and intelligible utterances as a

necessary condition for the interaction to even occur, and each must reconstruct the other's intentions (the deep structure) if there is to be coordinated social interaction.

2. The reciprocity of perspectives cannot operate unless additional procedures or sub-routines accompany its use. One sub-routine consists of the actor's ability to treat a given lexical item, category, or phrase, as an index of larger networks of meaning as in normative development of disease categories, colour categories, and kinship terms (Bar-Hillel, 1954; Cicourel, 1970a; Conklin, 1955; Frake, 1962; Garfinkel, 1967 and Sacks, 1967). The appearance of a particular lexical item presumes the speaker intended a larger set, and assumes the hearer 'fills-in' the larger set when deciding its meaning. A related sub-routine allows the actor to defer judgment on the item until additional information is forthcoming. Alternatively, an item or category may be assigned tentative meaning and then 'locked-in' with a larger collection of items retrospectively when a phrase appears later in the conversation. This *et cetera* procedure and its sub-routines permit the speaker-hearer to make normative sense of immediate settings by permitting temporary, suspended, or 'concrete' linkages with a short-term or long-term store of socially distributed knowledge.

3. To introduce a third interpretive property, the idea of *normal form* typifications, I quote again from Schutz:

But as I confront my fellow-man, I bring into each concrete situation a stock of preconstituted knowledge which includes a network of typifications of human individuals in general, of typical human motivations, goals, and action patterns. It also includes knowledge of expressive and interpretive schemes, of objective sign-systems and, in particular, of the vernacular language (Schutz, 1964, pp. 29–30).

Interaction participants presume normal forms of acceptable talk and appearances, or if discrepancies appear, attempt to normalize the action scene. The procedure provides the actor with a basis for rejecting or reducing a range of possible meanings to a collapsed typification of the social structures. The procedure instructs the actor to reject or recognize particular instances as acceptable representations of a more general normative set. The collapsing, typifying activity of immediate action scenes is context-bound, but enables the actor to make use of short and long-term store (socially distributed knowledge) so as to subsume the particulars of an unfolding setting under more general normative rules. Hence notions like status, role, and norm cannot be relevant to an understanding of everyday social interaction unless the actor possesses a procedure for recognizing normal forms or subsuming particulars under general normative or surface rules, and thus establishing a basis for concerted action. Asking the actor what he 'sees' or has 'seen' in experimental or field studies requires that the researcher know something about how the actor typifies his world, according to what kinds of linguistic categories and syntactic rules.

When the observer seeks to describe the interaction of two participants, the environment within his reach is congruent with that of the actors, and he is able to observe the face-to-face encounter, but he cannot presume that his experiences are identical to the actors: yet both actors assume their experiences are roughly identical for all practical purposes. It is difficult for the observer 'to verify his interpretation of the other's experiences by checking them against the other's own subjective interpretations', because while there exists a congruence between them, it is difficult to 'verify' his interpretation of the other's experiences unless he (the observer) becomes a 'partner' and/or seeks to question the other along particular lines (Schutz, 1964, p. 34). The observer is very likely to draw upon his own past experiences as a common-sense actor *and* scientific researcher to decide the character of the observed action scene. The context of our interpretations will thus be based upon 'logic-in-use' and 'reconstructed logic', and therefore include elements of common-sense typifications and theorizing.

The observer's scheme of interpretation cannot be identical, of course, with the interpretive scheme of either partner in the social relation observed. The modifications of attention which characterize the attitude of the observer cannot coincide with those of a participant in an ongoing social relation. For one thing, what he finds relevant is not identical with what they find relevant in the situation. Furthermore, the observer stands in a privileged position in one respect: he has the ongoing experiences of *both* partners under observation. On the other hand, the observer cannot legitimately interpret the 'in-order-to' motives of one participant as the 'because' motives of the other, as do the partners themselves, unless the interlocking of motives becomes explicitly manifested in the observable situation (1964, p. 36).

The complexity of perspectives involved in direct interaction and observation depend, therefore, upon subtle shifts by the researcher, requiring that he use interpretive procedures and common-sense typifications. The observer cannot avoid the use of interpretive procedures in research for he relies upon his member-acquired use of normal forms to recognize the relevance of behavioural displays for his theory. He can only objectify his observations by making explicit the properties of interpretive procedures and his reliance on them for carrying out his research activities.

When our interest in the sources of information provided by direct participation in interaction and observation is shifted to interaction by telephone, exchange of letters, messages we receive from third parties, read or hear about via the news media, the actor's perspective for 'knowing' his partner or 'other' narrows. If the telephone conversation is between acquaintances, friends or kinship elements our model of the actor must include the situation described by Schutz as follows:

I hold on to the familiar image I have of you. I take it for granted that you are as I have known you before. Until further notice I hold invariant that segment of my stock of knowledge which concerns you and which I have built up in face-to-face situations, that is, until I receive information to the contrary (1964, p. 39).

The ways in which the actor retains an image of the other based upon prior face-to-face experiences is a fundamental feature of how we can interpret interview material from respondents. Knowledge of what Schutz calls the 'constitutive traits' of the other by the actor is presupposed in making inferences about the meaning of respondents' utterances. Hence, when we become interested both in the actor's comprehension of a world divided into different sectors of immediacy, as opposed to others or objects not in face-to-face contact, then our theory and methodology must reflect the many transitional ways of 'knowing' for the actor which fall between 'direct' and 'indirect' experiences of others, objects, and events. The experience of others not in face-to-face contact Schutz refers to as the actor's perspective of a 'contemporary'. The mediate apprehension of the contemporary is accomplished by typifications, even though the 'other' may have been known in the past through face-to-face communication.

The act by which I apprehend the former fellowman as a contemporary is thus a typification in the sense that I hold invariant my previously gained knowledge, although my former fellowman has grown older in the meantime and must have necessarily gained new experiences. Of these experiences I have either no knowledge or only knowledge by inference or knowledge gained through fellowmen or other indirect sources (1964, p. 42).

Schutz's remarks suggest the elements necessary for understanding the basic processes that generate role behaviour or the actor's point of view *vis-à-vis* some 'other'. They also point to a more general model whereby we can decide how the observer-researcher obtains data about the actor-other, and how such data are to be interpreted. Schutz notes how the simultaneity of ongoing interaction means that the actor follows a step-by-step constitution of the other's conduct and its experienced meaning, and therefore, when faced with 'an accomplished act, artifact, or tool', the actor views the end-products 'as a pointer to such subjective step-by-step processes' experienced in direct interaction (1964, p. 43). The observer-researcher therefore, cannot always take utterances by respondents as evidence, unless he has some confidence that they can be shown to reflect the step-by-step processes of the original or mediate experiences thereby lessening the possibility that 'coded' substantive responses are distorting, altering or truncating the meaning of the activities, objects or events for the actor. Schutz comments on how the actor utilizes 'personal ideal types' as a means of comprehending what is experienced directly and indirectly. These provide the observer-researcher with a fundamental element for any model which seeks to understand how the actor manages to perceive and interpret his environment, in spite of apparent discrepancies and despite the fact that the 'norms' are not clearly understood 'directives to action' and that 'consensus' emerges through the constructions of participants using interpretive procedures in the course of interaction. The 'stability' of the world of contemporaries for the actor refers to the typifications employed by him and the fact that they are detached from an immediate and hence emergent subjective configuration of meaning because 'such processes – typical experiences of "someone" – *exhibit the idealizations* "again and again", i.e. of typical anonymous repeatability' (1964, p. 44). In the case of direct interaction the personal ideal types are modified by the concrete 'other' given in direct experience to the actor. Hence, the actor can deal effectively with an environment which carries with it ambiguity and gaps in 'directives to concrete action' because the typical is rendered homogeneous, non-problematical, and, therefore, taken for granted. The actor establishes equivalence classes subject to the modifications inherent in direct and indirect contacts with others. The observer-researcher's equivalence classes cannot be established without reference to the actor's use of interpretive procedures and the common-sense equivalence classes constructed during interaction.

Thus, when the observer-researcher questions respondents about the 'social structures', he must distinguish between various events and objects and how they are known to the actor. Schutz claims that a typifying scheme is inversely related to the level of generality of the actor's experiences, and the experiences are rooted in the stock of knowledge possessed by the actor, from which he derives the scheme.

These remarks make it obvious that each typification involves other typifications. The more substrata of typifying schemes are involved in a given ideal type, the more anonymous it is, and the larger is the region of things simply taken for granted in the application of the ideal type. The substrata, of course, are not explicitly grasped in clear and distinct acts of thought. This becomes evident if one takes social realities such as the state or the economic system or art and begins to explicate all the substrata of typifications upon which they are based (1964, p. 49).

If our observer-researcher is studying a family unit, a small village, a small group of elite leaders, he may interview A about X, where X may be an individual or some collectivity. The ideal-typical characterization of X by A keeps invariant A's direct experiences of X, making them typifications. A's description of X may be punctuated by examples designed as 'evidence' and motivated by various interests and stock of knowledge. The observer-researcher refers the information (depending upon how it is interpreted *vis-à-vis* the strata of meaning suspected and/or probed for) to his own stock of knowledge about X and his interest in X. The more removed (by 'institutionalized' law, by physical and social distance, by tradition) X is from A, the more standardized a given typifying scheme will be, the more careful will be the required probing and the inferences drawn. If the respondent A is referring to documents he has read, or his information is based upon others' interpretations of documents, the observer-researcher will have to decide the meaning of the sign-system used by A, for the 'distance' of the document is likely to lead to more 'objective' use of signs, that is, without benefit of 'inside' knowledge. If A was the member of some audience witnessing a village fight, and was face-to-face with the participants, his remarks shift to that of an observer as described earlier.

Summary

Throughout this chapter I have tried to discuss terms like status, role and norm within a general model for characterizing social interaction and the perspectives employed by participants. Everyday experience for the actor is at any particular moment partitioned into various domains of relevances whereby common-sense equivalence classes of typifications taken for granted are employed. The correspondence between the social analyst's terms, e.g., 'status', 'role', 'role-expectation', and the world as experienced by our constructed actor-type does not refer to the same sets of typifications, nor are the two sets of categories used by our actor and observer-researcher, or the experiences upon which they are based, arrived at by the same inferences and reasoning. In the ideal the actor and observer-researcher employ different kinds of constructs and their procedural rules are distinct. In actual practice, however, the actor's everyday theorizing is probably not much different from the observer-researcher. Both employ the same interpretive procedures and similar typifications, and they seldom clarify during interaction the particular vernacular or rules used to communicate the domains of relevance which each describes, nor do they delineate the strata or layers of meaning intended or suggested by the linguistic categories and connotations used. Differences between our 'practical theorist' and 'academic theorist' may all but disappear when both describe everyday activities. The observer-researcher must rely upon interpretive procedures when subsuming 'recognized' behavioural displays under concepts derived from his scientific vocabulary. Hence unless the researcher clarifies, conceptually and empirically, his reliance on interpretive procedures, he cannot make claims to 'objective' findings. Most of the above discussion can be summarized by the following remarks:

1. Participants in social interaction apparently 'understand' many things (by elaboration of verbal and nonverbal signals) even though such matters are not mentioned explicitly. The unspoken elements may be as important as the spoken ones.

2. The actors impute meanings which 'make sense' of what is being described or explained even though at any moment in clock-time the conversation may not be clear to the partner or independent observer by reference to the actual terms being used. Through the use of interpretive procedures the participants supply meanings and impute underlying patterns even though the surface content will not reveal these meanings to an observer unless his model is directed to such elaborations.

3. A common scheme of interpretation (the interpretive procedures) is assumed and selective background characteristics are invoked to account for and fill in apparent 'gaps' in what is described or explained. The participants seem to agree even though neither has indicated any explicit grounds or basis for the agreement. Each may choose to 'wait and see'.

4. The participants do not typically call each other's utterances into doubt, demanding independent evidence, so long as each assumes he can receive 'details' (or that 'details' are available) on discrepancies detected in the conversation. But even when there are doubts, the partner will seek to 'help' the other get through the conversation. Direct confrontations require radical shifts in the perspective each participant employs: but as a first approximation they both take for granted that each knows what they say and mean by their utterances.

5. The interpretive procedures activate short and long-term stored information (socially distributed knowledge) that enables the actor to articulate general normative rules with immediate interaction scenes. The interpretive procedures and surface (normative) rules provide the actor with a scheme for partitioning his environment into domains of relevance.

6. The interpretive procedures govern the sequencing of interaction and establish the conditions for evaluating and generating behaviour displays which the researcher labels as appropriate status and role attributes or conduct. The articulation of interpretive procedures and surface (normative) rules establish a basis for concerted interaction which we label the social structures.

7. Notions like status, role and norm, therefore, cannot be clarified unless the researcher's model explicitly provides for features enabling the actor to recognize and generate 'appropriate' behavioural displays. Nor can we explain the observer's ability to recognize behavioural displays as falling under such procedures and rules, unless we have a model of interaction that provides for interpretive procedures and their interaction with normative or surface rules.

2 The Acquisition of Social Structure: Towards a Developmental Sociology of Language and Meaning

How members of a society or culture make sense of, or assign sense to, their environment over time is central to the persistent problem of how social order is possible. Conventional introductory texts in sociology (Broom and Selznick, 1963) view the socialization of the child in standardized ways as basic for social control and the emergence of human society or social order. But these texts do not ask, or reveal how, the internalization of others' attitudes, and the inculcation of norms in the child, serve as 'blueprints for behaviour' in some developmental sense. The idea of 'adequate' socialization simply makes casual reference to the importance of social interaction and language. References to the emergence of a social self, norms, or rules for deciding appropriate and inappropriate behaviour according to vague but unspecified schedules of reward and punishment, do not ask what is 'normal' rule development. The conventional or 'normal' view (to use Kuhn's (1962) notion of normal science loosely) in sociology does not ask how language and meaning appear in children according to developmental stages, in order for a progressive sense of social structure or social organization to emerge as essential to conventional abstract theories about learning to follow the 'rules of the game' (Williams, 1960; Bierstedt, 1957; Gibbs, 1966). Nor do sociologists view the development of language and meaning as essential for deriving measures of everyday social organization.

Recent work in linguistics, language socialization, and research on the properties making up everyday practical reasoning suggest radical changes in conventional sociological conceptions of norms, socialization and the acquisition of rules by children. In this paper I will draw upon these advances to outline a sociological conception of the developmental acquisition of rules by children. Such a perspective is a necessary prerequisite to more precise measurement of social organization as opposed to measurement by fiat (Cicourel, 1964).

Theory of language and linguistic descriptions

The literature on language and linguistic analysis cannot be summarized in this paper, but some elementary notions are needed to reveal the sociologist's use of these materials in pursuing his concern with language and meaning in the measurement of social organization. A recent book by Katz (1966, pp.

110–12) provides a convenient statement of modern linguistic theory with which to commence the discussion.

The theory of language consists of three subtheories, each of which corresponds to one of the three components of a linguistic description and provides a statement of that organization of that component in a linguistic description. We use the terms *phonological theory*, *syntactic theory* (which together comprise *grammatical theory*), and *semantic theory* to refer to these subtheories. We use the terms *phonological component*, *syntactic component*, and *semantic component* to refer, respectively, to the three corresponding parts of a linguistic description. The phonological component is a statement of the rules by which a speaker deals with the speech sounds of his language; the syntactic component is a statement of the rules by which he organizes such sounds into sentential structures; and the semantic component is a statement of the rules by which he interprets sentences as meaningful messages.

The syntactic component of a linguistic description is a set of rules that generates an infinite class of abstract formal structures, each of which describes the syntactic organization of a sentence. It is the source of the inputs to both the phonological and semantic components. The phonological component operates on such formal objects to determine their phonetic shape, while the semantic component operates on them to determine their meaning. Both the phonological and semantic components are, therefore, purely interpretive: they relate the abstract formal structures underlying sentences to a scheme for pronunciation, on the one hand, and to a representation of conceptualization, on the other. The absence of a connection between the phonological and the semantic components accounts for the generally acknowledged fact about natural languages that sounds and meanings are arbitrarily related.

Particular linguistic descriptions must show how semantic interpretations are connected to phonetic representations of a given natural language. The elegance of modern linguistics for sociologists, however, cannot rest with ideal formulations about the tacit knowledge (Chomsky, 1965; Chomsky and Halle, 1965) actual speakers possess about their language, nor with the idealization assumed when ignoring distractions in speech, false starts, paralinguistic intonational features, jokes, memory limitation, antinomies, ironies, and the like. Chomsky's work on generative grammar refers to a system of rules to enable the linguist to assign structural descriptions to sentences under the assumption that a speaker who has mastered the language has internalized the grammar regardless of his awareness or potential awareness of the rules of grammar he has used. The concern, therefore, is not with the speaker's reports and viewpoints.

Thus a generative grammar attempts to specify what the speaker actually knows, not what he may report about his knowledge. Similarly, a theory of visual perception would attempt to account for what a person actually sees and the mechanisms that determine this rather than his statements about what he sees and why, though these statements may provide useful, in fact, compelling evidence for such a theory.

To avoid what has been a continuing misunderstanding, it is perhaps worth while to reiterate that a generative grammar is not a model for a speaker or a hearer. It attempts to characterize in the most neutral possible terms the knowledge of the language that provides the basis for actual use of language by a speaker-hearer. When we speak of a grammar as generating a sentence with a certain structural description, we mean simply that the grammar assigns this structural description to the sentence. When we say that a sentence has a certain derivation with respect to a particular generative grammar, we say nothing about how the speaker or hearer might proceed, in some practical or efficient way, to construct such a derivation. These questions belong to the theory of language use – the theory of performance (Chomsky, 1965, pp. 8–9).

In stressing what Katz calls the epistemology of linguistic descriptions and a theory of language, rather than performance (viewed as falling within psychology), Chomsky (1965, p. 10) relies heavily upon 'acceptable utterances', or what I will call a 'normal form' of everyday usage, or 'utterances that are perfectly natural and immediately comprehensible without paper-and-pencil analysis, and in no way bizarre or outlandish'. The sociologist, however, must be interested in competence *and* performance or situated usage, for it is the interaction of competence and performance that is essential for understanding everyday activities. Imputations of competence by members to each other and the recognition of this competence are integral elements of projected and 'successful' social action. Normal form social behaviour is comparable to the notion of 'acceptable utterances'. Chomsky's statement that generative grammar seeks to specify 'what the speaker actually knows' suggests a strong theory about everyday common knowledge. Yet such a notion remains vague and ambiguous in work on generative grammar, and is almost totally divorced from the socially organized settings of communication. The critical issue for the sociologist would be what everyday speaker-hearers assume 'everyone knows'. Thus members' tacit knowledge about 'what everyone knows' is integral to normal-form behaviour.

A central concept of the chapter is that 'interpretive procedures' as opposed to 'surface rules' (norms) are similar to, but in many ways different from, Chomsky's distinction between 'deep structure' (for rendering a semantic interpretation to sentences) and 'surface structure' (for designating phonetic interpretation to sentences), for interpretive procedures are constitutive of the member's sense of social structure or organization. The acquisition of interpretive procedures provides the actor with a basis for assigning meaning to his environment or a sense of social structure, thus orienting him to the relevance of 'surface rules' or norms. This fundamental distinction between interpretive procedures and surface rules is seldom recognized in conventional sociological theories. The conventional way of suggesting the existence of interpretive procedures is to refer to the notion of the 'definition of the situation'. But in using this phrase, the sociologist does not attempt to specify the structure of norms and attitudes, nor indicate how internalized norms and attitudes enable the actor to assign meaning to his environment nor how such norms and attitudes are developmentally acquired and assume regulated usage. The traditional strategy of the sociologist is to endow his model of the actor with the ability to assign meanings, but only after assuming that internalized attitudes and norms provide automatic guides to role-taking. The internalization of norms is assumed to lead to an automatic application of rules on appropriate occasions. Appropriateness, however, is not explained, nor is it viewed as developmentally and situationally constrained. When deviance is said to arise, it is deviance *vis-à-vis* the idealized surface rules as conceived by members and/or sociologists. But surface rules or norms presuppose interpretive procedures and can be consulted only after the fact (as written rules or social customs) for revealing the detection and labelling of deviance.

The problem of meaning or semantic interpretations of sentences (as bounded by formal grammatical rules or across open texts) is similar to the idea of inherently meaningful internalized norms and attitudes; there is an implication that a lexicon exists with obvious meanings for all competent users. But linguistic or philosophical constructions such as that presented by Fodor and Katz (1964), Katz and Postal (1964), or Katz (1966), are not very useful because lexical entries in dictionaries and search procedures for obtaining semantic categories of language are of little use to an anthropologist or sociologist dealing with members' natural speech, in which the attribution of meaning in everyday settings is by reliance upon 'what everyone knows'. Cryptic utterances are generated under the assumption that their situated meanings are obvious. In field and laboratory settings respondents or subjects and researchers continually use 'what everyone knows' to ask questions, give instructions, write down 'satisfactory' answers, and interpret the content of responses or conversations. Members in natural conversations obviously engage in similar uses of 'what everyone knows'. The reliance on assumed common knowledge facilitates practical exchanges. We are dealing with oral lexicons whose connection with written dictionaries is unknown and often remote or irrelevant. The acquisition of this oral lexicon by children, and a grammar that permits manipulations and efficient usage of the lexicon, are embedded in a semantic field that can be understood only by reference to the acquisition of interpretive procedures or a sense of social structure. The developmental acquisition of interpretive procedures presumes that a semantic input to sound and syntax means that initial or simplified interpretive procedures precede or accompany the acquisition of grammar.

Two problems require clarification here:

1. The establishment of a lexicon and rules for transforming lexical items into detached cognitive meanings (as opposed to situated or actual social scenes) must be separated from the interpretive procedures that make lexical items relevant in actual social contexts. The idea of performance requires an extension of dictionary meanings into their socially organized use in unfolding action scenes (cf. Gumperz, 1966).

2. Interpretive procedures are always operative within, or in reference to, social settings, and their necessary use in making norms recognizable and relevant in particular and general cases means that semantic issues are not independent of syntactic, phonological and ecological features, or of situated body movements and gestures. Further, the properties making up interpretive procedures are not hypothetical, but can be derived from behavioural manipulations of socially organized settings. Thus, interpretive procedures are not to be equated or confused with deep structure syntactic rules, despite a suggested similarity in function. Finally, the necessary reliance upon a corpus of common knowledge ('what anyone knows') is not to be confused with intended or truncated substantive issues that emerge in actual exchanges between members. The members' use of and reliance upon, this presumed corpus are invariant properties of interpretive procedures.

The acquisition of language and meaning

The problem of meaning for the anthropologist-sociologist can be stated as how members of a society or culture acquire a sense of social structure to enable them to negotiate everyday activities. But the developmental acquisition of interpretive procedures and surface rules by children cannot ignore a theory of language acquisition consistent with linguistic theory. Recent work (McNeill, 1966a; Lyons and Wales, 1966) stressing the necessity of coordinating the formulation of linguistic theory with studies of language acquisition requires supplementation by the anthropologist-sociologist; the semantic input to phonology and syntax becomes more than a function of an existing lexical domain formalized by a dictionary with appropriate search procedures for deciding or assigning meaning to utterances. A reference to the competence and performance activities of native speakers requires some commitment to how the former is detectable through the latter in empirical studies, and how both depend upon a developmental acquisition of interpretive procedures for acquiring and retrieving (or invoking) an appropriate vocabulary or terminology in actual encounters. Thus a child's vocabulary is filtered by his interpretive procedures and its retrieval depends upon the same structure *vis-à-vis* recognition decisions as to appropriateness in unfolding interaction. A reference to the child's exposure to, and imitation of, adult speech cannot ignore the role of interpretive procedures for assigning relevance to such speech and the retrieval of stored information triggered by auto stimulation and/or the perception and interpretation of an environment of objects over time.

The proposal that children acquire a rich and intricate grammatical competence in about thirty months (from around eighteen to forty-eight months of age), suggests the parallel assertion about the development of interpretive procedures prior to and during this period of language development. For the anthropologist-sociologist the semantic input to the phonological and syntactic components during the acquisition of grammar must go beyond a reference to:

1. Branching rules dealing with grammatical functions and grammatical relations.
2. Subcategorization rules dealing with syntactic features for subcategorizing lexical categories.

The syntactic component of a grammar is said to be made up of a base that generates deep structures. The deep structures take on semantic interpretations from lexical items in sentences and from the grammatical functions and relations the lexical items possess in the underlying structures. A transformational part of grammatical theory that is solely interpretive maps deep structures into surface structures. Chomsky (1965, pp. 141–2) provides a succinct statement of the form of grammar:

A grammar contains a syntactic component, a semantic component, and a phonological component. The latter two are purely interpretive; they play no part in the recursive generation of sentence structures. The syntactic component consists of a base and a transformational component. The base, in turn, consists of a categorical subcomponent and a lexicon. The base generates deep structures. A deep structure enters the semantic component and receives a semantic interpretation; it is mapped by the transformational rules into a surface structure, which is then given a phonetic interpretation by the rules of the phonological component. Thus the grammar assigns semantic interpretations to signals, this association being mediated by the recursive rules of the syntactic components.

The categorical subcomponent of the base consists of a sequence of context-free rewriting rules. The function of these rules is, in essence, to define a certain system of grammatical relations that determine semantic interpretation, and to specify an abstract underlying order of elements that makes possible the functioning of the transformational rules. . . .

The lexicon consists of an unordered set of lexical entries and certain redundancy rules. Each lexical entry is a set of features (but see note 15 of chapter 2 ['If we regard a lexical entry as a set of features, then items that are similar in sound, meaning, or syntactic function will not be related to one another in the lexicon']). Some of these are phonological features, drawn from a particular universal set of phonological features (the distinctive-features system). The set of phonological features in a lexical entry can be extracted and represented as a phonological matrix that bears the relation 'is a' to each of the specified syntactic features belonging to the lexical entry. Some of the features are semantic features. These, too, are presumably drawn from a universal 'alphabet', but little is known about this today, and nothing has been said about it here.

Chomsky's formulation stresses the role of the syntactic component of grammar for assigning meaning to the lexicon of its base and the signals produced by the transformation of deep structure into surface structure phonetic interpretations. If syntactic rules govern the lexicon and the context-free rewriting rules for defining the grammatical relations determining semantic interpretations, then the structure of social interaction (or the scenic features of social settings) would not possess independent status, but always be 'known' to members of a society *vis-à-vis* grammatical rules. Hence social reality would be generated by universal features of language possessed by all competent ('normal') humans. Cultural differences would presumably stem from some as yet unknown higher order grammatical rules that would permit variations in expression, but would remain consistent with universal features of a grammar's three components. The semantic component and its subservience to syntax in Chomsky's formulation is obscure and suffers from impoverished development. I shall assume it can be ignored and offer a different construction, one that claims an interaction between the particular grammatical forms actually used in daily social exchanges (not the ideal context-free forms used by some linguists), and the interpretations of language performance that can be made independently of syntactic structures, or where syntactic knowledge is either misleading or of limited use. Hence formal syntactic rules can be generated in cultural settings or can remain oral traditions: once they are available and used in socially prescribed and sanctioned ways, however, they constrain (although not completely) interpretations assigned by members. The existence or lack of constraints remains an empirical problem touched only barely by researchers. Rather than get involved in a Humboldt-Sapir-Whorf hypothesis discussion, I think the issue can be clarified if we ask how new recruits to a society are socialized and how they acquire a sense of social structure. The fact that recent work on developmental psycholinguistics has used a generative grammar model for studying the acquisition of syntax provides additional material for examining the syntax-semantic correspondence and for suggesting what properties an independent semantic component might contain.

The significance of taking a developmental approach to problems of interpretive procedures and surface rule acquisition is that adults are continually supplying children with lexical items or categories whose meaning can be decided only partially by reference to adult oral and written dictionaries, and where instructions by adults to children about meaning are not equivalent to an adult's use of written dictionaries. Oral dictionaries of the young child have been called 'holophrastic' (McNeill, 1966a, p. 63) because the words of such a corpus are presumed to stand for sentences. Such words reveal the necessity of a notion like interpretive procedures for understanding the child's ability to decide simple appropriateness. Instructions to a child require making problematic adult notions of 'what everyone knows'. Hence Chomsky's proposals can be examined in natural languages by treating the socialization process as an experimental setting within which performance generates exchanges useful for clarifying how competence might be attributed to children. Adult instructions, therefore, presume competence and syntactic, phonological and semantic relevances. Brown and Bellugi (1964) also suggest there is a world view (or culture-bound world view) communicated by these instructions, but they do not state how the child's conception of social structure is developed.

I am assuming that a world view is an observer's loose way of talking about culture-bound substantive attitudinal types of orientations to one's environment, and not a specification of universal properties of interpretive procedures for acquiring a general sense of social structure. It seems reasonable to propose that the particular substantive outcomes generated by interpretive procedures are culture-bound and permit the recognition of normal forms of objects and events, the presence of danger, a sense of fairness or injustice in cultural settings. Interpretive procedures prepare the environment for substantive or practical considerations in which a world view is presumed to be an abstract, central, orientational schema. But the world view (or related world views) of a particular culture is not an invariant orienting schema, and like the class of attainable grammars (Chomsky, 1965, p. 35) is not to be equated with universal features of interpretive procedures necessary for an adequate stipulation of how social order is possible and sustained over time. The generation or production of social structures, their maintenance and change over time, therefore, can be observed in the child's developmental and innovative acquisition of interpretive procedures and surface rules.

The view that the young child speaks an esoteric language fluently and does not merely produce an inadequate or incomplete adult language that can be analysed with categories of adult grammar (McNeill, 1966a, p. 16; 1966b) is relevant for describing the acquisition of interpretive procedures. The child's conception of the social world should not be studied by imposing as yet unclarified adult conceptions of normal social structures. Although initial interpretive procedures do not permit the child to comprehend adult humour, *double entendres*, antinomies, and the like, but do generate esoteric childhood social structures in which it is possible to fear stuffed animals on display in a museum, be whisked away by witches at night, and believe in the existence of Batman and Robin.

The sociologist cannot rest with a description of the child's performance in social settings; he must explain behavioural activities with a model of how the child's interpretive procedures and surface rule competence generate behavioural displays. The notion that the child possesses a simple grammar which generates telegraphic speech (Brown and Fraser, 1963; Brown and Bellugi, 1964; McNeill, 1966a) implies that the child's sense of social structure (his interpretive procedures and surface rule competence) generates childhood conceptions of social organization. It is difficult to convince the three- and four-year-old child that the 'monsters' and 'bad guys' are not going to 'somehow' inflict their nasty deeds upon him, in the same way that it is difficult to convince him of the dangers of crossing the street. The child initially acquires simple properties of interpretive procedures and surface rules which permit him to detect restricted classes of normal forms in voice intonation, physical appearance, facial expressions, cause and effect, story beginnings and endings, simple games, and the like; he finds it difficult if not impossible to understand exceptions and explanations of them which often terminate with 'that's the way it is'. Adult descriptions of the 'why' of everyday life to children provide a rich source of information on adult notions of simplified social structures. As has been suggested by McNeill (1966a, p. 51) with regard to the child's early speech – its severely limited grammatical competence which does not reflect the operation of transformational rules – the child's ability to comprehend subtleties in social organization, particularly surface rules involving possession of property, privacy, or the combined interpretive procedures and surface rule subtleties contained in antinomies and jokes, requires adult transformations of meaning. The child is forced to suspend the relevance of appearances, for example, when he is told that something is poisonous when it 'looks like candy'.

But I am only speculating about developmental problems in the acquisition of interpretive procedures and surface rules. We have little or no solid empirical information or even consistent and imaginative theoretical formulations about the child's acquisition of the properties of interpretive procedures. Therefore, a discussion of interpretive procedures from the vantage point of adult competence is necessary.

Some properties of interpretive procedures

The use of the term 'rules' (or legal and extra-legal norms) in everyday life usually means various prescriptive and proscriptive norms (Morris, 1956; Bierstedt, 1957; Williams, 1960; Gibbs, 1966). I have labelled such norms surface rules. In this paper I shall treat norms in everyday life and scientific rules of procedure as legal and extra-legal surface rules governing everyday conduct and scientific inquiry, in keeping with recent work in ethnomethodology (Garfinkel, 1967). By ethnomethodology I mean the study of interpretive procedures and surface rules in everyday social practices and scientific activities. Hence a concern with everyday practical reasoning becomes a study in how members employ interpretive procedures to recognize the relevance of surface rules and convert them into practised and enforced behaviour. Scientific research has its ideal or normative conceptions of how inquiry is conducted as well as implicit or intuitive strategies followed by individual researchers and promoted by different 'schools'. Paradigms of 'normal science' (Kuhn, 1962) emerge in different fields to define temporally enforceable strategies of research and bodies of acceptable propositions. As Michael Polanyi (1958) has argued, the scientist's success in his research relies heavily upon 'tacit knowledge' or unstated knowledge that cannot be articulated into surface rules. Interpretive procedures in everyday life and scientific research, however, are not 'rules' in the sense of such general policies or practices like operational definitions or legal and extra-legal norms, where a sense of a 'right' and 'wrong' pre- or proscriptive norm or practice is at issue. Instead they are part of all inquiry yet exhibit empirically defensible properties that 'advise' the member about an infinite collection of behavioural displays, and provide him with a sense of social structure (or, in the case of scientific activity, provide an intuitive orientation to an area of inquiry). I assume that interpretive and surface rules govern normal science in the same sense in which everyday social behaviour requires that members generate and use 'acceptable' descriptive accounts about their environments; scientists seek accounts that can be viewed and accepted as recognizable and intelligible displays of social reality. Scientific procedures orient the researcher's conception of normal science surface rules in normative or actual practice.

The child cannot be taught to understand and use surface rules unless he acquires a sense of social structure, a basis for assigning meaning to his environment. The acquisition of language rules is like the acquisition of norms; they both presuppose interpretive procedures. The child must learn to articulate a general rule or policy (a norm) with a particular event or case said to fall under the general rule (Rawls, 1955). There are no surface rules for instructing the child (or adult) on how the articulation is to be made.

Members of a society must acquire the competence to assign meaning to their environment so that surface rules and their articulation with particular cases can be made. Hence interpretive procedures are invariant properties of everyday practical reasoning necessary for assigning sense to the substantive rules sociologists usually call norms. Surface rules, therefore, always require some recognition and cognition about the particulars which would render given rules as appropriate and useful for understanding and dealing with actual behavioural displays. Hence all surface rules carry an open structure or horizon *vis-à-vis* some boundable collection of meanings until they are linked to particular cases by interpretative procedures.

Linking interpretive procedures and surface rules presumes a generative model in the sense of Chomsky's work on generative or transformational grammar. The interpretive procedures prepare and sustain an environment of objects for inference and action *vis-à-vis* a culture-bound world view and the written and 'known in common' surface rules. And just as a generative grammar is not a model for a speaker or a hearer (Chomsky, 1965, p. 9), but a basis for revealing how actual use is possible, the idea of generative or praxiological (Kotarbinski, 1962; Hix, 1954; Garfinkel, 1956) social structure is not a model for well socialized members of a society but an attempt to show:

1. How the acquisition of interpretive procedures and surface rules is necessary for understanding members' everyday activities.

2. How members and researchers assign structural descriptions to all forms of social organization.

An analogous generative or praxiological perspective is suggested in the remark by Goodenough (1964, p. 36): 'As I see it, a society's culture consists of whatever it is one has to know or believe in order to operate in a manner acceptable to its members, and to do so in any role that they accept for any one of themselves.' Stated another way, what must be known about the properties of interpretive procedures and surface rules in order to programme subjects' actions (in field and experimental settings) so that such behaviour can be recognized as 'normal' or routine (or unusual or bizarre) social activity by members?

Our present knowledge of the nature of interpretive procedures is sparse. I do not want to suggest or claim the existence of a 'complete' list (or of any 'list') but will simply describe a few properties to facilitate further discussion.

1. *The reciprocity of perspectives*. Schutz (1953, 1955) describes this property as consisting of

(a) the member's idealization of the interchangeability of standpoints, whereby the speaker and hearer both take for granted that each (A assumes it of B and assumes B assumes it of A, and vice versa) would probably have the same experiences of the immediate scene if they were to change places, and

(b) that until further notice (the emergence of counter-evidence) the speaker and hearer both assume that each can disregard, for the purpose at hand, any differences originating in their personal ways of assigning meaning to, and deciding the relevance of, everyday life activities, such that each can interpret the environment of objects they are both attending in an essentially identical manner for the practical action in question. A corollary of this property is that members assume, and assume others assume it of them, that their descriptive accounts or utterances will be intelligible and recognizable features of a world known in common and taken for granted. The speaker assumes the hearer will expect him to emit utterances that are recognizable and intelligible, and the speaker also assumes that his descriptive accounts are acceptable products and will be so received by the hearer. Finally, the hearer assumes that the speaker has assumed this property for the hearer, and expects to comply with the tacit but sanctioned behaviour of appearing to 'understand' what is being discussed.

2. *The et cetera assumption*. To suggest that speakers and hearers sanction the simulated 'understanding' of each other implies something more than a reciprocity of perspectives. Garfinkel (1964, pp. 247–8) suggests the understanding requires that a speaker and hearer 'fill in' or assume the existence of common understandings or relevances of what is being said on occasions when the descriptive accounts are seen as 'obvious' and even when not immediately obvious. The tolerance for utterances viewed as not obvious or not meaningful depends upon further properties and their reflexive features. The et cetera assumption serves the important function of allowing things to pass despite their ambiguity or vagueness, or allowing the treatment of particular instances as sufficiently relevant or understandable to permit viewing descriptive elements as 'appropriate'. What is critical about the et cetera assumption is its reliance upon particular elements of language itself (lexical items, phrases, idiomatic expressions or *double entendres*, for example) and paralinguistic features of exchanges for 'indexing' (Garfinkel, 1967) the course and meaning of the conversation. I return to this problem below. But notice that neither the reciprocity of perspectives nor the et cetera assumption imply that consensus exists or is necessary; rather, they indicate that a presumed 'agreement' to begin, sustain, and terminate interaction will occur despite the lack of conventional notions about the existence of substantive consensus to explain concerted action.

3. *Normal forms*. Reference to a reciprocity of perspectives and the et cetera assumption presumes the existence of certain normal forms of acceptable talk and appearances upon which members rely for assigning sense to their

environments. Thus, on occasions when the reciprocity of perspectives is in doubt (when the appearance of the speaker or hearer, or the talk itself, is not viewed as recognizable and intelligible such that the et cetera assumption cannot overcome discrepancies or ambiguities) efforts will be made by both speaker and hearer to normalize the presumed discrepancies (this is similar in sense to the reduction of dissonance or incongruity, cf. Festinger, 1957; Brown, 1962; 1965). But, unlike the social psychologist's interest in dissonance, the anthropologist-sociologist's attention must be directed to the recognition and description of normal forms, and to how members' linguistic and paralinguistic behaviour reveals the ways in which interpretive procedures and surface rules are called into question and the ways in which the social scene is sustained as dissonant or is restored to some sense of normality. Competent members (those who can expect to manage their affairs without interference and be treated as 'acceptable types') recognize and employ normal forms in daily interaction under the assumption that all communication is embedded within a body of common knowledge or 'what everyone knows' (Garfinkel, 1964, pp. 237–8).

4. *Retrospective-prospective sense of occurrence.* Routine conversation depends upon speakers and hearers waiting for later utterances to decide what was intended before. Speakers and hearers both assume that what each says to the other has, or will have at some subsequent moment, the effect of clarifying a presently ambiguous utterance or a descriptive account with promisory overtones. This property of interpretive procedures enables the speaker and hearer to maintain a sense of social structure despite deliberate or presumed vagueness on the part of the participants in an exchange. Waiting for later utterances (that may never come) to clarify present descriptive accounts, or 'discovering' that earlier remarks or incidents now clarify a present utterance, provide continuity to everyday communication.

The properties of interpretive procedures have been ignored because sociologists have taken them for granted when pursuing their own research, particularly research in their own society. Hence the sociologist invokes the properties of interpretive rules as a necessary part of making sense of the activities and environment of members he studies, and his use of these properties is derived from his own membership in the society, not from his professional training or from knowledge gained from research. Members use the properties of interpretive procedures to clarify and make routine sense of their own environments, and sociologists must view such activities (and their own work) as practical methods for constructing and sustaining social order.

Garfinkel (1966) has suggested that the properties of practical reasoning (what I am calling interpretive procedures) be viewed as a collection of instructions to members by members, and as a sort of continual (reflexive) feedback whereby members assign meaning to their environment. The interpretive procedures, therefore, have reflexive features linking their properties to actual scenes such that appropriate surface rules are seen as relevant for immediate or future inference and action. The reflexive features of talk can be viewed as saying that the properties of interpretive procedures, as a collection, are reflexive because they are necessary for members to orient themselves

(a) In the presence of, but not in contact with (for example, driving a car alone), other members.

(b) During face-to-face or telephone exchanges.

(c) In the absence of actual contact with others.

The properties of interpretive procedures provide members with a sense of social order during periods of solitary living, and they are integral to actual contact with others (though the contact may vary from walking alone in a crowded street, to sitting on a bus but not conversing, to actual exchanges with others). Within talk and in the absence of talk, reflexive features of interpretive procedures operate to provide a continuous feedback to members about the routine sense of what is happening. Hence physical features of the ecological scene, the members' presence or absence, the existence or absence, of conversation and features of talk within conversation, all provide the participants with continuous 'instructions' for orienting themselves to their environment and deciding appropriate inferences and action.

5. *Talk itself as reflexive*. Talk is reflexive to participants because it is seen as fundamental to 'normal' scenes. I am not referring to the content of talk but simply its presence during speech and the expectation that particular forms of speech will give a setting the appearance of something recognizable and intelligible. The timing of speech (as opposed to deliberate or random hesitation and alterations of normal-form intonational contours) and the timing of periods of silence or such occasional reminders of normal speech like the 'uh huh', 'I see', 'ah', 'oh', reflexively guide both speaker and hearer throughout exchanges. The observer must also make use of reflexive features to assign normal form significance to a scene or sequence of scenes as a condition for deciding the content of talk. Talk provides members with information about the appropriateness of occasions. Garfinkel notes that talk is a constituent feature of all settings because members count on its presence as an indication that 'all is well', and members also use talk as a built-in feature of some arrangement of activities to produce a descriptive account of those same arrangements. Thus the member's accounting of some arrangement relies upon the talk itself as a necessary way of communicating the recognizable and intelligible elements of the scene. Talk is con-

tinuously folded back upon itself so that the presence of 'proper' talk and further talk provide both a sense of 'all is well' and a basis for members to describe the arrangement successfully to each other.

6. *Descriptive vocabularies as indexical expressions.* In recommending further reflexive features of the properties of interpretive procedures I draw upon Garfinkel's discussion of how members take for granted their reliance upon the existence and use of descriptive vocabularies for handling bodies of information and activities, where the vocabularies themselves are constituent features of the experiences being described. The vocabularies are an index of the experience. But the experiences, in the course of being generated or transformed, acquire elements of the vocabularies as part of the generative process and permit the retrieval of information indexed by selected elements of the original vocabularies. Garfinkel uses catalogues in libraries as an example of this reflexive feature of practical reasoning. The titles used to index reports to facilitate a search for something, are invariably part of the vocabulary that went into the terminologies or vocabularies of the very experiences they describe. The catalogues are terminologies or vocabularies of the experiences they describe. Several years ago Bar-Hillel (1954) noted the necessity of indexical expressions in ordinary language, stating that context is essential but that different sentences might require knowing different common knowledge or presumed common knowledge to give them some kind of interpretation. Thus it might be necessary to know where the utterance was made, who made it, and its temporal character. The significance of conversational or written indexical expressions, however, cannot be stated as merely a problem in pragmatic context; rather it requires some reference to the role of 'what everyone knows' in deciding the indexicality of the utterance or some part of the utterance. The significance of descriptive vocabularies as indexical expressions lies in their providing both members and researchers with 'instructions' for recovering or retrieving the 'full' relevance of an utterance; suggesting what anyone must presume or 'fill in' in order to capture the fidelity of a truncated or indexical expression whose sense requires a specification of common assumptions about context (the time or occasion of the expression, who the speaker was, where the utterance was made, and the like). Brown and Bellugi (1964, pp. 146–7) suggest elements of this problem in discussing parental expansions of children's speech:

How does a mother decide on the correct expansion of one of her child's utterances? Consider the utterance 'Eve lunch'. So far as grammar is concerned this utterance could be appropriately expanded in any one of a number of ways: 'Eve is having lunch'; 'Eve had lunch'; 'Eve will have lunch'; 'Eve's lunch', and so forth. On the occasion when Eve produced the utterance, however, one expansion seemed more appropriate than any other. It was then the noon hour, Eve was sitting at the table with a plate of food before her and her spoon and fingers were busy. In these circumstances 'Eve lunch' had to mean 'Eve is having lunch'. A little later when the plate had been stacked in the sink and Eve was getting down from her chair the utterance 'Eve lunch' would have suggested the expansion 'Eve has had her lunch'. Most expansions are responsive not only to the child's words but also to the circumstances attending their utterance.

Brown and Bellugi are concerned with how the mother decides the appropriateness of expansions under situational constraints. But there are several problems here: the child's telegraphic utterance viewed as a reflection of a simple grammar of less complexity than adult grammar, thus endowing the child with limited competence; the adult expansion that encodes elements of social organization not coded by the child's telegraphic utterance; the child's utterance as indexical to children's grammar; and the adult's various expansions decided according to the indexicality deemed appropriate to the situational constraints or context. We should not confuse children's normal forms and the child's ability to recognize and use indexical expressions with the adult's stock of normal forms and typical usage of indexical expressions for encoding broader conceptions of social organization than those possessed by the child. When Brown and Bellugi (1964, pp. 147–8) suggest that a mother's expansion of a child's speech is more than teaching grammar, that it is providing the child with elements of a world view, there is the presumption of a developmental acquisition of social structure. Hence the child's creation of social meanings not provided by an adult model would parallel the creation of children's grammar not based exclusively upon a model provided by an adult but generated by innovative elements of the child's deep structure grammar. The child's creative attempts at constructing social reality or social structure and grammar can be viewed as generated by a simple conception of indexicality stemming from developmental stages in the acquisition of the properties of interpretive procedures and deep structure grammatical rules. The acquisition of interpretive procedures would parallel the acquisition of language, with the child's interpretive procedures gradually replaced or displaced by adult interpretive procedures.

A necessary condition of animal and human socialization, therefore, is the acquisition of interpretive procedures. Sufficient conditions for appropriate use of language and interpretive rules in actual settings include:

1. The acquisition of childhood rules (gradually transformed into adult surface rules).

2. Interpretive procedures and their reflexive features as instructions for negotiating social scenes over time.

Hence members are continually giving each other instructions (verbal and nonverbal cues and content) as to their intentions, social character, biographies, and the like. *The interpretive procedures and their reflexive features provide continuous instructions to participants such that members can be said to be programming each other's actions as the scene unfolds.* Whatever is built into the members as part of their normal socialization is activated by social scenes, but there is no automatic programming; the participants' interpretive procedures and reflexive features become instructions by processing the behavioural scene of appearances, physical movements, objects, gestures, sounds, into inferences that permit action. The progressive acquisition of interpretive procedures and surface rules is reflected in how children and adults interact, or how children interact with other children. Children continually rehearse their acquisition of social structure (and language) in ways reminiscent of adults rehearsing for a play or translating a written play into a live production. But in the latter cases the interpretive procedures and surface rules are already built-in elements of the actors, while in children it is possible to observe different stages of complexity over time. For example, the child's ability to learn surface rules governing a game follows a developmental sequence, and his ability to decide the relevance and applicability of surface rules is always a function of the development of interpretive procedures.

The child's conception of 'fairness' in games, play or family settings cannot be specified by reference to surface rules. Nor will any conception of norms now available in the sociological literature provide a basis for explaining how the child learns eventually to distinguish between games and their normal forms, and everyday life activities and their normal forms. What seems plausible despite little or no empirical evidence is that children acquire interpretive procedures prior to their use of language, and that they develop normal forms of voice intonation and expect their usage by others. Children are able to recognize and insist upon normal form spacing in speech and to develop their own indexical expressions.

The child's acquisition of social structure, therefore, begins with a simple conception of interpretive procedures and surface rules, and his stock of common knowledge is expressed initially in the form of single lexemes whose meaning by parents is usually judged by reference to imputations of childhood competence and adult meanings. Inasmuch as our knowledge of adult recognition and usage of meanings is unclear, a word about this problem is in order before going on to strategies for the semantic analysis of adult speech that could be useful for following the development of meaning in children.

Kernal and fringe meanings and their situational embeddedness

Earlier I remarked that members obviously are capable of carrying on conversations endlessly without recourse to a written dictionary by invoking an oral dictionary derived from common knowledge. The field researcher must obviously utilize the same oral dictionary in deciding the import of his observations despite the possibility of asking natives for definitions or referents. But in referring to an oral dictionary we lack a check as to its accuracy or the extent to which communicants actually refer to the 'same' oral dictionary. The child's acquisition of language, interpretive procedures and surface rules is complicated by exposure to limited oral dictionaries in different households, but we are still rather ignorant about the sequence of development here. I assume that the acquisition of meaning structures and the use of lexical items is governed by the development of interpretive procedures. Interpretive procedures, therefore, filter the acquisition and use of lexical items intended as indexical semantic inputs and outputs. Hence the use of an *etic* framework presupposes an *emic* perspective (following the usage by Pike, 1954); the researcher's use of formal grammatical or semantic (dictionary) categories provides an etic framework imposed upon unclarified emic elements used by both subjects and researcher. If we assume that children's language, interpretive procedures, surface rules, and common knowledge as opposed to adult conceptions, are contrastive sets that overlap because of developmental stages of acquisition, then our theories must include their developmental organization and reorganization as well as rules for their contrast. Modern approaches to the problem of meaning in philosophy, linguistics, psychology, and anthropology, however, do not deal with the problem of knowledge as socially distributed (Schutz, 1955, pp. 195–6).

Some things can be supposed as well known and self-explanatory and others as needing an explanation, depending upon whether I talk to a person of my sex, age, and occupation, or to somebody not sharing with me this common situation with society, or whether I talk to a member of my family, a neighbour, or to a stranger, to a partner or a nonparticipant in a particular venture, etc.

William James has already observed that a language does not merely consist in the content of an ideally complete dictionary and an ideally complete and arranged grammar. The dictionary gives us only the kernal of the meaning of the words which are surrounded by 'fringes'. We may add that these fringes are of various kinds: those originating in a particular personal use by the speaker, others originating in the context of speech in which the term is used, still others depending upon the addressee of my speech, or the situation in which the speech occurs, or the purpose of the communication, and, finally, upon the problem at hand to be solved.

Members' common knowledge permits typical imputations of behaving, dress, talking, motives, social standing and the like to others in everyday exchanges, and each developmental stage in the socialization process alters and utilizes interpretive procedures and surface rules, language, and non-verbal behaviour.

A characteristic feature of speech is its embeddedness or entification (Campbell, 1966) as the dialogue or written document unfolds. Initial use of speech presupposes kernals and fringes embedded in past experiences, or it may rely upon a written dictionary for structuring the assignment of meaning to early parts of exchanges and in later dialogue. I will mention only three general contexts within which the problem of embeddedness or entification is basic to semantic analysis.

1. The construction of written reports intended for general audiences or the preparation of a radio script or news broadcast does not permit immediate face-to-face exchanges between members; the use of embedded terms or phrases is usually restricted. Radio announcers with their own 'show' may presume an audience with whom embedded talk may be used, particularly if the programme consists of music designed for adolescent consumption. Radio stations with programmes directed to Negro audiences invariably presume their listeners are socialized to highly embedded speech. A news broadcast, therefore, would rely upon normal form speech.

2. Strangers meeting for the first time must rely upon appearances and a minimum of embedded speech, but interpretive procedures continually provide information as to the interpretation of appearances, initial speech, and nonverbal behaviour. The reflexive features become operational indicators of the sense of what is 'happening'. As strangers continue talking they may begin to develop embedded usage that can sustain particular relationships between them and evoke particular meanings with truncated expressions on later occasions. Embedded terms and phrases become indexical expressions carrying fringe information that encodes meaning structures considerably beyond kernal or denotative meanings. When strangers meet, therefore, conversations can remain superficial, relying upon appearances to make the setting recognizable and intelligible, or the exchanges can lead to progressive embeddings and elaborations that interlace the biographies of the speakers. The recursive folding back of speech by members that creates embedded talk is reflexive because such talk and accompanying nonverbal behaviour provide instructions indicating the relationship is or is not evolving into something more intimate. Embeddedness leads to the use of and reliance upon *double entendres*, antinomies, and parodies, thus enabling members to sanction indexical expressions as evidences of intimacy or 'friendlier' relations.

3. Acquaintances not only presuppose and use normal form expressions when conversing with each other, but demand embedded expressions to ensure and reaffirm the existence of past relationships. Treating embedded terms and phrases as indexical expressions enables members to talk about things not present (Hockett, 1959; Hockett and Ascher, 1964) and fill in 'what everyone knows' to create or sustain a normal form. Intimates' use of embedded speech relies upon connotative meanings built up over time. A componential analysis of such speech leading to denotative meanings presumes preliminary knowledge (or conjectures) by the researcher of interpretive procedures and surface rules. Members' use of terms from everyday social organization for the researcher's benefit become somewhat arbitrary abstractions or artificially constructed indexical expressions that are not clearly articulated with actual use by particular members on speci-fiable occasions of talk. If we wish to ask natives for denotative meanings about the use of kin terms it might be more appropriate to have them begin with childhood practices rather than with adult usage. The problem is similar to one posed by Brown and Bellugi on how we decide the appropri-ateness of a child's utterance; without contextual cues for deciding the sense of social structure required for inference and action the expression's rele-vance cannot be clarified. The elicitation procedures of componential analysts or ethno-semanticists are not always clear on this point. Frake (1961; 1964), however, does link abstract procedures to actual arrangements.

In each of the above general conversational settings members must assume the existence of an oral dictionary of 'what everyone knows'. The use of embedded terms and phrases in conversations generates meanings for indexing particular social relationships between members and becomes reflexive for members by instructing them on the unfolding relevance of lexical items in the course of attributing structure and 'sameness' to social objects and events. The measurement of social organization must include how embedded speech and its reflexive features enable members to mark off and identify settings into relevant categories for generating and deciding upon the appropriateness and meaning of communication. How members accomplish the task of assigning relevance to their environments enables the researcher to find measurement categories in everyday behaviour. In addition to how members employ categories signifying quantity (Churchill, 1966), the problem is also how members utilize particular social categories in situationally bounded sequences, under the assumption that normal forms of language and meaning prevail. The particular use of categories and the assumption of normal forms permits members to 'close' the stream of conversation such that sets are created permitting exclusion and inclusion of linguistic and paralinguistic behaviour into meaningful inferences about 'what happened'. The 'closing' operations presume members have 'frozen' temporally constituted imputations of meaning; interpretive procedures and their reflexive features generate a basis for 'freezing' surface structures into socially meaningful sets. Hence interpretive procedures and their reflexive features generate 'sameness' or equivalence in social objects and events in temporally and socially organized contexts according to the social relationships of participating members.

To summarize, members' linguistic and paralinguistic behaviour is transformed by interpretive procedures and their reflexive features into instructions to participants; the unfolding interaction leads to a continuous programming of members. Hence interpretive procedures and their reflexive features lead to behavioural outcomes within unfolding situational constraints. Members, therefore, impose 'measurement' on their environments by the articulation of interpretive procedures and their reflexive features with emergent social scenes.

The child's acquisition of social structure, therefore, begins with simple interpretive procedures and their reflexive features, facilitating the learning of lexical items and the development of an oral dictionary consisting of simple denotative meanings. The situated indexicality of early vocabulary is both grammatical and semantic, because it is assumed that the child with pivotal grammar is not using lexical items as indexical of adult sentences but is expressing telegraphic sentences of his ability to assume and refer to past experiences and/or objects not present. The researcher must restrain himself from imposing measurement categories intended for adults as relevant 'closings' for children's speech. This is difficult to avoid when we are not entirely clear about the nature of children's grammar and lexical domain. Attempts to develop measurement categories by examining the child's speech must follow the dictates of a developmental model and not simply what a researcher assumes is 'obvious' *vis-à-vis* adult meanings. Thus when adults seek to convince children that crossing the street can lead to dreadful consequences, the child's response or behaviour is not exactly unequivocal; the child may laugh at the suggestion. Attempts to explain death also pose difficult problems for adults because we are not clear when interpretive procedures development is adequate for the comprehension of death, especially when it involves the child or his parents. Recent developments, however, suggest some directions we might pursue in the analysis of conversational materials and I now turn to a brief examination of work that is sometimes called 'contrastive analysis'.

Contrastive analysis and the measurement of social organization

When the speaker commits himself to linguistic and social categories, he provides the hearer, himself, and an observer or researcher with information about what he intends. The commitment, however, may be a compromise between what the speaker felt had to be said, what he did not want to say, what he was incapable of saying because of limited vocabulary, intelligence, or the constraints of speaking with a stranger. Utterances ordinarily have a normal form, but the information they carry for all concerned are not unequivocal facts leading to direct and obvious analysis. The analysis will vary with the kind of theory utilized. I have argued for a developmental theory of social knowledge because a cross-section of adults in a particular culture or society does not reveal the invariant conditions making up members' utilization of social structure, for we are dealing with well built-in members who, like Chomsky's acceptable grammatical sentences, are usually committed to masking the ambiguity and problematic character of situational constraints that make up the construction of social reality.

In examining utterances or descriptive accounts of members of a culture or society it is important to recognize that our reliance upon 'what everyone knows', much less a written dictionary, presumes that a world view is built into the message. When logicians or philosophers of language analyse sentences disengaged from their context of occurrence and the biography of the speaker-hearer, the unstated presumption and reliance upon normal forms obscure the implicit ways in which the standardized character of the culture or society is presumed as obvious to members. The assumption of kernal or denotative relevance (but not fringe or connotative relevance) by logicians or philosophers of language (or science) seeks clarity by constructing social reality to fit the narrow form of analysis already judged to be logically adequate. The fringes that become attached because of the occasion of the utterance, the biography of the speaker-hearer, the social relationships assumed, and the like, presume a world view. The substantive content of the communication exchanged is built into the linguistic and social categories employed, as is the normal form of paralinguistic intonational contours emitted, the appearance of the participants, and so forth. The observer is provided a similar basis for assigning structural significance to the descriptive accounts. Our analysis presumes a theory that tightens the organizational space in which the exchange occurs; we can rule out certain contrast sets, include alternatives that are likely until further evidence is identified, and decide that the choice of categories by participants carries particular kernal and fringe meanings despite the restrictions of the code itself, the skills or lack of skills of the participants, and so on. The problem is similar to the parent expanding the child's utterance; the expansion must be responsive to the child's words as well as to the circumstances attending their utterance. Deciding appropriateness presumes knowing something about the parent's conjectures about the child's development. But in dealing with adults qua adults, we presume, as do participants, that each is a well built-in member of the society capable of producing 'acceptable' grammatical sentences in Chomsky's sense. Situational constraints can be simulated in experimental settings, but natural settings defy explicit preprogramming; members must use interpretive procedures and reflexive features as instructions for negotiating all scenes and programming each other successfully through encounters. Contrastive analyses must somehow deal with this problem of appropriateness.

Contrastive analysis has emerged in anthropology via ethnographic studies that depart from traditional ethnographies (Conklin, 1955; 1959; Goodenough, 1964; Lounsbury, 1956; Frake, 1961; 1962). Consider the following statement (Lounsbury, 1956, pp. 161–2):

1. Semantic features may be recognized in more than one way in a language. Some may be recognized overtly, with separate phonemic identities, while others may be recognized covertly, merged with other semantic features in various jointly and simultaneously shared phonemic identities.
2. For a single semantic feature there is sometimes a mixing of the two manners of linguistic recognition: some features emerge, so to speak, at some points to find separate identity in the segmental structure of a language, but are submerged at other points, being identifiable only as possible contrasts between various already irreducible segments. . . .
4. The description of the componential structure of contrasting forms is an important part of linguistic analysis, whether or not the contrasts have any correlates in the segmental structure of forms.

Both Lounsbury and Goodenough stress the importance of kernal or denotative meanings, while lacking a theory that would explain how researchers or members are capable of communicating denotative meanings in some pure form without necessary references to or use of fringe or connotative meanings and the interpretive procedures generating both. Hymes (1962) has suggested a more general framework when he describes the ingredients for developing an ethnography of speaking as knowledge of the kinds of things to be said, in specifiable message forms, to certain types of people, in appropriate situations. In describing the contrastive analysis developed by componential analysts or students of ethnographic semantics, I shall confine myself to Frake's (1964, p. 127) more general and useful viewpoint: 'Of course an ethnography of speaking cannot provide rules specifying exactly what message to select in a given situation. . . . But when a person selects a message, he does so from a set of appropriate alternatives. The task of an ethnographer of speaking is to specify what the appropriate alternatives are in a given situation and what the consequences are of selecting one alternative over another.' The specification of appropriate alternatives presupposes that natives used as informants are all competent members of the society and hence have acquired 'normal' interpretive procedures for deciding appropriateness and assigning relevance or a sense of social structure to situations. Specifying appropriate alternatives is a *post hoc* activity imposed by the researcher upon the actor's retrospective decisions about 'correct' choices.

Contrastiveness depends upon the temporal structuring attributed to unfolding scenes by members and upon members' use of social categories for linking the particulars of actual events to explanations provided by general rules. A further element needed for an ethnography of speaking is evident in the earlier quoted statement by Goodenough (1964, p. 36):

'As I see it, a society's culture consists of whatever it is one has to know or believe in order to operate in a manner acceptable to its members, and do so in any role that they accept for any one of themselves.' But there remains the problem of 'what anyone has to know or believe'.

The specification of alternatives and the presumed classes from which they are chosen require generating rules to structure and transform an environment of objects into meanings that 'close' the stream of behaviour into possible alternatives such that choice reflects both the member's and researcher's perspectives. To assume that the only valuable framework is one that imposes a denotative structure determined by the researcher and divorced from members' imputed intention and usage, reduces the actor to a rather simple 'dummy'. An example would be the child of three years, who is capable of simple grammatical construction and comprehension, telegraphic utterances, and interpretive procedures permitting only simple denotative comprehension of temporally impoverished social interaction, or a sense of social structure with little or no temporal continuity. Elicited denotative meanings would then generate indexical expressions disengaged from fringe meanings used by members in their generation, but the source of the researcher's structural descriptions of members' behaviour would be misleading though self-contained packages of meaning or 'blueprints for behaviour'. Situational constraints and unfolding contingencies are eliminated or minimized, and idealized normative structure becomes the ethnographic focus.

The general procedures leading to contrastive analysis have been stated by Frake (1961).

Analytic derivation of meanings ideally yields *distinctive features:* necessary and sufficient conditions by which an investigator can determine whether a newly encountered instance is or is not a member of a particular category. The procedure requires an independent. *etic* (Pike, 1954, p. 8) way of coding recorded instances of a category. Examples are the 'phone types' linguistics and the 'kin types' kinship analysis (Lounsbury, 1956, pp. 191–2). The investigator classifies his data into types of his own formulation, then compares 'types' *as though* they were instances of a concept. From information already coded in the definitions of his 'types', he derives the necessary and sufficient conditions of class membership. Thus by comparing the kin types of English 'uncle' (FaBr, MoBr, FaSiHu, etc.) with the kin types in every other English kin category, the analyst finds that by scoring 'uncle' for features along four dimensions of contrast (affinity, collaterality, generation, and sex) he can state succinctly how 'uncles' differ from every other category of kinsmen. . . . (When analytically derived features are probabilistically, rather than necessarily and sufficiently, associated with category membership, then we may speak of *correlates* rather than of distinctive features. A correlate of the uncle-nephew relation is that uncles are usually, but not necessarily, older than their nephews.)

To arrive at rules of use one can also direct attention to the actual stimulus discriminations made by informants when categorizing. . . . Perceptual attributes relevant to categorization, whether distinctive or probabilistic, are *cues*. Discovering cues in ethnographic settings requires as yet largely unformulated procedures of perceptual testing that do not replace the culturally relevant stimuli with artificial laboratory stimuli (cf. Conklin, 1955, p. 342).

When Frake notes that firstly, informants may be asked about meanings directly in each case he outlines above, and secondly a specific coding device constructed by the researcher is a necessary part of distinctive feature analysis, he presupposes that Goodenough's definition of culture has been satisfied, that the researcher knows how members operate in a manner acceptable to other members. To uncover 'cues', the researcher must have a firm grasp of 'what everyone knows' and takes for granted when conversing with members of the culture, or what members assume each 'knows' when conversing with each other. The elicitation procedure is designed to construct a written dictionary, but it ignores the necessary existence of a tacit oral dictionary for normal form social interaction. The researcher must acquire and use the culture's particular interpretive procedures (analogous to a particular language) and world view to decide the relevance of oral and written dictionaries; an oral dictionary is activated *vis-à-vis* situational constraints and the fringes that members attribute to actual scenes. The use of elicitation procedures to identify lexical items and their denotative meanings, and the initial learning of rules governing usage of lexical items are similar to how a child learns to be a bona fide member of his culture. The researcher, however, presumably learns at a faster rate of speed and acquires fringe meanings rapidly through day-to-day living; he has the ability to employ adult interpretive procedures in a different culture in a way the child cannot. Hence the initial elicitation procedures utilized when the researcher has only limited access to the native language and everyday practices give way more and more to an approximation of native interpretive procedures and surface rule usage.

The acquisition of the knowledge and skill enabling the researcher to perform 'like a native' makes it more and more difficult to employ simplified elicitation procedures and simultaneously, complicates the researcher's procedural rules for deciding 'what happened'. The more successfully the researcher can perform verbally and nonverbally like a native, the more he will take for granted and be exposed to practised and enforced rather than ideal normatively oriented everyday activities. The problem is like that of articulating general rules or policies with particular cases said to fall under general rules (Rawls, 1955). General rules are presented to children as general kernal or denotative meanings, diffuse as to application and requiring continual explanation in each specific case. The child's initial acquisition of interpretive procedures does not permit him to learn to make the necessary interpretations for linking general rules with particular cases except on a rote basis; he lacks the ability to justify the articulation according to adult procedures. Adults can make the articulation only by invoking implicit interpretive procedures, despite the common assumption that general surface rules are the basis for designating the conditions under which particular cases can be said to fall under the general case. The general rule cannot specify the many fringes, the contingencies surrounding the actual articulation. For example, laws pertaining to juveniles for deciding delinquency are linked to actual persons and events by the utilization of interpretive procedures by agents of social control (Cicourel, 1968). The initial etic coding procedures used by componential analysts for specifying denotative meanings generate an abstract skeleton; the perception and interpretation of particular cases as falling under initial general rules requires moving away from denotative meanings and incorporating more fringes based upon the use of interpretive procedures, and their reflexive features. The researcher relies upon 'what everyone knows' or upon his ability to perform as a competent member of the culture or society.

Frake was unable to use distinctive feature analysis for his work on the diagnosis of disease among the Subanun. He (Frake, 1961) proposes instead procedures parallel to those employed for determining a system of nomenclature: 'We collect contrasting answers to the questions the Subanun ask when diagnosing disease. By asking informants to describe differences between diseases, by asking why particular illnesses are diagnosed as such and such and not something else, by following discussions among the Subanun themselves when diagnosing cases, and by noticing corrections made of our own diagnostic efforts, we can isolate a limited number of diagnostic questions and critical answers.' Frake moved from a presumed etic formulation to an emic or member's perspective by following actual practices and normative descriptions, and therefore relies more and more upon 'what everyone knows'.

The Subanun ask 'Does it hurt?' (*mesait. ma*). The contrasting replies to this question are, first, an affirmative, 'yes, it hurts'; second a denial of pain followed by a specification of a contrasting, non-painful, but still abnormal sensation, 'No, it doesn't hurt; it itches'; and, third, a blanket negation implying no abnormal sensation. Thus the Subanun labels a number of contrasting types of sensation and uses them to characterize and differentiate diseases (Frake, 1961).

The outputs of contrastive analysis described by Frake are levels of terminological contrast, and the resulting tables are cross-tabulated outcomes obtained by running diagnostic questions (in the particular example discussed here) against a range of contrasting answers. Neither the elicitation strategies nor the terminology contrasts, however, specify procedures used by members for generating utterances that have their own built-in contrasts for competent members of the culture or society. The developmental question relevant here is how children construct and employ contrastive sets and recognize their appropriateness in actual settings. The elicitation procedures described by Frake suggest how the researcher cuts into a presumed adult normal flow to make contrastive sets explicit. Frake does not seek to pinpoint members' procedures for transforming social settings into 'instructions' for inference and further action, but a recent work does begin by making members rules central to the analysis.

Sacks (1966a) is interested in finding relationships that go beyond a recursive analysis of single sentences, attempting to link members' language categories by transcending sentences to include some indeterminate text ranging from one word to *n* pages. A central interest is how members 'do describing' and 'recognize a description'. The ways in which members produce and recognize descriptions are seen as necessary steps in arriving at criteria for 'correct sociological description'. Sacks's work, therefore, follows the tradition of insisting upon emic constructions as basic to etic descriptions.

The central notion in Sacks's work is called a membership categorization device. Devices consist of various categories, or a collection of categories (actually used and recognized by members as 'acceptable'), plus rules of application. The general idea is to pair a device (containing at least one category) with a population (containing at least one member). An example of a device would be 'sex', consisting of the categories male and female. A collection of categories is said to 'go together' because members 'recognize' them as such. The researcher, performing like a member, presumably follows members' relevances about 'what everyone knows' in deciding that a collection of categories 'go together'. Sacks uses the phrase 'members' knowledge' for Schutz's notion of 'what anyone knows' or socially distributed common knowledge. Thus Sacks implicitly employs the same concept of a 'well built-in' or a normally socialized member employing normal form kernal or denotative and fringe meanings. Sacks does not discuss it, but his analysis tacitly assumes that his subjects possess and successfully employ interpretive procedures, surface rules, and reflexive features. His research procedures appear inductive when seeking to show how members are likely to hear utterances in particular ways. The potential elegance of the formulation lies in the possibility of developing rules of application or what Sacks calls, for example, an 'economy rule', a 'consistency rule', 'hearers' maxims' 'viewers' maxims', and the like. Members' ability to connect different categories and thus arrive at meanings 'everyone knows' and sanctions suggest ways for revealing the application of interpretive procedures and surface rules within specific cultural or societal settings.

In a series of lecture notes (Sacks, 1966b), the above notions are illustrated with a two sentence story taken from a book on children's stories. The sentences, produced by a child of two years, nine months, are: 'The baby cried. The mummy picked it up.' Briefly, Sacks argues that native speakers of the English language will hear the two sentences as saying the mummy is the mummy of the baby, despite the absence of a genitive in the second sentence. The idea, however, is to discover ways of revealing how members' common knowledge about how things 'go together' enable the researcher to develop rules for explaining how members make sense of their environment and decide the referential adequacy of their utterances. Thus, the two sentences can be seen as an 'adequate description' because members will connect 'baby' with the device 'family' rather than, say, 'stage of life' (i.e. baby, child, pre-teen, teenager, young adult, etc.). 'Mummy' will also be connected with the device 'family', (i.e., mummy, daddy, brother, sister, baby, etc.), thus 'locking in' two categories from two different sentences on the assumption that the hearer constructs a coherent picture by the indicated pairings. A contrastive principle is presumed when Sacks notes that a hearer would not expect to hear 'short-stop' instead of 'mummy'. The notion of an 'economy rule' is coined to describe how a single category (from a device) is recognized by a member as being an adequate reference for a person. Thus 'baby' is presumed to be an adequate reference to some speaker-hearer. The 'consistency rule' states that if a population is being categorized, and one category from some device has been used to categorize a first member, and the same or other categories from the same collection can be used to categorize further members of the population, then the rule holds. Thus in the above two sentences the fact that 'baby' can be said to refer to the device 'family' leads to the use of the consistency rule, suggesting that the category 'mummy' is a relevant mapping by reference to the same device. A hearer's maxim would, therefore, direct a member to hear 'baby' and 'mummy' as belonging to the same device. Following my earlier remarks, norms or surface rules, therefore, are used by members to order (explain the particular) activities they observe, and are integral features of how rules of application are linked to the use of categories by members.

Sacks's procedures tacitly presuppose unstated normal form usage of interpretive procedures and their reflexive features; the various maxims and rules can be viewed as applied instructions for concrete social scenes. Sacks's formulation is similar to the notion of the indexicality of different categories; categorization devices reflect how members generate and recognize indexical expressions. A particular category serves as an index of unstated devices. Actual choices would then become realized in the course of interaction, and their measurement by the researcher would become a function of assumed linkage with other categories presumed to be distinctive features and contrastive sets. The speaker uses interpretive procedures and their reflexive features to generate appropriate categories and assign them situational relevance. The hearer receives instructions for programming his own attributions of meaning and generating responses. The identification of categories, and the connection between devices deemed appropriate by maxims and rules, can be viewed as a research strategy for operationalizing members' use of indexical expressions. When linked to the theoretical concepts of interpretive procedures, their reflexive features and the indexicality of expressions, Sacks's inductive procedure becomes a possible basis for measuring conversational material.

Sacks's work includes many additional features about conversations I cannot cover in this chapter: how characteristic beginnings and endings help members recognize their observations as intelligible; how different sequences of talk are tied together by characteristic locations in speech; and so forth. Contrasts sets are developed in the course of analysing the conversational material, and thus remain implicit until substance is designated by reference to a particular piece of conversation. Sacks draws upon his own common knowledge of how members are likely to 'hear' or 'see' things, and carefully examines hundreds of different texts for their opening lines, closing lines, ironies, antinomies, and the like, thus using the implicit notion of members' common knowledge as an inexhaustible reservoir of categorization devices for 'locking in' categories and how members make sense of their environment. The problem of what is 'heard' and the nonverbal elements of conversations are not explicit features of Sacks's analysis, but he relies upon these features when attempting to describe transcripts he has heard over and over again.

Although the strategies described above do not make explicit reference to the temporally constituted character of all exchanges, the use of normal forms, and the role of nonverbal cues, contrastive analysis provides the researcher with an empirical procedure for identifying (contrast sets and categorization devices during) different developmental stages in the acquisition of interpretive procedures and their reflexive features. A developmental model of how the child acquires and modifies the corpus of knowledge we have called an oral dictionary or 'what everyone knows', and of how he uses this knowledge in routine indexical expressions, should help unravel existing gaps in our knowledge of how competent adults construct and sustain social order through their everyday actions.

Concluding remarks

Throughout the chapter I have argued that interpretive procedures and their reflexive features provide us with basic elements for understanding how the child's acquisition of social structure makes social order possible. I assume that the properties making up interpretive procedures are analogous to claims about linguistic universals, acquired early in life and fused with the acquisition of language. I have tried to separate the acquisition of interpretive procedures from their development in a particular culture to stress their analytic status as paralleling the existence of linguistic universals independently of the learning of a particular language. The notion of world view and the acquisition of interpretive procedures in a particular culture suggest how the child becomes oriented to both generic and substantive cultural recognition and use of normal forms in his environment. Interpretive procedures and their reflexive features provide the child with a sense of social structure competence necessary for tackling the performance that includes the everyday usage of a particular language and world view. Actual performance means the transformation of verbal and nonverbal materials into instructions whereby members programme each other's unfolding action. Hence much of performance depends upon the unfolding social situation that cannot be automatically pre-programmed by built-in competence. The invariant status of interpretive procedures, for example, enables a normal child to acquire language in a family of deaf parents, and the interpretive procedures and their reflexive features enable deaf persons to acquire a sense of social structure that is nonverbal.

A developmental model suggests the problem can also be stated comparatively across species; pre-programmed competence and the acquisition of language and interpretive procedures become less and less determinate of performance as we encounter more complex organisms, with more and more emphasis placed upon expanding developmental stages of 'imprinting' and the contingencies of action scenes for structuring actual behaviour. Intra- and inter-cultural substantive differences in child-rearing must be separated from the invariant development stages of language and interpretive procedures.

Pursuing the developmental notion further I suggest that commonly held conceptions in anthropology and sociology about the fundamental role of a common value system require modification for explaining how social order is possible. The idea that concerted action is possible because norms and common value orientations generate consensus has been a long-standing thesis in the literature. The argument presented earlier states that members are quite capable of concerted action despite the absence of consensus, during explicit conflict, or as children where it is not clear that even norms are known or understood, much less elements of a common value system. I am not saying that values do not enter into the picture or that they are unnecessary, but that their role in generating, sustaining, or changing action scenes is always dependent upon the properties or interpretive procedures. The usual argument that a common value system exists and consists of an oral tradition in an esoteric society is also extended to pluralistic societies on the grounds that a common core of values also exists despite different ideological positions.

The idea of what is or should be desirable about objects, ideas, or practices is not invariant to concerted social interaction or social order. The relevance of general norms and values becomes central on ceremonial occasions or after conflict situations, where some attempt at structuring or re-structuring 'what happened' or 'what should have happened' becomes a key group activity. I am suggesting that values, like surface rules or norms or laws, are always general policies or practices whose articulation with particular cases remains an empirically problematic issue dependent on how interpretive procedures structure unfolding action scenes so as to generate bounded conceptions of 'what happened'. Thus actual choices between alternative courses of action, objects of interest, the morality of members' actions, desired ideals of life, and the like, occur within the context of interpretive procedures and their reflexive features. The interpretive procedures provide for a common scheme of interpretation that enables members to assign contextual relevance; norms and values are invoked to justify a course of action, 'find' the relevance of a course of action, enable the member to choose among particulars for constructing an interpretation others can agree to or an interpretation designed to satisfy the imputed interests or demands of others. The property of normal forms is invariant to a given culture or society, but its empirical relevance is always culture-bound and necessarily includes commitments to normative or value-oriented conceptions of appropriateness. Day-to-day living requires tacit commitment to some basic normative order; that order is built into what members assume to be known in common and taken for granted in their everyday activities.

References to norms and values in mundane activities is necessary for deciding which particulars of action scenes will be identified and used for articulating concrete cases with general policies or rules. The central developmental question becomes that of how adults routinely expose children to a practised and enforced order, as opposed to norms and values as idealized general policies or rules invoked after the fact to explain or justify activities governed by the contingencies of an unfolding action scene. The moment-to-moment programming each member accomplishes for himself and others re-establishes the normative order because of *post hoc* linking with general policies or rules. In attempting to socialize children this as yet ambiguous process of linking particular cases with general policies or rules becomes a perpetual laboratory for discovering how social organization is made possible through the child's acquisition of social structure.

3 Generative Semantics and the Structure of Social Interaction

When sociologists propose theories of social interaction, their conceptual apparatuses and research procedures presume that the language used to describe theoretical relationships, obtain, and describe data, is not a problematic feature of claims to knowledge. Language and non-oral elements of communication are always given some passing remarks as to their 'obvious' importance, but these elements are not independently studied and made essential conditions for the study of social interaction. How participants and researchers assign meanings to their own and others' thoughts, objects, and events remain taken-for-granted phenomena. The sociologist relies on his implicit knowledge of his own society's language and non-oral meanings to describe the outputs of human communication relevant to his interests in substantive research. The substantive terms used to describe the language outputs of social interaction presuppose that the recipient understands the society from the 'inside' as a native speaker-hearer. Hence the researcher relies on his unexplicated native competence to describe observations and verbal outputs, and the reader must presume or simulate this competence to interpret the results presented.

In this paper I propose some invariant presuppositions basic to the production of everyday social activities, and argue that these presuppositions constitute sociological cognitive elements of what I shall be calling a generative semantics central for an understanding of all human communication. Further, the explication of these presuppositions is fundamental to the development of sociolinguistics and an understanding of social interaction as contingent possibilities of specific settings.

Linguistic and philosophical perspectives

Recent linguistic concerns with semantics are rather extensive (Greenberg, 1966; Fodor and Katz, 1964; Bach and Harms, 1968). Here I wish to note only a few points about the linguist's approach to semantics and its relevance for the study of social interaction. A critical feature of linguistic theories dealing with semantics has to do with the emphasis on syntactic structure. A basic problem, the dependence on the sentence as a unit and then sub-units or constituents governed by context-free rules specifying different relationships among units and sub-units, leans heavily on the idea of a dictionary that is divorced from language usage in social interaction. The normative reliance on the syntactic structure of a sentence provides an elegant basis for linking and nesting the meaning of words, but idealizes the occasions within which native speakers of a language carry out the business of producing the social exchanges we call the social structures. More recent linguistic approaches to semantic analysis are less confining than in the work of logicians, but the linguist's preoccupation with a bounded sentence often means that he will ignore false starts and knowledge presumed by participants about in-group intonation patterns, visual cues relating to facial expressions, gestures and body movements, physical distance, dress, physical appearance, poorly formed sentence or utterance fragments, presumed social relationships, idioms, and in-group codes. Yet the sociologist cannot claim the same conceptual elegance of the linguist nor can he do much more than pay lip-service to what some linguists (at least for the present) prefer to ignore. But anthropological linguists like Gumperz and Hymes have made important contributions to the social context of language use by their study of language structures that go beyond the sentence to include notions like different codes in a language community, different linguistic repertoires in use, and the speaker-hearer's ability to switch from one code to another.

My stress on a generative semantics goes beyond deriving semantic components from lexical items and the syntactic categories used in their formation (Weinreich, 1966; Bendix, 1966), but clearly is similar to work done in componential analysis (Conklin, 1955; Goodenough, 1956; Frake, 1961), though perhaps more so to work in the related area of 'cognitive anthropology' (Geoghegan, 1968) and the 'ethnography of speaking' (Gumperz, 1966; Hymes, 1962; Blum and Gumperz, 1971). The work in ethnographic semantics or componential analysis involves the use of contrast sets obtained by an elicitation procedure and often implicit ethnographic knowledge by the researcher, and some comparison of elicited forms with usage in everyday interactional sequences. The present view is closely related to the work of anthropological linguists and the 'new ethnography', particularly where cognitive mechanisms and notions like linguistic repertoire, code, and code switching are stressed. But anthropological views do not always specify, nor make reference to a kind of base or invariant group of presuppositions or interpretive procedures that are basic to cultural meanings and the logic of common sense reasoning in everyday decision-making. I will describe these interpretive procedures below.

The reader will recognize that the work of Gestalt psychologists, particularly the more recent work in cognitive psychology (Bruner, 1957; Miller, Pribram, and Galanter, 1960; Brown, 1965) and psycholinguistics (Lenneberg, 1964; 1969; Brown, 1965; Smith and Miller, 1966) are important resources for the present work, but these theories are not concerned with the interaction between cognitive processes and normative rules as they structure social interaction.

I want to view syntactic and phonological structures as necessary but sometimes misleading devices for negotiating various forms of oral social interaction, and the preparation of written documents or letters. The critical elements of linguistic analysis include boundary conditions within which logical relationships are established, and rules which are developed for predicting the occurrence and co-occurrence of particular constituents. Within generative-transformational linguistic theory – the perspective I shall use as a resource in this paper – actual sentences can be viewed as having been produced by a 'deep structure', governed by 'phrase structure rules' and 'transformational rules' which change the outcomes of the phrase structure rules so as to produce the perceived sentences or surface structures. A critical feature of this theory is the notion that a finite set of rules is capable of generating an infinite number of strings, utterances or groupings that can be treated as bounded sentences. I propose to treat the linguist's and the member's creation of bounded sentences as a 'mechanical' normative system consisting of general rules that must be negotiated *vis-à-vis* particular social encounters. Linguistic features of speech bound the meanings exchanged only in a formal sense; thus there are obvious articulations between syntactic structures and semantic ones, but the syntax is also misleading because it conveys the impression that the formal appearances of bounded sentences are in close correspondence with interactional meaning structures. Linguistic theory does not address the larger horizons of meaning (codes, repertoires, code switching, choices available within repertoires) indexed by the syntax and intonational variations of talk invented or imagined by the participants for making speech socially relevant.

The behavioural scientist concerned with everyday dialogues cannot afford to treat linguistic theories as general theory describing 'natural' language structure. If universal elements of language exist, they must be examined within a cultural context that shapes the surface outputs of such universals by normative features particular to a culture, as well as invariant properties making up socially developed 'native intuition' or the logic of common-sense reasoning. The scientific traditions of western culture are difficult to separate from normative practices that emerged within particular cultural contexts. I prefer to treat phonological and syntactic rules and practices governing surface outputs as normative because it forces the student of sociolinguistics and social interaction to make explicit the psychological and sociological cognitive factors generating everyday social organization.

When we hear others, our search for meanings requires that we are not constrained by sentence boundaries, despite the fact that we are expected to use and orient ourselves to normative phonological and syntactic structures for locating roughly certain forms of talk and recognizing the appropriateness of the setting. The setting, however, also provides complex information for recognizing the relevance of particular forms of talk. Among persons who have established intimate social relationships a single lexical item can do the 'work' of a long paragraph, while accompanying gestures, body movement and intonation can provide a context that ten pages or five minutes of talk could not describe. Psychological and sociological cognitive processes enable us to link larger semantic wholes or meanings than do the formal syntactic structural frames provided by language, yet these frames provide their own cultural markers which are normatively important for bounding the stream of speech.

There is a common thread running through the above discussion which should be mentioned before proceeding – the notion of 'deep structure' in linguistics. Sociologists have used the term 'latent structure' to refer to something similar, but there are critical differences between the uses of 'latent' and 'deep' in sociology and linguistics. The sociologist's usage tends to be an implicit recognition of the cognitive problem of going beyond the information given by norms and values, but the theoretical discussions do not make problematic how the 'latent' structure comes to be generated, nor how this unexplicated underlying structure is connected to and produces the manifest structure. The linguist attempts to link the deep structure explicitly to the surface structure, first by developing rules for generating the deep structure, and then by developing transformation rules for producing the surface structure. Changes in linguistic theory revolve around the role of the deep structure in a grammar (McCawley, 1968a; 1968b; Lakoff, 1968a; Fillmore, 1968). In sociology ethnomethodologists (Garfinkel, 1967; Cicourel, 1968a; 1968b) have sought to indicate the necessity of notions like 'background expectancies', 'members' practices', or 'interpretive procedures' for making surface structures (the interaction scene) coherent or socially meaningful.

Notions like 'members' practices' and 'interpretive procedures' are implied in the writings of philosophers interested in everyday language. De Mauro (1967) historically contrasts Wittgenstein with many writers in tracing the emergence and shift in the formulations of language presented in the *Tractatus* and *Philosophical Investigations*. My interest in Wittgenstein lies in his remarks about the tacit information upon which the understanding of everyday language is based. Saussure, Martinet, and Wittgenstein stressed the importance of word use in a particular context.

An observation by De Mauro (1967, p. 40) is relevant to the views I develop later in the paper.

A phrase is not normally plurisemantic for the hearer, but for him the phrase is not isolated: he hears it in a precise setting made up of all he knows about the person who pronounces it, about his past experiences, his plans, about what the author of the phrase knows and thinks about those for whom the phrase is intended, and so forth (see also Ceccato, 1960, p. 19). This enormous bundle of information, not linguistically formalized, helps the rapid selection of the meaning best adapted to the situation in which the phrase was pronounced. Isolated from this framework every phrase may be plurisemantic.

By rejecting the idea that reality can be reduced to simple constituent parts, or that language can be viewed as a nomenclature, Wittgenstein develops the idea that the use of language is critical for understanding the simplicity or complexity of an object, particularly the experiences of the speaker-hearer and the coordinates he used when considering the object in question.

Man's past and present perception of his environment produces the relevant categories for his comprehension of activities over the course of the acts engaged in. Language provides the basis for specifying how we create simple or composite objects by our conversion of experiences into the categories available in the language (see Wittgenstein, 1953, paras 371–3, 378–84). According to this view linguistic forms are important structural conditions, but language usage, particular contexts, are critical for semantic descriptions (1953, paras 431–35).

De Mauro cites Calogero (1947) for his insistence that members are limited to particular meanings in their use of a term, because listeners have rights about what they can reasonably expect speakers to do with words and their intended meanings. De Mauro notes that Calogero recognizes the problem of an 'individualistic' conception of use, particularly since it could degenerate into a dialogue of 'What do you mean by . . . ?' and 'What do you mean by "what do you mean . . . ?"' Meaning does not depend on individual use, but on use by individuals belonging to the same historical community where normative constraints will operate (De Mauro, 1967, p. 49).

An important conclusion drawn by De Mauro (pp. 53–4) after discussing Wittgenstein and others is:

But in the measure in which you belong to my own community, you have been subjected to a linguistic and cultural training similar to my own and I have valid grounds for supposing that your propositions have a similar meaning for both of us. And the 'hypothesis' which I make when I hear you speak, and which you make speaking to me, is confirmed for both of us by both your and my total behaviour.

The work of Austin also develops the theme that everyday language (going beyond formal linguistic concerns) is central for understanding the meanings we intend in exchanges with others. Austin's general work (1961) cannot be described in the present paper, but I want to describe a few points relevant for any conception of generative semantics.

In his early papers, 'The Meaning of a Word' and 'Are There a Priori Concepts', Austin invokes the notion of the 'plain man', the man on the street, and his way of using and understanding everyday language. The importance of this notion can be found in the kind of language Austin claims the 'plain man' is capable of generating and receiving from others. The 'plain man' has an intuitive capacity or competence for producing and understanding utterances which defies attempts to explain this communicative competence by reference to a formal logical framework. What is critical here is Austin's continual reference to the 'plain man's' competence for making himself understood when talking to others like himself in everyday exchanges; his ability to know when the other person believed that one of his assertions was true. The concern with how we use words in particular situations, often regardless of the syntactic constraints presumably operative, was basic to Austin's feeling that no rigid separation should exist between syntactic and semantic considerations, and that despite the 'enslaving' character of words, the 'plain man' intends and comprehends thoughts that words fail to convey adequately (1961, pp. 35–6).

How the 'plain man' comes to doubt or trust others, to claim to know or recognize something because of 'seeing' or 'sensing' what is going on around him, can be discerned by examining his use of actual, everyday language. It is this concern with the 'plain man's' intuition and use of particular words or phrases, for example the use of 'because' when the speaker feels he can 'prove' his point and 'from' or 'by' when the speaker feels he 'knows' but cannot 'prove' his claims (1961, p. 54), that makes Austin's work so relevant to the development of a theory of generative semantics. The native speaker's intuition is a critical resource for his use of language, and Austin's reference to the native's mastery of his language has been criticized (Vendler, 1967, pp. 12–14, while discussing Cavell's work (1969, pp. 62–70) on the grounds that virtually no appeal to evidence is required for statements (categorical declaratives) discussed by ordinary language philosophers. But the sociolinguist must view the speaker-hearer's reliance upon invariant psychological and social presuppositions inherent in the notion of native competence as critical for an understanding of everyday language behaviour. It should be clear that both the philosopher and linguist rely, at every step, on an implicit usage of their own nativeness *vis-à-vis* their own language when engaged in ordinary language analysis or linguistic description. The notion of generative semantics developed below treats this nativeness as the basic resource for a general theory of communicative competence.

Normative rules and linguistic rules

All references to normative (or surface) rules in this paper intend the idea that we are dealing with a practice, policy, or institution which is justified by some collectivity or system of rules that confers powers and carries obligations which are binding upon some collectivity. Perceived adherence to the rules, practices or policies on the part of someone, implies the fulfilment of membership in the collectivity. Hence every interaction scene makes every actor's membership status in the collectivity potentially problematic; actual conduct presumably is evaluated against the contextual relevance of some system of normative rules. Normative rules, therefore, like syntactic, phonological, or semantic rules based on a dictionary, are divorced from occasions of practical use, and the members of a collectivity do not have ready access to lists of rules with which they evaluate each other's performance. The evaluation of performance is critical for attributing competence to members, yet it should be clear that more than simple references to the existence of normative rules are necessary if one's theory of society is not to remain static and ignorant of the contingencies of everyday interaction. A theory of norms presupposes a model of how the actor stores and processes information.

The study of normative rules is no different from the study of linguistic competence. We must account for the actor's ability to know implicitly about 'appropriate' everyday behaviour (as in everyday speech). The linguist wishes to discover the elements making up this implicit knowledge by studying the actor's competence 'as a system of rules that relate signals to semantic interpretations of these signals', and with the general goal 'to discover the general properties of any system of rules that may serve as the basis for a human language' (Chomsky, 1965, p. 3). The linguist's concern with the member's competence or implicit knowledge and performance or actual behaviour, states the sociologist's concern with normative rules and behaviour, for language competence and usage are a critical part of the structure of social interaction.

For the linguist it is the system of syntactic rules that determines the meaning of signals for the speaker-hearer. Meaning is produced by a dictionary with various entries and multiple meanings, and a set of 'projection rules' for specifying how grammatically constructed combinations of words produce or give meanings to words, and how the speaker-hearer is able to constrain the ambiguity of words in some context (Katz and Fodor, 1963). The speaker-hearer's reliance on his acquired native cultural ability as a tacit body of socially organized knowledge is not a variable condition of the linguist's theory for deciding meaning, but a 'given' feature of language competence and usage. A number of criticisms have been levelled against this theory of meaning (Weinreich, 1966), but I shall only mention two because of their importance in further discussion below: one point made by Weinreich is that the theory does not deal with the problem that the differentiation of submeanings in a dictionary might go on indefinitely, and secondly, that the concern with disambiguation does not explain the production of sentences intended as ambiguous by the speaker (Weinreich, 1966, p. 398). Despite differences among modern linguists about how to deal with the semantic component of a grammar, and what to do with the deep structure in alternative views, the problem of meaning depends upon sentential structure and its parts.

Discussions of normative rules in sociology also tend to be divorced from the interactional settings in which meanings are attributed to objects and events. Research instruments like questionnaires invariably pose hypothetical events or conditions for subjects in the same way as linguists propose sentences as candidates for grammaticality under a system of rules; both situations are divorced from the negotiated interaction scenes in which social organization is produced. The social conditions or sentences studied are given an ideal-typical character because they are stripped of the features or particulars and interpretive procedures members use to make general (normative, syntactic) rules creatively relevant to concrete settings. The production of concrete social settings is an on-going accomplishment of their participants. The phrase 'negotiated creativeness' is intended to underline the members' reliance on normative or syntactic general rules for finding and justifying the meaning of events as socially organized or as linguistically sensible. Despite the fact that the modern linguist's theory of deep structure is an elegant formulation, particularly in contrast with the sociologist's wastebasket usage of latent structure to disguise the inadequacies of his normative theory, both approaches to the idea of rules governing the production of grammatical utterances and social behaviour (treated as analytically distinct for the purposes of this paper) are deficient in their ability to account for the emergent, negotiated nature of meaning over the course of social interaction. The problem can be clarified if we discuss strategies of language research.

There is a vast difference, of course, between a field setting in an esoteric culture where the researcher does not have the help of a bilingual informant, and a situation where one is analysing a language native to his own speech. In the case of the former the researcher is lost unless he attempts to appreciate the native culture somewhat like a child, pointing to objects, and receiving responses that are difficult to segment phonetically. The researcher remains something of a stranger because he never acquires the language and ethnographic nativeness basic to an intuitive grasp of everyday activities. In the case of the research setting where a bilingual informant is available, the observer seeks to use conceptions of social organization from his own society learned implicitly and explicitly as a basis for describing kinship, legal, political, economic, and religious forms of activity. The researcher working with a bilingual or in his own culture tends to rely so heavily on his nativeness that it is not always clear whether one can claim he is developing a 'general theory' of language or syntax which is not culture-bound given that the researcher's native knowledge is treated as the primary resource for the formal rules derived.

The discovery of normative rules depends upon the researcher's use of his own nativeness with the language he knows intuitively, along with arbitrarily adopted phonemic and phonetic representations built into the analysis. The segmentation of continuous speech into chunks, pauses or whatever differentiating units the researcher seeks to impose, is central to the observer's framework for recognizing uniformities in language. The researcher's method of analysis, no matter how unstructured, imposes the conditions for finding order, measurement, or rules. This problem is compounded when many of the decisions made by the observer are never stated explicitly because:

1. They seemed obvious to him as a native speaker of the language.

2. Because his native informant withheld or took for granted the same kind of information.

3. Because as the only observer of an esoteric culture, he felt, after fourteen months of living with the natives, that he 'knew' the basis for some activity which he felt was a clear instance of something he could report or describe only partially in his own language.

The researcher's involvement in context-restricted encounters with natives, or his reliance on context-restricted information which he 'knows' as a native, are difficult to describe in detail when showing the development of rules designed to cross particular contexts.

The problem of the investigator's reliance on socially defined native competence in linguistic research seemed clear to me recently while participating in a linguistic course using generative-transformational theory to write grammatical rules for Indonesian using a native informant. The class participants were always forced to elicit ethnographic details when establishing syntactic rules, but this information was not integrated into the formalized properties of the grammar. Yet the ethnographic details were always necessary elements for generating and interpreting the syntactic rules though not part of the linguistic description. Hymes (1970) independently reports on the same problem. He notes how social factors are integral to the discovery of syntactic and phonological categories, yet the linguist or sociologist only describes one (linguistic or social) side of the research, never how both are necessary for understanding speech acts and structural relationships in language.

The early generative-transformational grammar work on syntax, which viewed semantic considerations as peripheral, as well as the more recent stress being given to semantics, differs from ethnographically based interests in sociolinguistics. The transformational view depends on the use of tacit normative rules, which the researcher has taken for granted as a native, for the discovery of syntactic rules which govern well-formed sentences or for revealing that any incomplete sentence can be shown to be part of one or more bounded sentences. The anthropological linguistic approach draws on implicit ethnographic features of social organization in ordering components and finding 'natural' clusters of social categories used by natives, and it cannot be restricted by the assumption of bounded sentences. The generative semantics I want to develop in this paper will not view sentence boundaries as 'natural', but as a particular normative practice that turns out to be rather convenient for developing and teaching rules of language. The 'mechanical' speech production, characterized as constituent units that can be bounded and called sentences, obscures the semantically generative features of language production and comprehension. The child's acquisition of language depends on powerful socialization practices imposed very early in childhood, with strong sanctions accompanying the development and competent use of phonological and syntactic norms. Parents and researchers both 'see' and 'find' this early development and 'order' in cooperation with the child, for if the child does not cooperate there are other normative remedies and conclusions about what is 'wrong' with him and what must be done to 'cure' him. Everyday social organization involving adult-child interaction is predicated on children being capable of mechanical speech production and segmentation. The question of how much of this production is comprehended by the child is not as clear, and I will say more about this problem later in the chapter.

How we use our native intuition to create and understand more formalized normative representations is not clear. In everyday speech our discovery of rules of a syntactic, phonological, or semantic type does not differentiate between those speech productions (and comprehension) said to be governed by the rules, and the intuitive, taken-for-granted elements we use tacitly when presumably acting in conformity with the rules. The member said to be acting in conformity with a rule responds to elements that are at best in weak correspondence with the features which an observer invokes when claiming a rule is being followed.

Normative elements like a particular orthography, phonemic standards, dictionary definitions, punctuation rules, and the spacing and identification of participants, produce and structure the sequencing presumed to be 'natural' in everyday conversations, and provide the researcher with a built-in order for his data. The data, therefore, are predigested in large part, and thus endowed with a considerable amount of structure for discovering new rules and reconfirming old rules in new materials.

One way of underscoring the unstated normative conditions both researcher and reader rely on when producing and evaluating research 'results' is to make more and more of these conditions problematic when contrasted with the 'normal' (predigested) way of analysing conversational materials. In a recent seminar, some of my students (Hugh Mehan, Kenneth Jennings, Sybillyn Jennings, and others) began treating previously transcribed tape-recorded conversations between an American parent and child by running together an arbitrary section (called 'enjambing' by the students) so as to mask distinctions of first and second speakers, pauses, punctuation, and so on. Giving the new, 'enjambed' conversation to someone unfamiliar with its initial segmentation and intent reveals what features are being taken for granted and built into the 'setting up' of a transcribed tape recording for analysis. Another strategy (by Jennings) is to begin an analysis by looking up each word in a dictionary to show how much reliance is placed on our tacit knowledge and contextual features for interpreting dictionary meanings. The transcriber of the tape recording uses his nativeness to endow the original conversation with considerable normative information upon which the researcher depends to 'begin' his analysis.

Researchers and the speaker-hearers they study, rely on the same forms of native intuition (psychological and sociological cognitive procedures) and assumptions about their own and others' socially distributed knowledge to sustain a 'sense of social structure' (Cicourel, 1968b) at all times. The researcher's and speaker-hearer's claims to knowledge depend on a tacit understanding and use of predigested conceptions and cognitive procedures. Unless we make such tacit practices objects of study, we cannot understand the researcher's claims to 'objective research findings', nor the speaker-hearer's routine generation of meaning structures in everyday life.

Interpretive procedures and the member's sense of social structure

Phonological, syntactic, or dictionary markers which the member is capable of identifying and utilizing for comprehending what happened, must be linked to context-restricted settings which the speaker-hearer must generate by invoking particular features that assign normatively acceptable sense to what is observed, read or heard. The speaker-hearer's descriptive accounts must reflect normative rules he feels would be viewed as 'normal' or reasonable to others receiving the account. But normative rules are not self-contained instructions for assigning meaning to an environment of objects and events. The child must learn to articulate general rules or policies with particular objects and events so as to show that the context-restricted features experienced can be accounted for by the claim that they are governed by the general rules or policies (Rawls, 1955; Cicourel, 1968a). Notice, however, that normative rules do not exist for providing the speaker-hearer with instructions on how this articulation occurs between particular features experienced, and the general rules or policies said to govern the adequate explanation or meaning of the particular objects and events. The competence necessary for articulating general rules and the particular social activities that emerge in everyday interaction obviously must include some facility with language and non-oral features of communication, just as it must include cognitive features involving memory operations, the creation of object constancy, causality, attention, or the more general problem of information processing.

To handle the problem of articulating general rules with particular social settings, I have used the notion of interpretive procedures as invariant properties or principles which allow members to assign meaning or sense to substantive rules called social norms. Psychological cognitive processes are not sufficient conditions for generating a sense of social structure; cognitive psychological theory does not reveal how we articulate particular (socially structured) thoughts and perceived displays of objects and events with more general social rules or norms. The actor's search for the appropriate norms that would provide acceptable accounts for others enables him to bound the objects, events and experiences, to achieve a basis for common-sense measurement, using descriptive terms that force activities into ostensibly bounded sets. By creating such sets the member is able to categorize objects and events in a seemingly definitive way; definitive for the practical purposes at hand, as Schutz (1964) has noted. Dictionary meanings, despite their context-sensitive creation, are formalized into recipes that can be used as general normative rules to locate the relevance of emergent experiences. Deciding that a dictionary entry is relevant resolves an immediate practical problem because the user does not have to provide logical criteria to defend his choice of lexical items, instead he utilizes an unstated negotiation process for deciding which features justify lexical choice.

The general principles or interpretive procedures I view as sociological cognitive elements, that go beyond psychological processes but obviously include them, can be described in a rough way as follows (and documented *vis-à-vis* other literature in Cicourel, 1968b).

1. *The reciprocity of perspectives.* This principle states the child must acquire the ability to orient himself to partners in communication so as to assume that they share the same social setting. This means assuming that:

(a) Each would have the same experience if they were to change places.

(b) That until further notice they can disregard any differences that might arise from their respective personal ways of assigning meaning to objects and events.

Thus the participants assume they employ a standardized native orientation to the immediate scene; they are both receiving the same kinds of information, recognizing the same kinds of features that are presumed to carry the same 'obvious' and subtle meanings for both. The fact that particular members may recognize that discrepancies exist between their interpretations and those of their partner is not the critical issue, but that both participants will adopt the idealized standpoint of assuming reciprocally shared experiences, and the same principle for assigning meaning or relevance to their immediate environments (Schutz, 1964).

A consequence of the reciprocity of perspectives principle is that members will assume, and assume others assume it of them, that their descriptive accounts or utterances will be intelligible and recognizable features of an environment which they know in common and take for granted as the 'same' for all practical purposes.

2. *Normal forms.* The interpretive procedure here termed 'normal forms' builds on the reciprocity principle because this principle instructs the participants to expect (and demand) that each assume the other emit recognizable and intelligible utterances regardless of discrepancies that could be noted by one or other speaker. The tacit but sanctioned behaviour of appearing to 'understand' what is being discussed or reacted to assumes that both participants possess similar (normal form) repertoires of what constitutes normal appearances in their culture. The reciprocity principle instructs the actor to impose an idealized interchangeability of standpoints during interaction and to follow a similar procedure for assigning meaning or relevance, but when discrepancies or ambiguities appear, speakers and hearers will attempt to normalize the presumed discrepancies (similar to the reduction of dissonance or incongruity as in Festinger, 1957; Brown, 1962; 1965). This sociological cognitive principle differs from psychological notions in the 'known in common and taken for granted assumption' which members have about appearances; that everyday appearances are essentially the 'same' for 'everyone'. The sociological conception presumes that this common-sense principle provides each member with instructions for unwittingly (and sometimes deliberately) evaluating and striving for a reciprocally assumed normal form judgment of his utterances and perceptions. The member's unwitting acquisition and use of these principles provide a common and standardized system of implicit signals and coding rules. Without such principles everyday interaction would be impossible for nothing could pass as 'known' or 'obvious', and all dialogue would become an infinite regress of doubts. Demonstrating one's competence as a normal member of

the society requires the unwitting following of the above principles. Forcing members of a culture to justify 'objectively' any use of implicit or explicit rules is impossible unless the above and following principles are utilized in a taken-for-granted way.

3. *The et cetera principle.* The reciprocity and normal form procedures require that the member presume critical features of a common culture, assumed to be standardized for practical purposes, without specifying that consensus exists or is necessary. It is the *presumption* that everyday participants in social life are operating under the same principles, 'playing the same game', that is critical. Phonological and syntactic principles extracted from his environment by the child are not sufficient for linking different utterance chunks over clock and experienced time with contextual features being observed, remembered or imagined. The participants to a conversation must 'fill in' meanings throughout the exchange (and after the exchange, when attempting to recall or reconstruct what happened) because of the inadequacies of oral and non-oral communication, and the routine practice of leaving many intentions unstated (Garfinkel, 1964). Vague or ambiguous or truncated expressions are located by members, given meaning contextually and across contexts, by their *retrospective-prospective sense of occurrence*. Present utterances or descriptive accounts that contain ambiguous or promissory overtones can be examined prospectively by the speaker-hearer for their possible meaning in some future sense under the assumption of filling in meanings now and imagining the kinds of intentions that can be expected later. Alternatively, past remarks can now be seen as clarifying present utterances. The filling in and connecting principles enable the actor to maintain a sense of social structure over clock and experienced time despite deliberate or presumed vagueness and minimal information conveyed by participants during exchanges.

4. *Descriptive vocabularies as indexical expressions.* The normal form appearances of objects, events, speech and non-oral behaviour which require the actor to go beyond the information given so as to fill in meanings and make 'firm' and tentative connections prospectively and retrospectively, are partially reflected in the accounts members use for describing their experiences. The descriptive vocabularies are indexes of earlier (and present) experiences and thus reflect elements of the original context so as to permit the retrieval of information that would locate the activities in a broader horizon of meaning than contained in treating each lexical item as a dictionary entry (Garfinkel, 1966). The actor relies upon an undiscussed variety of elements to locate the conversation in which he gives an account of past experiences. The talk he and others provide, their respective timing, hesitation, intonation, physical distance and postures assumed, all signal that

even while giving an account of some past activity, things are 'going well' (or poorly) at present. The necessity of indexical expressions (that require the attribution of meaning beyond the surface form, Bar-Hillel, 1954) in ordinary language usage is essential because different utterances presume differentially distributed common knowledge (Schutz, 1964). For the speaker-hearer to understand what is being said, he must rely on his tacit knowledge and imaginative construction of normal forms. The descriptive vocabularies that make up indexical expressions help the speaker retrieve the experiences they describe, and the principles of reciprocity, normal forms, and et cetera require the speaker to assume that others interpret his expressions similarly. Particular descriptive vocabularies are important for members of an in-group because of the context-sensitive meanings these expressions retrieve. But indexical expressions force all members to retrieve by recall or invention particular ethnographic features from context-sensitive settings that will provide acceptable normative meanings to present activities and accounts of past activities. The general significance of indexical expressions, therefore, is to be found in their use by members for locating speech and non-oral communication within a larger context of meaning by instructing the speaker-hearer to link an expression to the clock-time; the type of occasion in which it occurred; the speaker and relevant biographical information about him; the place; the intentions of the speaker; and the kinds of presumed common or special knowledge required for endowing the expression with obvious and subtle meanings. Thus the socially distributed knowledge presupposed in the principle of normal forms takes on normative substantive significance by forcing the speaker-hearer to make various oral and non-oral commitments about his understanding of everyday social organization.

The above analytic description of interpretive procedures tends to obscure their continuous interaction for the speaker-hearer such that their use becomes an embedded feature of an exchange, providing a reflexive feedback by which the member assigns meaning to his environment. The principles outlined above are generative in the sense that they constitute a few (but not exhaustive) procedures interacting together so as to produce instructions for the speaker-hearer for assigning infinitely possible meanings to unfolding social scenes. The socially organized settings that are produced require the cooperation of the speaker-hearer with another (at least imagined) participant so that each provides the other with information that can be processed by the interpretive procedures.

Remarks on the generative semantic process

Earlier in the chapter I used the phrase 'mechanical production' of speech to characterize the role of phonology and syntax in generating everyday meanings. My reasons for using this phrase are not motivated by any intention to dismiss the importance of these key components of language. I am trying to stress the tacit, taken-for-granted characteristics of phonology and syntax as normative rules designed to force everyday behaviour into normal forms that permit the assumption that relatively unambiguous decisions about meaning are being made from the perspective of the user and some intended audience. The 'unambiguous' nature of such decisions must be understood as practical activities geared to specific occasions. The more ceremonial or ritualized the interaction (in the sense of members making some effort to subscribe to formal normative rules of grammar), the greater the likelihood of observing the use of logical consistency in arranging sentences, in using lexical items and phrases consistently within bounded sentences, and thus a more self-conscious use of language as in the case of particular usage for a 'known' audience. Everyday speech in rather mundane settings like family households, informal social gatherings and the like, always includes many incomplete sentences, considerable ellipsis, and a pronounced use of context-sensitive utterances although formal markers are present and in constant use.

Despite the fact that psycholinguists have convincing evidence to show distinct developmental stages of production, it is not clear what kind of control and comprehension over his output the child possesses before and after each stage. Some tentative results from research I am doing with Kenneth and Sybillyn Jennings suggest that we should carefully re-examine differences between production skills (particularly the appearance of such skills) and comprehension, and make problematic the kinds of tests to be used in deciding adequate comprehension. We are using different variations of standard sentences with normal form and bizarre constructions for assessing the child's ability to distinguish between the implied actor and the receiver of the action in sentences containing various direct and indirect object constructions. One method for revealing this ability requires the child to act out the sentence in conjunction with a partner his age. We are using subjects from ages three to twelve, and our preliminary observations suggest a re-examination of how we are to decide the relationship between a given level of production and its controlled use and understanding by the child.

The assertion of mechanical production in the child's speech is designed to emphasize the importance of the negotiated use of interpretive procedures in the contextual setting for assigning meanings. The interpretive procedures must instruct the speaker-hearer as to the social conditions relevant for appropriate speech production and comprehension. A twelve-year-old child seems to have rather firm control over complex speech production when asked to act out and then explain the information contained in various standard American-English active and passive constructions. The demand for this kind of production, like that demanded of adults with elementary school or even high school educational levels in bureaucratic settings, leads to somewhat strained and uncomfortable usage. Adults who are forced routinely into more formal conversations and correspondence because of occupational duties become proficient with speech production so as to become sensitive to its standard use in everyday conversations. Formal usage is not simply a function of educational level and experience; a critical factor is the social relationship between participants. Most persons talk freely and often when among others with whom they feel comfortable, taking many liberties *vis-à-vis* their speech style (Gumperz, 1966; Blum and Gumperz, 1971). The linguist tends to be somewhat of a captive of his own source of data; usually his analysis depends on his own native production of isolated sentences that always manage to be well-bounded and only occasionally ambiguous *vis-à-vis* dictionary meanings and current linguistic models. Even when using native informants the elicitation procedure deals with single sentences. Everyday social interaction would probably be rather limited and rather boring if most speaker-hearers had to employ the kinds of sentences that linguists generate for analysis by relying on their own native competence.

The history of semantics has continually stressed the view that language can be viewed as a picture of reality. This view preoccupied Wittgenstein in his early work (De Mauro, 1967). The idea that a proposition can serve as a picture of reality because of a correspondence between its parts and elements in everyday environmental settings remains a preoccupation of linguists who rely on dictionary descriptions of meaning for lexical items. The pictorial idea combined with the notion of distinctive features (like animate–inanimate, number, masculine–feminine–neuter) provide a basis for bounding a lexical item so as to create measurement values or unique bundles of information for different items. The use of distinctive features has been proposed in a more general but vague sense to handle the problem of how speaker-hearers and researchers use descriptive vocabularies to assign meaning in everyday social interaction, but there is a difference in the way such features or particulars are employed. My view of this notion of particulars, seen as indexical properties of natural language, stresses

1. The idea that the clarity and specifics of an expression (without necessarily specifying its actual lexical content) are to be found in the consequences of its use, without claiming distinctive features acting as a boundary.

2. The additional point that the collection of descriptive possibilities that are produced by the use of an expression becomes a phenomenon subject to indefinite elaboration of meaning and submeanings under different contextual circumstances.

The notational particulars for describing the meaning of some sentence become critical features for understanding the researcher's attempt to provide himself and others with an account of what he is trying to do. These particulars do not stand as analytic elements to be divorced from the researcher's intentions, the audience he presumes, or what he treats as 'obvious', but instead they must be viewed as indexical. The notational particulars do not stand as obvious depictions of an explanation, but as relevant only if the reader can supply information about the researcher's competence and intentions, about what preceded the discussion taking place, a knowledge of certain conventions being used implicitly and explicitly by the researcher, and so on. The notion of particulars having indexical properties strongly underlines the point that attempts to find and describe formal structures of the speaker-hearer's natural language usage are difficult to achieve with formal linguistic methods currently in use, because interpretive procedures used by the researcher for his scientific measurement remain an unexplicated resource for justifying his results.

The term 'particular' is seldom described by ethnomethodologists (though Garfinkel and Sacks, 1969, have called 'looking ahead' and 'watching something go by' particulars). Discussions of the notion of 'indexical particulars' are difficult to follow, yet the use of traditional substantive terms is avoided because they imply a blind commitment to measurement theories and normative theory that is divorced from language use and the logic of common sense reasoning. I have tried to elaborate my own view below.

Traditional measurement seeks to assign numerals to objects and events according to some explicit set of rules or coding practices. In making such assignments researchers make use of interpretive procedures that remain an unwitting resource to them. Their coding practices are unavoidably embedded in a context-restricted setting having indexical properties. Thus studying the researcher's coding practices becomes indistinguishable from studying speaker-hearer's use of interpretive procedures. By studying members' practices for assigning meaning during everyday interaction we simultaneously discover something about the problems all researchers encounter when they take for granted their own nativeness in trying to develop a system of measurement. The researcher's native or intuitive use of language while studying language behaviour in speaker-hearers, becomes an integral part of his research problem and theory. The availability of phonological and syntactic normative rules and their sanctioned use by natives and researchers is seen to be an indication of universal organization in languages spoken by humans. Our ability to locate syntactic rules, phonological rules, and discrete lexical items in all languages known to linguists (where the lexical items are viewed as consisting of linear sequences of sound segments) is taken as evidence of the universal nature of spoken languages. I want to treat such universal features of language as the formalization of culture-bound normative outcomes developed by Western linguists and scholars over many centuries and conveniently used for practical business, social pedagogical and scientific purposes by increasing numbers of persons in bureaucratically developed civilizations. Such 'universal' practices, therefore, are indexically governed when used in everyday interaction, ceremonial occasions and scientific activities.

The speaker-hearer, like the researcher engaged in measurement or coding practices, seeks to attend his everyday world as an environment known in common with others. In taking the world for granted, the speaker-hearer attempts to create language categories that seem to fit his conception of what he experiences, even when normative syntactic rules have to be violated. The speaker-hearer and researcher produce expressions that appear unequivocal because indexical properties are not made explicit when used to provide others with accounts of activities, for it is assumed that others will utilize 'appropriate' features or particulars for retrieving what the speaker intended.

The notion of particulars used here differs from the notion of distinctive features in at least two important ways: almost anything the member attends can be a particular; and no grouping of particulars crosses specific settings to form measurable sets of features unique to different objects and events to which meaning is assigned. The resulting 'openness', ambiguity, and uncertainty will strike most readers as absurd because it robs him of the kind of measurement procedures considered the hallmark of rigorous research in the behavioural and social sciences. Yet the open character of such a theory of meaning suggests the basis for misunderstanding in everyday communication, as well as its unique flexibility. The researcher's attempts to specify semantic features traditionally presume that the member is oriented to similar criteria used by the researcher as when one tries to describe bundles of features making up different sound patterns.

Studying an esoteric language forces us to seek information about the native's cultural perspective in his use of language, for even the researcher studying the formal properties of his own language cannot avoid a reliance on features that remain unstated and basic to a native's socialization experiences. Any set of semantic features we designate as distinctive in traditional measurement is embedded in a native's tacit knowledge and use of interpretive procedures as a collection of instructions. Like a native speaker-hearer, the researcher's use of coding practices are practical exigencies necessary for describing a normal report to colleagues. Cutting off the indefinite elaboration of possible submeanings remains a practical agreement in specific contexts that forces each participant to fill in meanings during and after the interaction. The assignment of numerals to semantic features creates a special language game embedded in a world of taken-for-granted common-sense meanings.

Basic to the idea of a generative semantics is the necessity for a theory that would incorporate members' use of interpretive procedures to assign a negotiated sense of meaning, that becomes a concretized appearance (actual commitments are made to lexical items and syntactic constructions which are assumed to be clear) during a specific exchange. Our task is to find ways of making these interpretive procedures visible during experiments with everyday speech exchanges, or, by using field settings, reveal the principles during routine encounters. In current research with children we are finding convincing ways of using video- and audio-tape equipment for detecting the acquisition (over time) and use of interpretive procedures and indexical particulars in specific situations.

Members use interpretive procedures for generating context-sensitive measurement sets consisting of identifiable normative lexical items, grunts, gestures, conversational chunks, body movements and intonational shifts which have indexical constraints throughout the exchange, but which nevertheless produce 'clear, understandable, and relevant' meanings for the participants' practical goals in the interaction. The choice of words, phrases, gestures, intonation and so on, provides the speaker-hearer with a basis for justifying the interpretation of what is happening, and what is to be done next or at some future time. The member's choice of surface representations for communicating his experiences can never convey the ramified thoughts which reflexively give him feedback about unfolding objects and events, and thus endow all communication with an 'openness' of meaning.

Current theories of language do not specify how the speaker-hearer is to evaluate the oral and non-oral particulars of an observable scene, to which he brings socially constituted knowledge. The speaker-hearer must articulate what he experiences with the possible choices among lexical items and their different submeanings (and potential indefinite elaboration by cross-reference). Dictionaries can only be used by presuming the psychological and sociological cognitive processes the mind uses for processing information. Historically, the teaching of language has led to the normative construction of dictionaries and grammatical rules designed for general, practical purposes. Future research must link the use of dictionaries and grammatical rules to psychological and sociological cognitive processes presupposed in language acquisition, use, and change.

Oral and non-oral meanings

The qualitative stages of a child's language development permit him to impose changing constructions and transformations on his perceived and imagined environment. We assume that his comprehension of objects and events around him is partially marked by oral and non-oral particulars. These markings, however, do not consist solely of classes of distinctive features made up of unique sets governed by context-free rules for identifying or assigning meanings, but are specific to actual occasions of use. These particulars take on concrete partial identification when the speaker-hearer refers to his own talk (or gestures) for clarifying what he intends. Participants assume they 'know' (as they assume others 'know' and that others are assuming the same of them) what unstated particulars mean and which ones are relevant for a given context. If participants are called upon to explain their terms, facial expressions and the like, formally established dictionary features may be cited, but such accounting practices are not likely and are usually avoided because they produce negative sanctions among persons on a first-name basis. Logically explicit features are neither expected nor available to most participants in everyday exchanges. The use of specific lexical items or intonation seems to be carried over (observable say, because of repeated tape-recordings of the same parent-child pairs over clock-time) to different contexts. The sign vehicle (lexical item, phrase, intonation, gesture) that is adopted as a context-sensitive measure on one occasion but then employed in other situations, will not evoke the same surface (observable) particulars each time, although the users must presume that their respective ethnographic constructions for 'understanding' what is intended retrieve similar or adequate unstated particulars for the practical purposes at hand. Our 'check-out' of others' use of standardized sign vehicles does not consist of interrogation or pulling a dictionary out of our pockets or purses, but of (often unwittingly) processing the surface signs against a wider horizon of assumed social meanings (an 'oral' dictionary) invoked for the occasion.

The discussion of interpretive procedures can help us understand the speaker-hearer's production and comprehension of non-oral communication, and in particular the manual signing and finger-spelling of the deaf. The hearing child's acquisition of non-oral features of communication is viewed as natural and integral to his acquisition of oral speech, suggesting that such features are as basic as, if not prior to, the child's facility with oral communication (Cicourel and Boese, 1972a). The generative nature of sign language usage for the deaf and the use of non-oral features of communication among hearing persons are not viewed as being tied to a syntactic rule production system, but as having features that mark sign language as a qualitatively distinctive system for the deaf, and as a residual system for the hearing that either adds supplementary information to oral speech or can transcend such speech and serve as an independent channel of communication (Cicourel and Boese, 1972b). I am assuming that the hearing child first learns a rather primitive signal system consisting of gestures, quasi-manual signs and vocal cues. As his speech production grows more sophisticated, the use of the signal system becomes residual and subject to minimal control. If speech is not encouraged or is blocked, the manual sign system would emerge as the basic form of communication. I am asserting that the generative semantic principles underlying both hearing and deaf systems of communication are the same.

The use of manual sign language probably affords a better example for revealing how the member's use of particulars (without claiming distinctive features) operates to produce linguistic change and social change in general. The guiding principle remains that of invariant interpretive procedures; instructions for the imposition of common-sense normative typifications on contingent interaction scenes. Young, hearing children around 12 months of age and adults who do not speak the same language will rely heavily on grunts, pointing to objects, pantomime, and something that might be called primitive manual signs to communicate their intentions. Two deaf persons interacting for an hour or more will begin to develop a generative system between them by building on a simple use of signs or arbitrary arm, hand, and general body movements, while pointing to objects or trying to describe some event, and many of these signs will be linked to the user's ideas about some of the particulars which he feels depict an initial iconic version of the activity in question (which becomes more schematic over time). As in the case of hearing persons using an oral language, the two persons will develop signs whose particulars are restricted to the contexts of interaction, and the unstated attributions of meaning each assumes the other 'knows' in common. But the above description applies to native sign language users who have learned to sign spontaneously in the same sense as hearing children learn to speak spontaneously. Second language signers who have learned formal sign language that is in correspondence with American-English and the American-English alphabet and can be finger-spelled (Cicourel and Boese, 1972a), would be able to identify grammatical normative rules and the linguist could refer to distinctive features, because second language signs have been constructed in accordance with oral language syntax. But it is very difficult for a second language signer to acquire the native sign system or understand it as a native.

The generative principle rests on the idea that the use of particular signs depends on the unstated common knowledge that embellishes the surface signs governed by indexical properties. A third signer who comes on the scene will experience some difficulty in pinpointing the meanings intended by the two original signers, because of the contextual constraints, but if he is a native signer he should have no difficulty developing a general sense of what is going on. A non-native signer would be rather disoriented. Everyday meanings are generative in the sense that interpretive procedures and the indexical properties governing oral and non-oral signs rely on a common body of unstated knowledge that is socially distributed and which participants depend on for recalling, imagining or inventing ethnographic particulars for locating the sanctionable normative character of their experiences.

Researchers of manual sign language and some deaf persons, as well as those interested in ignoring manual signs and finger-spelling in favour of an all-oral method for deaf persons, tend to assume that sign language is not 'really' a natural 'language' because it does not seem to possess the same kind of syntactic normative rule system as oral languages. Despite an important exception (Schlesinger, n.d.) psycholinguists interested in sign language as another natural language often impose oral syntactic rules assuming that the latter model must be relevant because no other can be conceived possible. The idea of a sign language with a different normative rule structure, from oral language, perhaps more basic to primate and human communication from an evolutionary point of view, does not seem to be possible for linguists and psycholinguists who seek to *find* syntactic rules by asking questions that could only lead to *imposing* such rules on native sign language.

When first and second language signers (respectively, those who learn it spontaneously, and those who learn it after having learned an oral system as hearers) use the 'same' signs, it is not clear that they are perceiving and attributing identically describable and unstated particulars. Each tends to favour one system over the other, and thus one system remains basic as a translator. When using manual signs each seems to put a different stress on different para-language information (Cicourel and Boese, 1972b).

I want to suggest, therefore, that the non-oral particulars used by speaker-hearers retain a kind of primitive sign system basis which resembles that of native sign users, but which differs because the signs or non-oral particulars are continually translated into surface (observable) and unstated meanings mediated by an oral system of communication. I am suggesting that we characterize non-oral communication among speaker-hearers by borrowing conceptual elements from native sign users so as to retain some independence for the non-oral particulars used in everyday speech, which are difficult to describe with phonological and syntactic normative rules. If the oral system of communication is being used for representing non-oral particulars, then we are probably losing information about speaker-hearers' implicit reliance on non-oral features that may be based on a primitive intuitive understanding of native sign language. The notion of a 'silent language' (Hall, 1959) would be examined from the point of view of native users of an actual silent language. We can incorporate the study of native sign language into the developing field of sociolinguistics, for both oral and sign language must have the same psychological and sociological cognitive basis, despite the fact that each may have quite different normative grammatical systems for representing the member's experiences.

Summary

In this paper I have urged the adoption of a semantic theory that begins with the member's everyday world as the basic source for assigning meaning to objects and events. The member's common-sense stock of knowledge and his information processing interpretive procedures provide the basis for developing an invariant set of conditions for understanding how speaker-hearers and deaf persons assign meanings to their respective environments. The interpretive procedures and the indexical properties of the particulars they process become a basis for measurement and a resource for the researcher in his studies of language behaviour. The researcher cannot ignore his reliance on these procedures for his own research activities.

Several closely related ideas are basic to the idea of a generative semantics as discussed in this paper.

1. The child acquires a group of abstract principles which enable him to 'discover' the sense of his oral and non-oral activities during the process of creating 'acceptable' exchanges with others. The term 'acceptable' cannot be made precise here because it is always tied to context-restricted information (utilized by the participants) for deciding the adequacy of what is generated over the course of an exchange.

2. The member's ability to monitor his own output and the output of others involves a reflexive embedding of thoughts, perceptions, and spontaneous acts into subsequent outputs. Simultaneously, the speaker-hearer projects this reflective activity prospectively and retrospectively so as to create 'traces' and 'glimpses' of what was intended by participants, including the speaker-hearer himself. Thus 'errors' and 'good' or embarrassing points, elements irrelevant to the present conversation, thoughts about other problems, past encounters with present participants, all become embedded in the experiences which make up some sequence of activities that is often terminated by practical exigencies like a lunch bell, another appointment, feeling bored, and so on.

3. The member experiences far more than he can describe, far more than he can react to, and more than he wants to react to; and his descriptions of what happened carry the presumption that others will attribute unstated elements to his remarks. The description must provide the speaker and hearer with a basis for recovering or imagining the experiences that went into the creation of the account. Native speakers and hearers are well-versed

in recalling, inventing or imagining the acceptable normative elements which shaped the descriptive account, despite the fact that the analytic linguistic components, e.g. phonological, syntactic, semantic (dictionary), lack the precision needed for portraying what happened, even if such formal elements are known to the participants explicitly.

Social change (including linguistic change) is recorded when we use some form of communication to convey new thoughts and experiences. Variable reliance on different particulars across social contexts is mirrored partially in the slower change in normative rules governing social interaction. These changes derive from the use of interpretive procedures and the indexical properties of oral and non-oral communication in context-sensitive settings. The historical process, whereby surface and unstated particulars are added and dropped by speaker-hearers' everyday language use, provides an important basis for studying sociolinguistic changes.

4 Ethnomethodology

The term 'ethnomethodology' was coined by Harold Garfinkel (1967) to index the study of everyday practical reasoning as constitutive of all human activities. A basic consideration in the study of practical reasoning is members' use of everyday talk or accounts to describe the factual status of their experiences and activities. This abstract opening statement is not intended as a crisp explanation of the term 'ethnomethodology', but a delaying action so that a more elaborate discussion will evolve gradually in later sections.

In this chapter I restrict myself to selected aspects of generative-transformational linguistics in order to address more general issues in the problem of meaning. The term 'linguistics', however, is to be used in a generic way despite my more narrow reference to some features of generative-transformational grammar. I will trade on a presumed knowledge by the reader of current issues in generative-transformational linguistics in my development of ethnomethodology and its perspective on language and meaning.

The ethnomethodologist is interested in the modern linguist's use of speech or talk to construct a grammar that will describe the structure of language. But this interest in the linguist's activities assumes that every attempt to describe the structure of language relies on practical reasoning as a tacit and unexamined resource for finding in talk (but primarily idealized talk) an innovative but rule-governed structure (competence) that is said to transcend actual displays (performance). The ethnomethodologist's central concern is the study of members' necessary reliance on practical or mundane reasoning to communicate with others, and the fact that members count on this tacit use of practical reasoning for more abstract activities like constructing mathematical proofs or developing rewrite rules in linguistics.

Ethnomethodologists and linguists employ somewhat different conceptions of meaning, but both rely on the production of speech or accounts as a point of departure. For the linguist, the meaning of speech becomes fairly restricted; it is tied to the establishment of relationships and reference in speech, through the use of formal types of reasoning that seeks to produce determinate outcomes. For the ethnomethodologist, talk and action are produced and understood as indexical displays of the everyday world (Bar-Hillel, 1954; Garfinkel, 1967; Cicourel, 1968b). The linguist relies heavily on a conception of meaning based on syntax, while the ethnomethodologist addresses the interpretive abilities presupposed by the necessary interplay between competence and situated performance. This chapter relies on elements of linguistic theory to present an ethnomethodological view of the problem of meaning. A partial outline follows.

Linguistic and ethnomethodological approaches to the problem of meaning differ markedly. The former has stressed formal properties of language which would be relevant for the development of logical relationships and rules to describe the association between sound patterns and the objects, events or experiences to which they refer. The latter approach has been concerned with the process whereby rules said to cover interactional settings are constructed, as well as with the assessment of claimed measurement of the actual implementation of rules in specific circumstances. Ethnomethodology emphasizes the interpretive work required to recognize that an abstract rule exists which could fit a particular occasion, while linguists minimize the relevance of interactional context-sensitive features when stressing the importance of syntactic rules for semantic analysis. Recent work on generative semantics (Lakoff, 1968b; McCawley, 1968a and b and Ross, forthcoming) has been moving towards including the consideration of context and presuppositions as developed in philosophical studies of language and anthropological linguistics, and these works have been helpful in formulating the present chapter.

The ethnomethodologist views meaning as situated, self-organizing and reflexive interaction between the organization of memory, practical reasoning, and talk. Linguistic rules are seen as normative constructions divorced from the cognitive reflection and ethnographic settings in which speech is produced and understood. Universal grammatical structures inferred from proscribed and prescribed forms of talk can be described as general rules, policies or practices, under which situated innovative language displays of familiar forms are subsumed. Syntactic and phonological rules provide linguists with carefully constructed normative ideals that can be studied and described independently of actual use in social settings. The researcher's context-free description or account, however, presumes and tacitly relies on an intuitive use of ethnographic particulars and interpretive procedures that are never made explicit, though occasionally touched upon in an abstract way.

The term generative semantics, therefore, is not, for the ethnomethodologist, a syntax-based theory of meaning and reference. The acquisition and use of general rules of syntax and phonology presuppose a tacit reliance on cognitive activities embedded in the organization of memory within an interactional setting. Settings or some kind of imagery must be recalled, invented, or imagined to make utterances, stripped of their situated occurrence, appear plausible. There is a continual reflexive monitoring by the speaker-hearer to provide self-organizing information processing during activities like reading a text or discussing a setting different from the one being experienced. The conception of generative semantics proposed here assumes that the speaker-hearer selectively consults and intuitively presupposes features or particulars in a setting to invoke the tacit or explicit phonological, syntactic, lexical, social, or legal rules to order and justify his speech.

The use of memory and interpretive procedures (Cicourel, 1968b; 1970b) for recoding or chunking activities illustrates how practical reasoning requires indexical procedures for expressing reflexive thoughts that interact with visual and auditory particulars in a setting. In contrast, the notion of a rule of grammar, like any normative practice or policy, is invoked to construct a correspondence theory that minimizes the role of intuitive reasoning in linking a rule or practice with particular occasions of speech usage. Those particulars remembered or selectively witnessed (intended) are tied to standardized conceptions of meaning so that categorization by rule can simulate a sense of adequacy for intended meanings and reference. Linguistic analyses and studies of artificial intelligence achieve their elegance by examining utterances which are divested of the non-syntactic particulars presupposed in their production. These utterances, while not as 'purified' as those constructed by logicians, are conveniently produced by the linguist by drawing on his native abilities with the language, or by making use of elicitation procedures that guarantee the selectivity necessary for fitting utterances to idealized syntactic or phonological rules. The student of artificial intelligence and the linguist achieve elegant description by relying on idealized utterances and their practical reasoning and intuitive knowledge of language to legislate non-syntactic ambiguity and contradictions out of their constructed realities.

A recent study of children in quasi-experimental and natural classroom settings is discussed in the final section to clarify issues in the problem of meaning by revealing how situated reconstructions of past experiences, and unfolding auditory and visual cues are central for the child's production of oral expressions which adults evaluate as phonologically, syntactically, and semantically 'correct'. The child's understanding of presumed 'clear' stimulus sentences by an experimenter or teacher does not always coincide with the adult's conception of a correct correspondence between a stimulus and a response.

Additional work on manual sign language provides an even broader theoretical and empirical basis for suggesting that the problem of meaning in a general theory of communication cannot be conceived as part of an oral language tradition that is syntactically organized. Many versions of sign language emerge depending on the frequency of interaction between participants as dyads or in larger groups. The self-organizing nature of sign activity among deaf strangers underlines the situated basis of meaning because there are no standard rules of orthography and grammar which force members to express themselves via idealized or rule-modified constructions that have been divested of non-syntactic particulars. Only when signs are set up in correspondence with oral language grammatical structures and a standardized lexicon does sign language give any appearance of having formal context-free properties.

Recent linguistic work (Lakoff, 1968b) suggests that one version of the generative semantics proposed by syntactically-oriented generative-transformational linguists will be forced to adopt more of a situated interactional approach to meaning if notions like counterpart theory, and the idea of sentences containing contradictory references to different possible worlds, are pursued. One consequence of adopting an interactional perspective wherein syntactic rules play a minor role in problems of meaning and doing reference, is that current reliance on sentence boundaries and a static lexicon of the 'look-up' sort will have to be altered radically. The notion of 'sentence' is being re-examined in response to recent work on performative theory and embedding in phrase structure rules. Unless the syntactic basis for meaning is altered we must view the linguist as a judge: he would be a specialist for interpreting a highly formal system of rules, practices, or policies so that these rules could be invoked to justify the claim that a particular instance of speech can be said to fall under a rule, practice or policy (Rawls, 1955; Cicourel, 1967; 1968a). The analogy between judges and linguists is central to my argument because in each case the features or particulars which serve as empirical displays (e.g. the details of a police report, the intent of an action that leads to bodily harm, the sentences offered as candidates for grammaticality, lexical items assigned meaning by reference to a dictionary and classificatory bundles of features) are always idealized accounts whose 'legality' is decided by the judge or linguist by consulting a rule structure he has imposed on the ambiguity and looseness of everyday language. The judge and linguist assign normative sense to sentences or their structure and thus detach utterances from their common sense and situated meaning, transforming them into context-free claims about social reality. The linguist, of course, would claim that many of his judgements (e.g. number agreement) render context irrelevant.

When lawyers are taught about legal activities by the use of textbook materials that include the 'facts' of a case, a large number of contingencies or particulars are eliminated so that a coherent story appears which reduces possible ambiguities in the description of an unfolding scene over clock-time. The language of the lawyer's argument is a carefully edited grammatical text whose structure is managed, just as a linguist's candidate sentences are edited or the informant's utterances constrained through the linguist's elicitation procedures. The utterances used by linguists for constructing rules that account for linguistic descriptions are generally posed as context-free. The self-contained or bounded nature of these utterances eliminates the ambiguities that members must incorporate into their production of speech when carrying out everyday conversations. In actual exchanges editing is constrained by a concern for chaining sequences, but can also trade on visual and auditory information.

If we view a speaker-hearer's utterances as accounts that are situated, edited versions of information that is being processed, then fragments of utterances, pauses, ellipsis, auditory and visual information not verbalized, can no longer be ignored but must be incorporated into the linguist's theories. The differentials in meaning emerge within the contingencies of an interaction setting where the ethnographic context, the biographies of the participants, and subtleties of voice intonation, gestures, and body posturing all contribute to the information that is continually being processed while utterances are being produced. To include such contingencies would obviously go beyond the goals of most linguists. The linguist is dealing with an 'idealized speaker-hearer' who often turns out to be himself or his wife turned informant, someone who is tacitly reflective at least about sentences he dreams up or is asked to assess. This reflective activity divorces the formal sense of the utterance from the contingencies mentioned above, while simultaneously producing a tacit (but suppressed) ethnographic context that could yield the utterance. But even this tacit context is often irrelevant for the linguist interested in showing what sentences must look like if rules that seem to hold for one class of sentences must also cover another sentence whose structure seems a bit odd. The linguist makes explicit use of his own or an esoteric informant's native intuition or 'feel' for the language without addressing the cognitive aspects of his production of language.

We can illustrate some of the problems mentioned above by discussing Lakoff's paper (1968b) on the problem of reference. He proposes two readings of the following sentence (Lakoff's numbering):

2. 'I dreamed that I was playing the piano.'

The first reading is called the 'participant reading' and Lakoff describes this as a feeling that he is sitting at a piano, seeing the keyboard, with his fingers hitting the keys. He adds an 'etc.' to his description to imply further particulars are possible. In the second reading (called the 'observer reading'), he sees himself (or someone like himself) sitting at the piano, playing it, as if he were sitting in a movie watching himself perform. What is of interest in Lakoff's distinction between participant and observer readings of a sentence is that all readings imply perspectival views of possible speaker-hearers, and the kinds of ethnographic conditions that might render these readings (or others) plausible. The ethnographic particulars are integral to the interpretations offered. A consequence of including specific ethnographic conditions is that sentences can be seen as meaningful and also satisfying syntactic rules, yet a dictionary look-up of each lexical item can only locate the sentence for a reader by tacitly trading on a native's intuitive reasoning and conception of ethnographic particulars. In situated everyday conversation, however, we also have many sentences which are either grammatically improper or not understandable by reference to a dictionary. My concern is to show that as soon as the linguist entertains alternative possible readings he tacitly invokes situated circumstances that render problematic the context-free readings possible by reference to syntactic rules and a dictionary. Each reader can supply many features or particulars that are privileged to the perspectival view or account of the observer to justify a specific reading of an utterance.

Lakoff then presents two additional sentences that are said to represent participant and observer readings of the same action:

3. 'I enjoyed robbing the bank.'
4. 'I enjoyed my robbing the bank.'

Sentence (3) is said to be a participant reading which refers to an enjoyment of a bank robbing experience, while (4) is said to be an observer reading where there is a reflexive observing or possible contemplation of an event. To call the act reflexive suggests that the speaker-hearer's thoughts provide a self-organizing basis for the intended reference. His thoughts may be only partially indexed by the utterance produced, making it difficult for an observer to determine the intended referent. Lakoff is interested in showing that sentences like (5), (6), (7), (8), (9), and (10) cannot be handled by the theory of referential indices (if two noun phases (NPs) have the same referential indices, they have the same 'intended reference'), for sentences like (9) and (10) would have the same underlying or deep structure, yet include two different semantic references (asterisk indicates an ungrammatical sentence).

5.   'As a participant, I enjoyed robbing the bank.'
6.* 'As an outside observer, I enjoyed robbing the bank.'
7.* 'As a participant, I enjoyed my robbing the bank.'
8.   'As an outside observer, I enjoyed my robbing the bank.'

9. 'I imagined robbing the bank.' (participant)
10. 'I imagined myself robbing the bank.' (observer)

The point being stressed by Lakoff is that syntactic distinctions cannot handle the problem of the 'same' intended reference within the same sentence or different sentences where both participant and observer readings refer to different kinds of discourse or possible worlds. The subjects of (9) and (10) have the same reference in the same world, while the subjects of the verbs *imagine* and *rob* have the same physical reference but the worlds (participant and observer) are different. Lakoff's distinction can be extended by noting that imagining presupposes not only my participating but also observing myself as a participant. Thus Lakoff (referring to another sentence) distinguishes between the actual world in which one can do dreaming activity, and the world of the dream itself. A person's identity must be referenced differently when different realities are entertained and the person assumes two identities because the actual world (read: the world within my reach or grasp) is conceived as two possible worlds (read: the world within my reach and the world within my dreams, cf. Schutz, 1964). Lakoff presents another sentence to show how two types of people (read: with ideological differences) in one possible world are reduced to a single individual in another possible world (read: the ideological world reconstructed by the speaker-hearer).

15. 'You think that Nixon and Humphrey are different people and that *they* will campaign against each other and one of *them* will lose, but I think that Nixon and Humphrey are the same person and that *he* will win.'

Lakoff has touched upon the construction of multiple realities by members (be they informants or researchers) described more extensively by Schutz (1962), by recognizing that generative transformational grammar cannot handle the complicated problems of reference posed by different possible worlds. The same syntactic markers confuse different possible worlds in the surface or deep structure constructions, but it is clear that the speaker-hearer (informant and researcher) must supply meanings that must be attributed on the basis of what seems 'obvious' or what 'anyone knows' to be the intentions of the speaker-hearer.

When Lakoff argues that within the first half of the same sentence (15) Nixon and Humphrey have different referential indices, and therefore cannot have the same index in the second half of the sentence, he wants to show that syntactic grounds for doing reference are inadequate. The possible semantic solution suggested by Lakoff would require a logic through which different possible worlds can be represented, such that a single entity in one world can be represented as two different entities in another world. By insisting on a normative system of rules to gloss what members in everyday life resolve routinely despite syntactic limitations, the linguist or logician seeks to organize our speech acts such that linguistics or logic becomes a policy science. Natural ways developed by members for coping with inherent gaps and inconsistencies in lay theories of language use would be ignored, while more elegant rule systems would be constructed that could logically hope to resolve the ambiguities of doing reference as outlined in the work by Lakoff. Much of language can be viewed as normatively learned, in that existing forms of speech become progressively reified and standardized by historical accidents and power relationships within a community or country. The result of normative language legislation is that some forms are rewarded or honoured more as marks of social achievement or intellectual status, and other forms of speech are justified by reference to scientifically-based psychological theories of learning and testing.

Linguists insist that the acquisition and use of natural language is miraculous because it is characterized by the ability to understand and produce an indefinite number of expressions which are new to one's experience. Chomsky (n.d.) notes the creative nature of language and the independence of its appropriate use from any clear-cut stimulus configurations in some conditioned sense. He suggests these very characteristics may preclude detailed knowledge about the human use of language as an instrument for expressing thought and feeling. He goes on to discuss several other important issues which I want to link to Lakoff's paper and to the problem of meaning as situated phenomena that require the interaction of the speaker-hearer's (a) standardized or typified use of information to provide for memory generalization and the resolution of ambiguity; and (b) continual reflexiveness of thought, talk, and situation.

Doubts about the phonetic representation are expressed by Chomsky in the same argument by raising the question of the legitimacy of this abstraction process. He raises the issue of whether our understanding of the use of language must go beyond grammatical structure when we use formal rules for interpreting surface structure as phonetic form. Anyone who has done field research with children and adults in his own and foreign communities will recognize the difficulties of locating phonetic representations for many sounds. We utilize phonetic categories as normative rules that we force on materials. By incorporating scientific knowledge into our everyday use of language as well as our teaching children how they are to represent themselves through sound patterns, the linguist ignores the interaction between what is learned normatively and what is claimed as linguistic universals or an acquisition device.

Linguists do not study the abstraction process itself when they devise notions like deep and surface structures, phonetic and semantic representations. Yet these abstractions are employed as descriptions of language competence and use. Notions like deep and surface structure cannot alone recover the abstraction 'everyday language' because the pragmatics of everyday language use is always embedded reflexively in the setting of its production. Some of these situated and reflexive features are illustrated by Lakoff's distinction between participant and observer readings of a sentence and the idea of different possible worlds which cannot be referenced by the theory of referential indices. Deep structure is an arbitrary notion (but heuristically useful) constructed by the linguist to deal with the fact that surface structure is indexical; it always implies more information than is displayed. Proposing transformational rules to link deep and surface structures does not alter the arbitrariness of deep structure which the linguist constructs by selectively consulting the particulars of a setting and his own reflections about how a given utterance may have been produced.

Despite his expressed cautions about the abstraction process, Chomsky shifts from a treatment of the formal rules of grammar as describing the structure of language to a reification of the grammar as characterizing part of the speaker-hearer's knowledge of a language. The linguist's heuristically useful constructs for depicting an ideal speaker-hearer have become rules that a person who has learned a language has mastered. The linguist's heuristically developed rules constitute the person's knowledge of the language.

The claims about what constitutes a person's knowledge of a language are presented by Chomsky in the context of showing how certain sentences appear to have deep and surface structures that are similar, if not identical, while other sentences differ in their deep and surface representation. He goes on to alter previous formulations by noting how surface structure can be important in determining the semantic interpretation of a sentence. This observation requires a discussion of how different meanings are presupposed in the surface structure of a sentence in the sense outlined by Lakoff when he talks of different possible worlds, and the readings possible by a participant as opposed to an observer, or both readings in the same sentence. Chomsky has further modified earlier versions of his theory by noting how different intonational contours can alter the surface meaning of a sentence. Differences of intonation can lead to complicated conceptions of the presuppositions involved. Speaker-hearers make use of presuppositions on every occasion of speech. The serious question discussed in more detail later in the chapter is how the presuppositions are to be located by reference to a rather rigid system of rules claimed for the speaker-hearer. Alternatively, how are we to locate presuppositions by reference to intonational contours that influence the way that information is processed and then presumably indexed by sound patterns? Much of contemporary linguistics operates within a theory of grammar characterized by three components – the phonological, syntactic, and semantic – along with an elusive lexicon. By introducing the idea of presupposition and treating intonation seriously, the linguist, whatever his view of the interrelations among these components, will find it hard to avoid bringing in additional types of information that have been glossed with the label 'pragmatics'.

The picture that emerges from Chomsky's paper is that deep structure endows an utterance with predication and modifications which enter into the problem of determining meaning, while the surface structure in part handles matters of focus and presupposition, pronominal reference, and topic, among others. Recalling Lakoff's remarks that possible worlds can contain contradictions, the fascinating changes taking place within generative semantics lead one to ask if linguists can hold on to the formal syntactic distinctions (like sentence boundaries) as both observers' rules for explaining speaker-hearers' utterances, and as claims that the formal notions are also part of universal grammar and the speaker-hearer's mental structures?

The idea of a deep structure with transformational rules that provide for a surface structure is an important heuristic device because it calls attention to the indexicality of everyday language; however, it also raises serious questions about the term 'natural' in referring to language use. The naturalness of language becomes problematic because it is not clear how linguists' formulations, teachers' curricula, educational psychologists' and psycho-linguists' assessment tests, and educated adults' models, interact in a speech community. The linguist's use of elicitation procedures to discover evidence of linguistic universals presupposes an ideal language structure. Speech acts may be called 'natural' by an observer when he senses that members appear to be oblivious to 'correct' or ungrammatical usage. We have, however, little knowledge about uneducated everyday language use (even in non-literate societies) despite many field studies. In addition, we ignore the extent to which our studies of competence and use are continually infused with formal normative elements that derive from monitoring one's own output or having it monitored by others. What seems to be natural about everyday speech is that groups have always developed various kinds of normative rules or conventions for such purposes as determining kinship relationships, performing public ceremonies, and interpersonal address.

The linguistic expert uses his own capabilities as a native speaker-hearer or those of an informant to formulate the grammatical utterances of a language. The idealized sentences produced are the work of an expert, even when the sentences are elicited from an informant prompted about what he is expected to say. Using his own native competence (or that of an informant) the linguist provides us with conceptions of what is possible or believable about an utterance up for grammatical or semantic review. He will note that we cannot ignore the universal character of disjunctions as underlying yes–no questions, or that imperatives have second person subjects, and the like. But these conceptions or presuppositions (like participant and observer readings or intonational stress) must be in agreement with the normatively constructed logical schema adopted for representing syntactic relationships.

Lakoff's distinctions are important because he attempts to push the syntactic framework to its limits to show that it cannot cover reference work which endows the speaker-hearer with the ability to live with apparent contradictions and multiple realities which defy traditional two-valued logic. Logical frameworks are subdomains of everyday language which have been cleansed of difficulties that would confound the correspondence theory necessary for idealized outcomes. Therefore, grammatical or logical utterances retain their rule-governed structure because they have been cleansed and divorced from their occasions of use, and other particulars about the biographies of the participants, the features of the setting tacitly taken into account, the reflexive thinking and use of talk, and so on. For the linguist the book he is now reading is proof that language behaviour can be understood independently of the occasions that produced it. The speaker-hearer (linguist, logician) can consult his own speech for evidence that his enterprise is a success because his mastery of the formal normative framework becomes a referential schema or system of general rules to justify claims that utterances he produces or those of a native informant can be described by reference to these rules. The linguist constructs a self-validating circle that tacitly utilizes unexplicated common knowledge as a basic resource for recognizing topics, constructing appropriate presuppositions, and eliminating possible alternatives not suggested by the logical possibilities of idealized normative rules.

Linguists prefer to live with different kinds of conveniently constructed glosses, while the ethnomethodologist prefers to treat the glossing itself as an activity that becomes the phenomenon of interest while recognizing that no one can escape some level of glossing in order to claim knowledge about something. But this claim to knowledge, this use of some level of glossing for communication, is also a claim for a privileged position. Different levels of glossing produce different self-validating circles and hence different claims about what is known. We can perhaps achieve glimpses of our glossing activity by making it clear that every attempt to simulate or avoid the glossing activity is itself a glossing operation. This means showing the absurdity of efforts to be uncompromisingly literal in our descriptions of observed events or activities in which we participate.

In this section I rely on selected topics in recent work on visual and linguistic memory organization and studies of artificial intelligence to provide a more general framework for examining the semantic issues addressed in the first section. Ethnomethodology and semantic issues in linguistics both presuppose that cognition and thought are central for understanding linguistic competence, but employ different models of the speaker-hearer. Linguists imply that the same mechanisms govern both the production and comprehension of speech. The ethnomethodologist seeks to locate the comprehension of speech in an emergent interactional setting that makes speech production both a topic and a resource for the participant. This section explores the treatment of everyday language as an abstract topic for creating strong rule systems to justify claims about grammaticality and meaning by linguists and cognitively oriented students of artificial intelligence, and their failure within these enterprises to study how everyday language and meaning are and remain *tacit* resources for applying and interpreting these systems. The constructed rule system guarantees that a correspondence theory of measurement will be constitutive of utterances which are candidates for grammaticality or computer procedures which are intended to establish artificial constructions of meaning and reference.

A central issue in studies of artificial intelligence is how to deal with the short- and long-term storage of information. Linguists have not given the problem of memory much attention because recall and recognition are not problematic issues in discussions of deep and surface structure and the transformational rules that link them. The linguist claims a certain kind of immunity from contamination by memory problems largely by ignoring performance issues and focusing on a corpus of materials that is divorced from interactional settings. The linguists, however, share with the students of artificial intelligence an interest in syntactic, semantic, and lexical problems, and the use of edited sentences generated primarily by a native speaker-hearer who is either the researcher himself, or an informant who acts like a research assistant. Recent work in artificial intelligence has posed interaction between a machine programmed to generate English sentences, and a native-speaking subject or informant-researcher (Greenberger, 1962; Reitman, 1965; Minsky, 1968; and Simon, 1969). Ethnomethodologists (Garfinkel, 1967) have used a kind of 'talking-out-loud' procedure similar to those used by students of artificial intelligence (De Groot, 1965; Quillian, 1968; Simon and Barenfeld, 1969) for generating material designed to make visible how language and meaning are embedded in and created by a cognitive information processing system. Quillian (1968), Colby *et al.* (1969) and Simon and Barenfeld (1969) study information processing by having the speaker-hearer engage in some task like thinking out loud about chess moves, stating and justifying beliefs, or having a coder-subject encode sentences of English text into the format of a previously created memory model. The authors of these studies view the protocols as displays of information processing. Yet the task alters the routine ways in which humans confront such problems by asking for explicit statements of activities seldom discussed while actually being experienced.

The ethnomethodologist collects talking-out-loud protocols and employs them to reveal the taken-for-granted features of daily activities after making everyday routines appear strange to subjects. Garfinkel (1967) demonstrated this idea by having subjects ask questions of a 'counsellor' about their problems. The counsellor's 'answers', however, were randomized 'yes' and 'no' responses. Subjects were able to reorient their thinking to absorb apparent contradictions and ambiguities. Another procedure is to have persons give accounts of some recent activity and then show each subject an audio or video tape of the activity while asking for another account of the activity. The ethnomethodologist sees these constructed accounts as indefinite elaborations of ostensibly the 'same' scene, where various accounts produce different outputs. Specifying that someone did the task 'correctly', made a 'proper' chess move, or reasoned 'correctly' is not a goal of ethnomethodological analysis. Instead there is a deep concern with treating the temporally constituted production and comprehension processes as the phenomena of interest. This means that the grammatical structure of speech acts is merely one part of indexical activity or the production process, and no more 'natural' than raising or lowering the voice, stepping closer to or farther from someone during a conversation, or relying on facial expressions and body movements to communicate the intent of one's thinking.

The use of grammatical rules to order speech provides an elegant and powerful tool for organizing and standardizing the production of verbal acts that index cognition and thought. Rules of grammar and programmes of artificial intelligence are designed to eliminate ambiguities and contradictions and to produce outcomes that are internally consistent. The production of rule-governed utterances or programmes are normative constructions subject to specifiable constraints if they are to code and recode or chunk information according to specifiable search procedures or algorithms (Miller, 1956; Norman, 1969). Our human experiences continually outstrip our ability to express them in speech acts. We must assume that a number of tacit properties are operative or plausible when we code, recode and then use information to communicate with others. The organization of memory and the intuitive procedures we use to interpret an interactional setting are strained by the indexical structure of language. Our ability to assign meaning to utterances is contingent on an understanding of various possible sources of information in a complex setting. Syntactic rules do not appear to be central but are clearly useful for achieving normative agreement.

The organization of memory can only be meaningful *vis-à-vis* the settings in which speech and non-oral communication occur. The setting is not merely a passive vehicle for witnessing universals of language; the setting is constitutive of how properties of cognition as displays of practical reasoning render a scene sensible or socially meaningful. Speech, like one's social and personal identity, requires continuous performances if rules or attributes said to transcend the setting (like presumed personality traits said to be somehow embedded in the actor) are to be recognized as operative. If we seldom speak to others in public settings our performances suffer, and we avoid such occasions. If we do not write often then even a simple letter becomes difficult, while a governmental form proves torturous. Persons who become deaf after adolescence quickly lose their ability to speak like natives because the reflexive feedback of a temporally constituted scene that includes intonation, body movements, gestures, visual and auditory details, is altered as a source of information. The organization of cognition which served us on previous occasions is reconstituted in each new setting while we normatively reconstruct our speech, our social identity, and culture itself. The discovery of constancies reflects the normative organization of everyday experience by an inescapable reliance on memory and practical reasoning.

Speech as used in everyday conversations provides the native with his own measurement system because some members ritualize certain forms of speech. The more obvious examples of normative features of speech are to be found in ceremonies and rituals, which we call religious or developmental as in rites of passage, or legal as in marriage or judicial activities. Thus, everyday talk indexically constitutes its own explication on each occasion of use. As a measurement system of cognitive activity, speech indexes some particulars, but we must feel, perceive, recover, invent, or imagine many more particulars in order to assign sense to a setting. Some set of phrase structure rules and transformational rules does not produce language; we must ask how the particulars of language production as a situated accomplishment of each occasion can be linked reflexively by speaker-hearers to some normative system of grammatical, legal, or other rules. We examine our talk in order to find, among other things, its normative character.

Chunking or recoding is a way of describing formal indexical activity. Miller's (1956) work on the span of immediate memory is important for showing that regardless of the information content (which limits absolute judgement) of different items, our immediate memory seems to be limited by the number of items. Miller distinguishes between *bits* of information that seem to be constant for absolute judgement, and *chunks* of information that seem to be constant for immediate memory span. Miller reports that by regrouping two or more digits into code items that remained at seven or less, subjects could extend the number of digits that could be retained in immediate memory. This efficient regrouping or recoding of old items into new items is called *chunking* by Miller. We expand the number of items we can remember by building larger and larger chunks so that each chunk contains more information than previously. The span of immediate memory appears to be independent of the number of bits that can be grouped into a chunk.

The term 'short-term memory', however, seems to refer to a type of psychological experiment rather than to describe the recoding process as it operates in humans (Norman, 1969). We are not very clear about how members carry out chunking because most of the recoding experiments have been done with fairly simple stimuli. Miller notes that we engage in recoding operations continuously on objects, facts, images, arguments, and events told as stories, and that these operations are more complicated than the presumed unidimensional stimuli used in psychological experiments. We continuously recode our experiences into verbal reports that we remember, and then use the verbal recall as a way of recovering the events recoded, or to give accounts to others about our experiences. Miller suggests that particular speaker-hearers develop idiosyncratic ways of recoding which become embedded in their life history.

All language use seems to reflect some kind of underlying competence and also represents at least two kinds of compromise which the speaker-hearer must negotiate:

1. The language employed is part of an indexical process whose most primitive formal output can be loosely characterized as chunked or recoded information.

2. The products of chunking are normative displays that are culture-specific and also constrained by differential abilities, educational training, use, or occupation.

The negotiation means that, within the indexicality of language, actual use can always vary in different contexts or occasions; variations emerge because participants locate and elaborate particulars differently by relying on speech, visual and auditory information, biographical information, and a reflexive elaboration of their own memory or general cognitive procedures.

Language chunking or recoding constitutes our efforts to express our experiences. The role of rules for generating admissible sound patterns expressed logically as bundles of features and strings of words normatively segmented into logically constructed units called sentences, is only one (though often useful) element among various chunks of particulars that convey meaning and do reference in everyday exchanges. To say that something is rule-governed presupposes that members will agree that certain behaviours or activities are being followed correctly or incorrectly. This means that indexical expressions (Bar-Hillel, 1954; Garfinkel, 1967; Cicourel, 1968b; Garfinkel and Sacks, 1969) or any given instance verbalized (or produced non-orally) as a chunk of particulars must be subsumed under general rules such that the speaker-hearer will presume that others would agree with his reasoning and recognize the instance, event or object as falling under a class, policy, practice, or general rule (Rawls, 1955; Hart, 1961; Cicourel, 1967; 1968a).

Linguists have advanced a convincing argument for biologically based universals of language (Chomsky, 1965). I do not wish to quarrel with the biological foundations of language (Lenneberg, 1968) here, but do wish to question the idea of 'linguistic universals'. The linguistic argument states that every human group studied has a spoken language with a lexicon and a grammar, where the lexicon seems to be organized into normatively consistent bits and chunks. Each language provides for pronominal displays, contains notions of time, space and number, as well as notions like true and false, and can be described as having phonological and syntactic levels of structure. It seems clear that biological competence is presupposed in these activities. But we can also call the 'universals' normative constructions imposed initially by certain 'experts' in a tribe or linguists in a society or nation-state. The idea is that forms of communication other than oral language can convey these activities. This view argues that 'linguistic universals' are cultural products of normative chunking or recoding activities. A linguist would want to argue that the *same* linguistic norms keep turning up in different languages. He would claim that this consistency cannot be dismissed as the product of the researchers' methods for discovering language regularities.

I want to treat each linguistic universal as a particular kind of gloss imposed by the ingenious constructions of the researcher (and lay scribes and grammarians). Each glossing practice (Garfinkel and Sacks, 1969) represents the researcher's native ability to begin with any level of indexicality designated as 'correct' speech or any language display in conformity with some general rule or practice. The researcher then seeks to reduce the chunk or gloss to constituent or basic elements. I do not think that work in acoustical phonetics alters this assertion because the native intuition of a speaker-hearer is essential for recognizing meaningful patterns in physical displays of human speech. Normative grammatical constructions we learn as natives help us find noun phrases and verb phrases in all languages, or we can train members to use an alphabet in such a way that the sounds of any language will fall under the general rules involving vowels and consonants. Similarly, we can use a case system to find that all languages can be forced into this kind of construction providing we are willing to employ the handy notion of ellipsis or presuppositions about tacit knowledge. The use of speech or talk is a tacit presupposition of common sense or mundane reasoning for speaker hearers. Hence we rely on an intuitive use of talk as a constitutive self-organizing feature of practical reasoning in order to examine talk reflexively as a resource for claiming that we have discovered universals in every normatively organized society.

Linguistic rules are one of the formal ways humans have normatively discovered to construct chunking or recoding procedures for handling verbal information that indexes a variety of experiences embedded in an interactional scene. The construction of meaning and reference can be facilitated by such rules for generating and processing information in everyday interaction, even when the information is produced and stored independently of oral language. But meaning and reference can be generated and communicated by modes other than oral language.

A consequence of treating linguistic universals as normative constructions is that solutions to the problems of meaning and reference can be facilitated because the idea of universals forces a wide variety of complex experiences and information processing procedures into a social framework for displaying ostensible forms of agreement, consensus, or understanding. But the ability to produce grammatical and ungrammatical strings of sound patterns that can be coded into a standard orthography tells very little about the more difficult problem of how the child is able to index information and assign meanings in specific contexts. The central issues in the biological argument are that a child must be able to acquire the language in question despite the fact that his parents do not know how to teach it to him in some systematic way that would include schedules of reward and punishment. The child must possess the ability to learn to produce a wide variety of utterances that others will be able to comprehend, and to understand an unlimited number of diverse utterances he has never heard before. Humans' species-specific cognitive properties which permit the production and understanding of unlimited utterances preclude a conditioning argument for the acquisition of language, but the normative construction of rules means that mistakes are recognizable and, therefore, conditioning successes *are* possible.

Our ability to create subdomains of everyday language by eliminating or deleting particulars that create ambiguity or contradictions (e.g. logical or mathematical systems) also gives rise to conceptions of language production based on the notion of rule-governed linguistic universals. But how we understand what we can produce seems to extend beyond the way the linguist conceives of the grammar of phrase structure and transformational rules (Quillian, 1968). We find we can attribute children's capabilities to imitate sentences given by adults (in the home, in the classroom, in a psycholinguistic experiment) to the idea of a short-term store or primary memory that requires rehearsal if it is to be transferred to a long-term store or secondary memory (Norman, 1969). The ways in which we decide that the child understands what he can produce or what adults produce is not very clear. Much of what is attributed to linguistic competence is based on the child's ability to generate or produce utterances. Neither the biological foundations of language nor the biological basis of cognition, need be questioned to understand that the production of utterances seems to be dependent on the cognitive ability to learn and use normative linguistic rules. Rehearsal is essential for discussions of primary and secondary memory regardless of whether or not one believes in a unitary theory or prefers to distinguish short-term and long-term storage mechanisms. The idea of rehearsal must include reflexive exchanges with others where the individual's own thoughts become the object of rehearsal and elaboration or situated indexical activity.

The problem becomes more complicated when we recognize the role of visual perception in remembering and planning (Miller, Galanter, and Pribram, 1960). An interactional setting complicates the use and understanding of language because of visual and auditory information and reflexive thoughts by speaker-hearers. The idea of one kind of memory for pictorial material and another for linguistic material (Haber, 1968; 1969; 1970) suggests that pictorial and linguistic material are interactionally productive features of understanding in all settings. Subjects seem to remember pictures better than a name associated with a picture. We can extend this point to say that we can understand more than we can formulate according to normatively (grammatically) correct rules and appropriate lexical designations for objects and events. Haber's experiments suggest that subjects retain information about fine details of pictures even though these details may not be routinely available to the subject for reporting to the experimenter. After viewing a detailed picture subjects are given a word-association task initially linked with a blank projection screen and then are asked nondirective questions about the picture. The subjects' first ten spoken words are used to elicit additional associations that appear to facilitate his later recall of details absent from the earlier report. Haber concludes that the pictures were not stored by the subjects in the form of words, but that the pictures and their details had to be attached to words during a period of intense associative activity. Thus, because pictures are not stored in or coded initially into words, their particulars cannot be recalled in detail through words unless the memory of the subject is aided by an activity like the free-association exercise. Haber notes that we could probably improve recall considerably if we could increase the attachment of words to visual images. This suggests that the recoding or indexical activities of pictorial and linguistic memory can be linked, resulting in an improved ability to remember pictures or feelings not associated with words. Having demonstrated that the iconic image is visual, Haber and his associates conclude that the visual image is accurately conveyed to the short-term memory and locate the source of errors in later processing stages of memory.

An interesting problem raised by the work of Haber and his associates inheres in the language subjects use to describe the visual images. Apparently the experimenter had no difficulty deciding that subjects had accurately reported and recalled the initial stimulus presented, and that the image was conveyed by the subject's visual processing system to his memory system. Subjects achieve perfect recall at the instant after they are shown an array of letters tachistoscopically. The subject must extract information from visual stimuli and then attach linguistic terms or glosses to this visual coding process. Haber implies we have the ability to retain all the 'relevant' information of an iconic sort for a matter of milliseconds effecting a transfer to short-term store. Haber notes that words are remembered as ideas. The subject's linguistic reports therefore become further indexical expressions of reported perceptual memory. The researcher and subject employ normatively organized linguistic indexical expressions of recorded perceptual information to convince each other that agreement has been attained.

How do we represent iconic information linguistically? How do we recover the indexical particulars that escape perception due to the subject's limited capacity to retain all of the items or details in a display? The problem is not merely one of information loss, but of information transformation and distortion that only the subject can partially monitor. How do we account for the description of the normative recoding process itself, so as not to fall into the trap of believing that our procedures elicit all 'relevant' particulars because what is available to the subject is thought to be controlled experimentally? The limitation of memory capacity is only describable within the constraints of the experimenter's limitations as a native speaker-hearer.

This problem will be discussed *vis-à-vis* the deaf (and could also include the blind) in the last section of the chapter in order to emphasize the normative organization of manual signs when one is deaf (or verbal displays when one is blind) and cannot speak, or can speak but without auditory feedback. Even with children who can hear, speak and see, psycholinguistic research makes limited use of visual and auditory information processing ideas and 'substantive' findings for understanding that the child is using more than linguistic rules and responding to considerably more than a presumed controlled auditory stimulus sentence. The setting itself provides a self-organizing collection of particulars that the child selectively invokes and reorganizes to process the experimenter's linguistic stimulus.

Recent work on artificial intelligence studies reveals how much more complicated the linguistic model must become to describe understanding in an actual setting. Researches by De Groot (1965; 1966), Simon (1969), and Simon and Barenfeld (1969) articulate information processing theories using computer simulation with formal human problem solving by examining the substantive problem of chess move choices. Simon and Barenfeld go beyond problem-solving heuristic search procedures by demonstrating that subjects impose considerable structure on the problem situation in the course of the first few seconds of exposure. Not linguistic but perceptual information processing is central to the Simon and Barenfeld research. Simon and Barenfeld monitor subjects' eye movements during the initial few seconds after the problems have been presented to them by the experimenter. This is combined with an attempt to test the subjects' abilities to extract and retain information from the complex visual displays of a chess board within a few seconds of exposure. Simon and Barenfeld stress that the game player seems preoccupied with extracting information about position so as to generate possible moves and understand their consequences, rather than with trying to find actual solutions. Thus a combination of eye fixation and peripheral vision provides reflexive information about the subject's relative attention to specific and more distant squares. The experimenter must discover the possible squares perceived and those from which information was extracted by the retention test. According to the authors there is consistency in the research results of Russian, Dutch, and American subjects' abilities to extract information while moving from one to another square of the chess board. The maximum rate is estimated at about four fixations per second.

The Simon and Barenfeld work presumes that relations among the squares, between squares and pieces, and among pieces are extracted from the board by eye movements and some level of expertise carried in short- and long-term perceptual storage. The authors discuss the chess perception programme called 'perceiver', in which the machine simulates the initial sequences of eye movements of human subjects, and the programme posits relations among pieces on the board as well as processes that will generate these perceptions in some particular sequence. Thus the machine programme can specify what should and will be done under some sort of optimal human conditions, but the machine operates under an all-or-none principle in extracting information, while the human player relies on momentary and past indexical experience to decide what is 'important'. Past reflexive experience is central for humans. A grand master or master chess player is capable of reproducing a chess position without error after a few seconds of exposure. A random board reduces a grand master to the level of a weaker player.

The Simon and Barenfeld paper is central to our earlier discussion because the chess player's ability to place pieces correctly is linked to the role of short- and long-term memory. The chess player must chunk or recode information (Miller, 1956) if his expertise is to be maintained. The transfer of information from short- to long-term store has been estimated to be a matter of five seconds. Therefore short-term store is probably operative in order to make maximum use of information that is limited by fixation time. What constitutes a 'chunk' of information is not clear. Simon and Barenfeld say that it means 'any configuration that is familiar to the subject'.

I will summarize my use of Miller, Haber, and Simon and Barenfeld to indicate how these works help to clarify related issues about meaning and reference. The role of perceptual processes and their primary and secondary memory do not necessarily involve ever speaking to another participant in a chess game. Encounters in everyday life may only require a few seconds devoted to extracting information from a setting to generate action, but without any necessary recourse to speaking. The experimenter creates an artificial problem by having the subjects produce talking-out-loud protocols to monitor perceptual processes, information extraction, and storage in primary memory. This forced linguistic information processing may involve a different memory mechanism and a transformation or distortion of the presumed 'basic' data.

There are many activities accomplished each day that do not have to be described verbally. Our experiences of the everyday world are not always mapped into verbal constructions, yet we may assume that speaker-hearers proficient in the normative use of language probably incorporate normative rules of language use into their thinking and thus are able to describe experiences as if the verbal categories were constitutive of the experiences. But if we follow Haber's work (and the research he builds on and cites), then visual information processing must also include a linguistic operation, involving an inherent tacit recoding, if information is to be reportable to others, including experimenters. In playing chess, it may never be necessary to report the nature of one's move, and we would therefore expect players to be incapable of describing all of the information they may have situationally recognized as relevant and extracted from the board by a sequence of visual fixations. The reflexive elaboration of information continually extracted while attending the board with the help of short- and long-term memory means that these experiences retain a sense of vagueness because the player must rely on verbal expressions of perceptual activities. Forcing a player to transform his chess thinking experiences into verbal reports means producing glosses which experimenters call basic data.

Studying visual memory by requiring the subject to demonstrate recognition of previously exposed photographic slides or their mirror images by pressing a button, avoids total reliance on verbal reports of pictorial memory. Similarly, when subjects are asked to draw in the details of a previously shown photograph (Haber, 1970), we obtain some idea of aspects of pictorial memory that can be retrieved, but not easily obtained, through verbal reports. Such a measure cannot be used with children, however, for their ability to draw is not developed and the researcher must employ everyday language as if it were neutral to the description of pictorial memory that he seeks.

When children (ages five to six years) are given sentences to imitate, they sometimes repeat the sentences perfectly, but when they are asked to act out what the sentences intend they cannot (by adult conceptions) always carry out the 'correct' activity. We also find that sentences that seem to be acted out 'properly' are not imitated 'properly' (Jennings, 1969). Finally, some sentences that are imitated and/or acted out properly (again by adult conceptions of what is 'proper') may not be understood according to adult conceptions when the child is asked to explain what is supposed to happen. When the imitation involves objects and activities that may be strange to the child or which are innovative, the researcher cannot be certain what imagery the sentences arouse. The production of imitated sentences may be 'mechanical' (Cicourel, 1970b) because perceptual information (including cues the child attributes to the experimenter) at the child's disposal may be more significant in the carrying out of a verbal stimulus than the child's understanding of the grammatical rules that are supposedly being tested. The child's eye movements and fixations are seldom a concern of the developmental psycholinguist (though of central interest to his colleagues in perceptual development), nor does the psycholinguist concern himself with how verbal categories get attached to perceptual and auditory experiences. The particular occasion presupposes cognitive abilities that are invariant to, but must also incorporate, the complexity of the setting.

Researchers may find that they must continually consult the child's response in order to learn something about the possible world their stimulus questions may have produced. The child's interpretation of what he is expected to do remains somewhat foreign to the researcher's conception of language acquisition. An adult's world is presupposed to provide the frames for transforming the unknown world of the child into a presumed measurable enterprise. The researcher's questions provide the frames for establishing correct and incorrect responses that can stand independently of the possible worlds the child constructs.

If a sentence generates imagery that is seldom verbalized, then the elegant syntactic rules in the linguist's conception of language structure will not help unless the recipient of the sentence is practised in the ways of attaching verbal categories to such experiences in normatively acceptable constructions. But skilled speaker-hearers recognize the indexicality of their constructions. When subjects are requested to provide more and more detailed accounts, we create frustrating and often insurmountable difficulties. Yet every account seems to be amenable to indefinite elaboration.

We force experimental subjects to chunk their (selective) experiences to capture how they process information. But we also make the linguist's mistake in such experiments by treating the verbal reports as if they were basic data rather than expressions whose understanding requires going beyond linguistic information. This glossing process is not understood to be the heart of meaning and reference and thus is not examined.

Notice that Lakoff's sentences like (2) and (9) involve activities which presuppose experiences imagined or recalled and a visual ethnographic context integral to any discussion of meaning and reference. The details of imagery derived from visual stimulation which are relived when one goes to bed hours after the original experience, have, Hebb (1968) notes, a convincing realism except in one respect – the fine detail is missing. When the linguist asks us to consider various sentences which can be generated by our facility with rules, he is not concerned with the way in which the sentences may stimulate our short- and long-term memory or strain it reflexively as we attempt to create and process information derived from complex settings.

An objective statement or expression, therefore, can be viewed as one which has been idealized in regard to its inherent indexicality. Contextual particulars are ignored, while logically consistent assumptions are constructed and made explicit. Objective and indexical expressions are both constructions in that they include only elements that presume the recipient is a 'well-socialized' speaker-hearer who will interpret the utterances in specific and predictable ways. Logical, mathematical, or scientific constructions, despite monitoring to eliminate contradiction, are like everyday expressions because they presume that the reader or speaker-hearer has been socialized to the utterances produced and can be counted on to assign them specific rule-governed meanings.

Simon's (1969) statement that man is a simple behaving system which generates complex behaviour largely because of the complexity of his environment, implies that because behaviour is adapted to goals stimulated by the environment and man's thinking about his environment, behaviour is an artificial construction. Simon remarks that there is an inner environment (biologically limiting) that places constraints on the kinds of information processing of which the organism is capable. My treatment of indexicality and reflexivity in this chapter is also at issue in Simon's (1969, pp. 51–2) conclusion that the relationship between language and thinking can be stated as an 'overstrong' Whorfian hypothesis: 'Only the expressible is thinkable'. Simon then says that if this can be accepted: 'Only the thinkable is expressible'. This can be interpreted as saying that despite the biological basis of language, its actual expression is artificial in a normative rule-governed sense. However, if only the expressible is thinkable, then our normative constructions (ideal syntactically organized utterances, logical and mathematical subdomains) reflexively fold back on our thinking to make thinking compatible with our attempts to communicate inter-subjectively. Language generates its own system of measurement, and every expression of language would contain only those particulars that reflect the thoughts that led to the expressions. Innovative ways of thinking would always appear in innovative expressions.

The generative transformational linguistic view states that the syntactic component is the fundamental link between the phonological and semantic components. Remarks by Quillian (1968) and others cited above state that our memory includes what can be said in language, what is sensed in perception, and properties and relationships of thinking more general than syntactic rules could reflect. The attribution of meaning may not be expressible in all instances of communication. The speaker-hearer must recognize that multiple meanings can exist for different expressions or their sub-parts. The information that is created and processed is embedded in and constitutive of the context of interaction. A sentence that is formally syntactically or semantically anomalous need not be anomalous for the speaker-hearer. And as Quillian notes, even if we honour the transformational linguists' model for the production of utterances, we will need a more complex model to study the understanding of sentences.

Simon must ask how the expressible and thinkable can be so interrelated if our understanding of the expressible is only partially dependent on the production of the expressible. What is expressed in an account suffers from the same difficulties as the language itself because no language can ever mark or provide for those particulars necessary for its production *and* comprehension. Hence even as we speak of these difficulties we count on the reader supplying particulars that the language does not and cannot carry in some 'obvious' or clearcut way. Much of language production can be mechanical in the sense that it is rule-governed because of the normative constraints imposed on the speaker, but our understanding of interactional scenes or texts is not entirely reliant on what is expressible, for what is thinkable can only be expressed indexically if at all.

I have tried to discuss ethnomethodological ideas within the framework of cognition or information processing and information generation. But beyond the scope of this framework the ethnomethodologist proposes that invariant properties of cognition and thought are plausible only within a world taken for granted and known through a self-preserving practical reasoning or a 'mundaneity principle' (Pollner, 1970). Operating within the mundaneity principle, the speaker-hearer seeks to create and sustain coherence by organizing information into practical chunks and normatively acceptable categories. The theories of linguists and students of artificial intelligence examined operate within the mundaneity principle but are correspondence schemes carved out of practical reasoning and selective displays of everyday language. They rely on an unexamined nativeness that provides for a world that is self-organizing and pre-constituted. This nativeness cannot be discovered and examined if it is treated as an obvious phenomenon within a correspondence theory of reality; the latter does not recognize this nativeness as constitutive of knowledge processes, a precondition of our inquiries, and an endless, tacit resource for everything we do.

The ethnomethodologist also employs glosses while operating within the mundaneity principle at different levels, and these glosses forever remain a member's account of practices said to make up the properties of mundane reasoning. Because these glosses recommend that a sense of 'stepping back' is possible to obtain a perhaps absurd and hence 'objective' view of the world, the ethnomethodologist is also vulnerable to the charge of having adopted a privileged position. In recognizing that we can generate only different glosses of our experiences, the ethnomethodologist tries to underline the pitfalls of viewing indexical expressions as if they could be repaired and thus transformed into context-free objective statements. Our inquiries, therefore, cannot ignore the mundaneity principle when dealing with substantive outcomes or claims about the structure of syntactic rules, the nature of information processing, the organization of perceptual and linguistic memory, or the elegance of linguistic productions. What is of interest is how language, memory and our senses can be seen to preserve the mundaneity principle and provide the ways by which members create what Simon calls the sciences of the artificial. The sciences of the artificial (standardized or grammatically correct versions of language, logical or mathematical systems, and scientific theories about the universe) generate a dialectic between science and practical reasoning (Schutz, 1964; Garfinkel, 1967; Pollner, 1970) that proposes science as a superior way of discovering truth. The sciences of the artificial presuppose mundane reasoning, and this practical reasoning is a constant resource for constructing a meaningful and viable science. The everyday world is an indispensable tacit resource for the creator of the sciences of the artificial, but is seldom a topic of inquiry (Zimmerman and Pollner, 1970).

I, with several of my graduate students, have conducted a series of studies into the acquisition and use of oral language and manual sign language at home and communicative competence in the school. Central questions in our work are how the world comes to be formulated and reformulated by and for the child in terms of an adult's conception of clock-time; and how the very existence of this world depends on adult formulations of the child's reasoning and language acquisition. There are two kinds of glosses here:

1. Those used by parents, teachers, and clinicians for describing normal development.

2. Those employed by researchers for demonstrating that child development and language acquisition are descriptive sciences.

In the research we seek a kind of 'indefinite triangulation' procedure that would reveal the irreparable but practical nature of accounts used by subjects and researchers. I use the expression 'indefinite triangulation' to suggest that every procedure that seems to 'lock in' evidence, thus to claim a level of adequacy, can itself be subjected to the same sort of analysis that will in turn produce yet another indefinite arrangement of new particulars or a rearrangement of previously established particulars in 'authoritative', 'final', 'formal' accounts. The indefinite triangulation notion attempts to make visible the practicality and inherent reflexivity of everyday accounts. The elaboration of circumstances and particulars of an occasion can be subjected to an indefinite re-elaboration of the 'same' or 'new' circumstances and particulars.

The triangulation procedure varies with the research problem. When gathering information on language acquisition in the home setting we left a tape recorder for about one hour during lunch. A transcription of the tape was done by a typist who had been instructed to render a verbatim record. Then the transcript, the first version of this scene, was read by the mother while she listened to the tape; her comments produced another version of the interaction. The typist was next asked to listen again to the tape and to describe what she thought was 'going on', correcting her original transcript as she deemed necessary. In this elaboration and correction a different version of the scene was always produced. My phonetic transcription of the tapes created still another version. With a number of different versions of an interaction scene, the problem is deciding which version captures the child's language, the child's referencing ability, the parent's constructions, and so on.

The reader could now say that we should have simply combined the different versions to produce the 'best' one possible, but the point is that different versions could have been produced indefinitely by simply hiring different typists and providing the mother with different transcripts. The mother could not always remember the context in which the interaction occurred especially if we waited several days before playing the tape for her. The mother's equivocation about the meaning of the child's utterances or her own statements, because of her inability to recall the ethnographic particulars available at the time of the interaction, points to the situated nature of meaning.

In another study with Kenneth and Sybillyn Jennings (Cicourel *et al.*, in press) we employed a procedure in which sentences having direct and indirect object constructions (in active and passive voice) were acted out and imitated by pairs of pre-school and kindergarten children (aged three to six years). There was a table of toys beside the children which they identified before the test began. The sentences typically require one child to give an object to, or receive an object from, the other child. Child A, upon recognizing that he is the agent, must convert the information from the sentence into a search procedure that requires him to scan the table and pick out an appropriate object and then give it to child B.

We used video tapes to show from a different view the problem indexicality raises for language acquisition studies. Multiple versions of the scene become apparent when the researcher finds that although a forced coding of the child's responses can be made at the time of presenting the stimulus sentences, subsequent viewings of the tape reveal that the original coding was often ambiguous and could be changed (Jennings, 1969). By coding the child's responses as if they were motivated only by the stimulus sentence, psycholinguists might typically infer that the child does or does not have an internalized rule for comprehending active and passive and direct and indirect object constructions. But repeated tests of different children and repeated viewings of the tapes revealed that various schemes of interpretation and analysis could emerge and be supported. The conclusion of this discussion is that repeated viewings of the tapes provide the researcher with different versions of the phenomenon because different particulars are noticed each time even though some particulars may be remembered over several occasions. Each hearing of the oral part suggests new inferences because closer attention is paid to intonational features. Concentrating on any particular aspect of the scene such as watching the child's eyes provides a basis for additional conjectures.

Children generate their own interpretations of the setting and search the setting for additional information. If child A starts to move first, child B may not move because he may assume that child A 'knows better' what to do. If child A moves with the first NP, then child B may not even pay attention to the rest of the stimulus sentence. This suggests that the stimulus sentence may not be retained long enough for the child to process the oral stimulus and link it to the perceptual information he needs to carry out the task. The child may be responding to the noun he hears first, regardless of the noun's assignment in a deep structure. He may receive only a selective version or some fragment of the sentence due to a form of interference generated by himself, his partner, or the experimenter.

Still other problems emerged when it was found that some sentences could be imitated accurately but not acted out 'appropriately' while other sentences could not always be imitated accurately but could be acted out 'correctly'. Psycholinguists do not always treat such problems as part of a more general information processing task where the interplay between perceptual and linguistic memory and routine interference from the experiment can reduce the number of chunks the child has to process. It seems clear that the issue is not simply one of testing the child's internalization of grammatical rules. Rather it points out once again that syntax is only one among several factors that the child must attend in deciding the meaning of an utterance in an interactional setting.

When the child is asked to explain his actions or the intended actions of a stimulus sentence he may be forced to generate linguistic constructions or information that is not in one-to-one correspondence with his perceptual memory or the immediate perceptual display as it is selectively organized by him. We investigated the 'naturalness' of the stimulus sentence by asking four children (seven, nine, ten and twelve years) to act out some 'bizarre' sentences. A few weeks later we sought explanations from the children in an interview. The stimulus sentence seemed to provide the child with an occasion to explore reflexively various possibilities that could possess what for him seemed to constitute reasonable accounts to justify his interpretation of the stimulus sentence. This sometimes meant that a bizarre sentence was rejected by the child because the surface subject of the sentence which was taken to be the agent lacked features deemed appropriate to the action, for example, 'A lampost can't give a table a book'. In other cases the child carried out the instruction reporting that he was, say, the fire hydrant. The syntactic structure of the stimulus sentence obviously provides valuable information to the child, but this information may not be central to his performance because of the influence of the interactional particulars experienced reflexively in the setting or imagined as relevant.

When I assisted Marshall Shumsky with his dissertation we worked out another variation of the indefinite triangulation procedure to generate different accounts of the 'same' scene. Several conditions of differential participation in one session of Shumsky's on-going encounter group were arranged. Some experienced participants who came only infrequently were specifically asked to be at the video session. A member with limited experience in the group was to come when the session was well underway. One of the older members, the member who came late, and the participant who had joined most recently were interrogated about their experiences in the day's session. We were interested in obtaining each participant's reconstruction of the group experience and comparing the vocabulary the older and newer group members used to express their opinions and feelings.

Shumsky placed one of the older members on the 'hot seat' of intensive group focus soon after the session began. As soon as attention was diverted from him, he was removed from the session and asked to provide an account of what had occurred in the group to that point. After this account was audio-taped, he was shown portions of the video tape which depicted his 'hot seat' experience, and he was again asked to address particulars identified by the interviewer.

The group member with limited experience arrived an hour and a half after the group started. She was allowed to participate for about ten minutes, then she was removed from the group and was interrogated in the way described above. Of particular interest here was the way she described the part of the session she did not experience directly but saw on video tape. Finally, the participant with the least experience in the group was interviewed. One month later the same group members were interviewed independently of each other. They were asked to provide initial reconstructions, and then they were shown the same video segments they had seen before.

The participants' conceptions of the group experience, the motives they attributed to others, were all varied and often contradictory. With each interview individual utterances or fragments were used as different particulars to provide different meanings of 'what happened'. The expressions utilized could not be examined to recover the particulars used during each interview. Some knowledge about the recoding process and the role of memory and general information processing activity can be gained by observing how subjects reconstruct their expressions of what happened. When participants were repeatedly shown a video-tape of the session they provided new interpretations because on different viewings they noticed someone's intonational shifts, his facial expressions, his use of particular lexical items, changes in body position, the movement of the eyes, and the like.

Participants in group interaction (as in the perceptual experiments described by Haber) receive more information than they are aware of or can possibly verbalize. It is not clear how selective particulars (ignored, stored, or available only by prodding or by verbal associations) are utilized to construct accounts, nor how perceptual, somaesthetic, kinaesthetic, and auditory information become selectively processed by a reflexive self. The speaker-hearer must process information so as always to be 'seeing' the meaning or intentions of his own actions, as well as the actions of others, in a retrospective and prospective way that is situated and is contingent on an open horizon of unfolding possibilities (Schutz, 1964; Garfinkel, 1967; Cicourel, 1968b). The meaning of any lexical item or string of items can be described by reference to syntactic rules and constraints. The meaning of any received or produced utterance for the speaker-hearer is embedded in a larger context that is activated and deepened by the complexity of the setting, and the reflexive availability of short-term and long-term store that are themselves influenced by normative linguistic and non-linguistic social practices. Memory can be seen as socially organized information that members learn to store as idealized normal forms or typifications of their experiences. These normal forms are socially distributed among any population and available as a stock of knowledge for assigning and reassigning meanings, but must link with situated social interaction (Schutz, 1964).

Ease and facility of expression in a given context are contingent upon the ability to transcend one's own talk and the talk of others, while making use of information generating and information processing procedures. These procedures include syntactic and phonological rules and dictionary information as normal form expressions embedded in a complex environmental context. Thus many of the utterances of the encounter group do not provide grammatically relevant information for understanding what seems to be going on. The grammatical structures available provide information for the linguist, but are not clear resources for participants or observers. The verbal accounts given of what happened are contingent displays whose indexicality cannot be repaired by coding devices for making data more 'precise' or improving methods of research by additional experimental controls.

In research being done with MacKay, Mehan, and Roth, studying communicative competence and language use in the classroom, we have been using another variation of the indefinite triangulation procedure. Two first grade classes in two elementary schools with different mixtures of Anglo, Chicano, and Black students have been observed for eight months. Various standard psycholinguistic, reading and intelligence tests, and specially designed variations on them, have been used to assess children's understanding of general classroom instructions and materials presented in lesson form and on tests. A major task of the research is the examination of assumptions which test constructors must make about the child's world in order to develop measures of intelligence and general knowledge.

Triangulation was used as a research strategy by obtaining the teacher's account of her plans and expectations for a lesson she was to present. Then, both the lesson presented to the class and the teacher's subsequent assessment of the impact of the lesson in interaction with some of the children were videotaped. We also observed the lesson and asked several children about their conception of what the lesson was about. A brief, general overview of the lesson was gathered from the teacher. After a few days the teacher was interviewed about the lesson once again. She was first asked to reconstruct the lesson, its purpose and goals, then she was shown a video tape of the lesson and asked to describe aspects of the lesson and the children's reactions towards it.

As in the encounter group study and the study of language acquisition in the home, different accounts of the 'same' scene were obtained. The different accounts reveal the difficulty of trying to repair each glossed level of information to claim 'adequate' objectivity because these glosses too can be infinitely changed and expanded. Each account draws upon both stated and unstated particulars and is contingent on the social constraints of the actual lesson. One's selective storage, or changing memory of the setting, or a selective or changing audio- or video-taped recovery of the setting provides an important basis for indefinite accounts of the 'same' scene.

When we contrast the teacher's accounts with the children's accounts it is sometimes difficult to recognize that everyone presumably witnessed the 'same' event. The children seem to receive and organize the lesson in terms of their own orientations at the time of the event. Interferences are routine and may be self-generated, initiated by other students, or by the teacher in response to a particular student. Where each child sits, who sits next to him, and the teacher's ability to follow his gaze contribute both to the parts of the lesson the child picks up and to the teacher's conception of what the child has assimilated.

The classroom research is too extensive to describe adequately here. The work, however, underlines the problems mentioned earlier about the child's ability to utilize perceptual experiences, or his memory of these experiences, in contexts where verbal expressions are necessary for the teacher to assess the child's ability and achievement. It becomes impossible to separate competence from performance because the linguist's and psycholinguist's models are not realistically based on the ways in which children seem to develop and display cognitive abilities that transcend language use itself. The child may be forced to process information couched in grammatically correct sentences produced by the teacher as a way of satisfying educational goals, but this does not constitute a test of how the child receives, organizes, and generates information nor is it a test of what he understands about the setting or task. The teacher's utterances and intentions in combination with the use of perceptual materials for conveying a lesson may appear to be ambiguous and/or contradictory for the child. The child's ability to produce utterances recognized by the psycholinguist and teacher as grammatically adequate may not index his ability to understand the syntactic or lexical complexities of his productions, or how he processes the complexities the teacher or researcher produces.

Our bilingual Chicano subjects present a more complicated situation because these children appear to have learned two grammars and two phonological systems that are not integrated. For some tasks the children may understand similar instructions in both Spanish and English, yet not be able to produce utterances that convey what they seem to know. The children seem capable of switching from one language to the other to indicate their intentions, but they are not always capable of translating from one language into the other. Depending on the initial structure of an utterance, adults seem capable of starting in Spanish, while inserting English items within the Spanish grammatical frame, and vice versa. Our subjects were unable to engage consistently in this form of systematic switching, yet a few of them seemed to be moving in this direction. The bilingual child who relies on pointing and gesturing appears to be attempting to transcend his apparent inability to make his knowledge, thinking, and intentions comprehensible by normative verbal reports.

In describing the last research project, being done in collaboration with Boese, I must trade somewhat more on the reader's imagination because the material derives from a study of manual sign language used by deaf adults and hearing children born to deaf adults. The two children we studied (called Freddy and Andy) were video-taped in the home when they were one to two and two to three years of age.

To orient the reader to the study of manual sign language, we distinguish, for example, between native sign language as a first language, whose initial normative structure seems to be a product of the interactional scenes of only those persons who communicate with each other frequently in a household setting, relying on primary and secondary memory in order to recreate signs that can be recognizable as the 'same' across different occasions (Cicourel, 1970b; Cicourel and Boese, 1972a and b; Boese, 1971) and signing learned as a second language. As soon as deaf persons move out of a family setting into a deaf community or into contact with speaker-hearers, the picture can change considerably if the hearing society or culture has developed a standardized orthographic system, a normative grammar, and a lexicon. Deaf persons who have been taught to speak and read lips as a second language may also create normative signs by establishing a correspondence between a native sign and a lexical item in the oral language. Hearing persons who have learned to sign as a second language have been instrumental in creating this correspondence.

Because many speaker-hearers have learned to use manual signs and have helped to standardize many native signs so that they are in correspondence with oral lexical items, we must distinguish between:

1. Native signers who have had no contact with oral language in its standardized normative form.

2. Native signers exposed to oral language who have standardized normative signs in their repertoire in correspondence with an oral lexicon.

3. Second language signers who have first learned an oral language as speaker-hearers and then acquired a knowledge of standardized normative and perhaps some native signs which they incorporate into their conception of language as an oral-written system of communication.

Second language signers, therefore, do not *think* in terms of an (as yet unknown) competence to generate and understand signs in situated contexts.

As speaker-hearers, we may never know how to understand this competence which deaf persons rely on tacitly. We might imagine deaf linguists, relying on a standardized idiographic normative sign language developed by deaf scholars, someday attempting to describe this competence just as oralists attempt to describe the competence-performance of a speaker-hearer.

Speaker-hearers concerned with teaching the deaf how to speak, read lips, and read and write oral language often cite the fact that manual sign language has few, if any, of the characteristics of oral language. They cite particularly the absence of inflections and order constraints, considered necessary for oral language, but ignore the absence of many of these normative constructions in other oral languages. The detailed standardization found in oral languages is lacking in sign language and clearly limits the power of sign language. A normative system that is generalized as rules is a powerful way of generating abstract meanings and doing complicated reference. Some sort of standardized idiographic system is not precluded for sign language, though the ones that have been attempted thus far have always used oral language as the point of departure. Despite the powerful generative system of rules said to describe oral language, the translation of signs into oral reports compounds the indexicality problem. Contextual features are central in sign language, but we are poorly informed about communication that depends extensively on seldom-studied perceptual, kinaesthetic, and somaesthetic information. Because signs are not ordered in ways associated with normative uses of oral language, serious questions may be raised about syntactically based linguistic universals (Schlesinger, n.d.).

To argue that the uneducated deaf are dependent on kinaesthetic, somaesthetic, and perceptual information articulated with non-linguistic primary and secondary memory, means that standardized oral syntax plays a minimal role in communication within this group. The educated deaf person making use of manual signs which have been set in correspondence with an oral lexicon does not utilize an intuitive understanding of oral syntax for signing, but will convert information obtained from the oral system into his sign system (Cicourel and Boese, 1972a). Finger spelling and lip movements will be seen as signs even though they have a direct correspondence with oral letters of the alphabet and words (sound patterns). The argument is similar to saying that an adult who learns a second language as a non-native will always tend to translate the second language into his own as a means of understanding this second language. The native signer's dependence on his perceptual, somaesthetic, and kinaesthetic memory to generate and understand manual signs emphasizes the deep involvement of all communication in the unfolding context of interaction despite the existence of abstract powerful normative systems of oral language syntax. This means oral language syntax is of limited value to deaf persons using manual signs who cannot experience oral language as speaker-hearers do. The feedback necessary for monitoring output and understanding inputs based on intonational differences is lacking.

Before closing this section and the chapter, I want to present a limited amount of data from our study of two hearing children. Freddy and Andy were born to deaf parents whose primary language during the course of our research was sign. There are many problems inherent in understanding manual sign language because oral language glosses must be used to further index signs whose meanings are themselves embedded in different experiences and memory and in a complex interactional setting. Our attempts to reconstruct and attribute meaning to the video tapes were hampered by an unexpected realization that it was very difficult to recapture the contextual cues used at the time of the initial recording. The fact that so much of the meaning was tied to the setting itself made it imperative that we reconstruct some of the unstated conditions of the context for even a poor beginning.

Some serious consequences and rewards emerged from our somewhat embarrassed realization that the video tapes were very difficult to understand six to eight months after participating in the interaction we recorded. Our involvement in the setting at the time of the filming seemed 'routine', and our understanding of what appeared to be 'happening' seemed rather 'obvious'. But the observation that understanding the video tape was quite difficult underlines the central argument of this chapter: that the researchers, as participants are heavily dependent on tacit contextual particulars for producing an account of the setting. The video tape does not capture the way participants' situated experiences produce emergent meanings as a reflexive accomplishment. Our memories were not adequate for recovering the sense of social structure experienced at the time of recording, and our glosses of what happened required considerable intensive viewing in order to reconstruct a plausible account. This translation problem might lead the reader to conclude that if there had been a simultaneous translation by a sign/oral language 'bilingual' interpreter the matter could have been resolved. But a simultaneous verbal gloss (translation) at the time of the original signing interaction, even by a bilingual who is a native signer, does not guarantee as much accuracy as might be expected. It is like the problem of attaching verbal expressions to perceptual experiences and memory; the information lost and transformed by the recoding process is difficult to recover much less identify.

Several layers of glossing occur, each with its own indexicality or chunking operations which mask particulars integral to each layer. The rendition of an oral gloss of the manual signs is a recoding problem that poses many difficulties because thinking in sign language as a native can not readily be transformed into an oral gloss. The interpretation of thinking-out-loud protocols is difficult enough; adding the manual sign activity only compounds our problem.

One way of trying to repair the reflexivity and indexicality problems posed by the translation from one medium to another, would be to analyse the normative signs used by the deaf mother or father with the child. One could observe how the child modifies these normative signs while creating his own signs. But such repair work presupposes some understanding of how sign language is generated independently of imposing oral syntax as a schema of analysis. The translation of parent–child interaction by a bilingual interpreter at the time of actual interaction merely transforms the problem of how signs can be viewed as a generative semantics qua sign language, into a traditional problem in developmental, oral language psycholinguistics. The translation and simultaneous transformation of the problem into an oral psycholinguistic one permits the researcher to find 'pivot structures', noun phrases and verb phrases, uses of the active voice, direct object constructions, and the like, but these glosses are created by the translator for the benefit of an oral or speaking-hearing audience interested in demonstrating that linguistic universals as constructed (normatively) for oral language, 'must exist' for the deaf as well.

The perplexing difficulties of the problem can be illustrated by the following materials from our study of manual sign language acquisition. The material on the left hand side of the page was translated by a native signer (Robert Boese) whose parents were both deaf though he is a speaker-hearer, while the right side was translated by a second-language signer (Marian Boese). Robert Boese learned to speak and understand verbal sound patterns when he began attending public school around seven or eight years of age. This phenomenon of hearing children of deaf parents learning to speak without difficulty is reported by Lenneberg (1964; 1967; 1969). The signing was done by Freddy at two years of age.

Tape 3, Translation, video segment 240–53, 1 April 1970

Native signer	*Second language signer*
First viewing:	*First viewing*:
253: 'Come.'	Nothing recorded.
Second viewing:	*Second viewing*:
Nothing recorded.	243: 'car, car, car.'
	250: 'bird, outside.'
Third viewing:	*Third viewing*:
243: 'Oh, I hear a truck, I hear something out there there now is a truck moving out there, there is a car, truck.'	243: 'car, car.'
	249: 'stopped, stopped.'

246: 'Oh, now there is a car out there, a truck, and
it is moving.'
250: 'A bird, there is a bird out there, flying very
fast, high bird.'
253: 'Come.'

Fourth viewing:
243: 'Oh, I hear out there a sound, a truck, I hear
something outside, car out there, moving.'
246: 'Car out there, car outside, car moving; car
outside, like a dump-truck; there is a truck out there
(247), and it is a kind of (248) dump-truck; I hear it,
you hear it, it is a dump-truck, it makes (249) a big
noise, and it is dumping things out there; a truck
out there, it is dumping something, it makes a fast
stop; there is a truck there, and it is dumping things,
it dumps the things out, and then it stops.'
250: 'Oh, bird, bird out there, bird.'

Fifth viewing:
243: 'Car, truck, accelerator, beep-beep; I hear,
down the hill, (244) there is a car out there; there is
a truck moving back and forth there; I hear a car
out there, beep, it is moving, there is a car out there,
a truck, moving.'
245: 'Steering wheel.'
246: 'There is a car out there, a truck; there is a car
out there, (247) dumps the things down, and hears
the stop and opens up, and (248) stops.'
250: 'Bird is flying in the air, bird is flying very
hard; (251) it is a bird, bird out there, come, come
[moves toward window]; it is a (252) bird, there is a
bird flying out there, there, out there (253) oh, I
heard a sound, hear the truck, come on, come over
here.'

Sixth viewing:
Not attempted.

Fourth viewing:
Nothing recorded.

Fifth viewing:
Nothing recorded.

Sixth viewing:
250: 'Bird, bird, bird.'

There is an obvious discrepancy in these free translations between the
first and second language signers' attribution of particulars to a video scene
of about thirty seconds duration. The native signer took many liberties in
his translation and inserted articles freely as well as verb inflections and
adverbs. It was difficult to synchronize the two readings because of technical
problems such as the tape stretching and the difficulty of accurately noting

the reading of the counter each time. But there were other kinds of inferences, for example, a facial expression would be recorded as an 'oh'; meanings would be attributed to the signers and included in the translation on the basis of body movements integral to the native translator's use of tacit knowledge in signing. The interpretation of a sign or series of signs is always embedded in the total context wherein the observer or participant makes reflexive use of memory. While studying the present burst of signing it was not clear initially what Freddy was trying to express until we accidentally turned up the volume (thought to be irrelevant at the time) of the video recorder and discovered what sounded like a big truck.

The reader might claim (from even a quick glance at the translations) that there is consistency in interpretation even though there are many variations in the ways the translations are expressed each time. We could transform the materials of the free verbal gloss into sentences that are normatively ideal for a linguistic analysis and thus 'clean up' the transcript to produce bounded sentences that seem to 'make sense'. But such tidy sentences would merely satisfy our preconceptions of the 'correct' utterances we should be able to find if we are to lend support to the linguistic universals' thesis as formulated by speaking-hearing linguists for oral language.

There are two substantive points the reader should attend to:

1. The native translator reports 'I hear out there, a sound, a truck . . .' and 'it makes a big noise'. The translation suggests the child is relying on his hearing, but this interpretation did not occur until after we accidentally heard the noise of the truck apparently passing by outside. If we had relied only on the signs, the elaboration reported would have taken a different form.

2. Difficulties in translation may be attributable to the vagueness of the child's signing ability as occurs in oral 'baby talk'. We have also found that translations of adult signing do not alter this problem, particularly when native signs are used extensively.

We encountered two other problems:

(a) The translator's use of short- and long-term memory of the original setting and video tape to create consistency in his analysis across successive interpretations of roughly the 'same' video scene.
(b) The extent to which the elaboration of particulars was produced to satisfy the translator's desire to communicate with a speaking-hearing audience.

We are convinced that an independent native signer would have considerable difficulty coming up with even a free gloss of minimal coherency unless he was told many ethnographic particulars about the setting and the kinds of signs taught to (and modified by) the child, as well as the signs invented by the child almost daily. The verbal gloss attributed to the above burst of signing contains all the features necessary for claiming grammaticality in oral language (word order, NPs, VPs (verb phases), agreement between subject and predicate, etc.), but these features cannot be found as 'natural' structures of sign language unless negotiated and imposed by establishing an arbitrary correspondence between oral syntax, an oral lexicon, and manual signs. Such an imposition tells us nothing about how native signers generate meanings and do reference with a system of signs embedded in each contextual setting, rather it suggests how a bilingual native signer can provide a translation intelligible to speaker-hearers.

It might be easier to understand the difficulties of repairing the indexicality of translating signs into oral glosses that would satisfy syntactic rules or a standardized lexicon, if we examine attempts to provide verbal glosses for a presumed literal description of the signing itself.

Tape 3, Verbal gloss of literal description, segment 240–53

Native signer:

240: 'Freddy sitting position, legs apart, arms down, hands (241) close together, twisting and turning his fingers, index (242) and thumb together.'

243: 'Freddy turns his head, his head was down, and now he turns his head to his right and upwards and looks at mother. Then he looks straight ahead, moving head to upright position, his head pointed in front of him with eyes facing straight ahead of him.'

243: [Repeating of numbers indicates rewinding the tape] 'He moves his hand, with his index finger, other fingers kind of closed, points with arm half stretched out in front of himself, his index finger, as well as his other fingers, but mainly his index finger, points towards his ear, moves head towards me, slightly to the left, head shifting to the right, right hand with palm open, 45 degree angle, and

Second language signer:

242: 'Freddy looks up and looks towards Bob and Mother and he looks towards his Father, looks back towards Bob.'

242: [Rewinds tape] 'He looks up, he looks towards his father.' (I just realized that I have to stop the machine faster than that because by the time I have said 'he looks up' and 'by the time he looks over to his mother', he has already said a whole string of thoughts and that is almost up to 243).

242: (missed it that time.)

242: 'Freddy looks over to Bob and his mother, to his father, back again and there are, I would say, five separable signs to 243.'

242: (I feel hampered by the equipment and feel really frustrated by the equipment . . . It stops it and then jiggles all the tape and I want to stop it faster and I find the lever very hard to work.)

jerking hand motion up and down, vibrating it, kind of like the accelerator motion, and then points again, with his index finger, and then partially closes his hand, his right hand, all motion with right hand, giving an up and down motion, as if holding on to a steering wheel, with movement going slightly up and down, with arm in front of him, moving it up and down.'

243: 'With his index finger, he points back and forth, back and forth, with his right hand, touches his mother, having turned his head from down to up and right, then points to me with his right hand, having moved a bit to the left, and both hands, with both of them he does hands clenched, a grip-like hold, attempts to draw, as if holding imaginary steering wheel, grasping each other.'

242: 'He looks up, and the first sign or movement, let's not say signs anymore, the first movement he does is something like he has hands both in front of him at the point of looking up from them. I still haven't decided where he looks first.'

243: 'He is looking up, looks at his mother and down, back to his mother and in looking towards his mother, at 242 1/2; so he looks to his mother, his dad, then his mother, and then looking back to his mother he signs at the same time this time. Then his first motion is: he takes his hands, his right hand away from the object that he has just above his lap, as he is sitting on the couch. The left hand and the object, in the same position, and takes the right hand, lifts the right hand up, and does something with it towards his chest, his upper chest, that is all between 242 1/2 and 243.'

242: 'Towards chest, away from chest, up towards mother, with that same right hand.'

242: 'He looks up, looks back, . . . I do not know how to describe that, that burst of motion.'

I have arbitrarily cut off the amount of detail that can be presented. A more elaborate account can be found in Cicourel and Boese (1972b) and Boese (1971). Yet I hope the illustration is sufficient to give the reader a sense of the problem. It is quite difficult to match a segment of the free oral gloss with the segment of verbal gloss of the literal description. Each translator encountered rapid bursts which were resistant to description as physical movements. Trying to describe them verbally often seemed ridiculous unless many liberties could be taken. Note that the native signer provides a kind of detail different from the second language signer. He addresses details of body movement, notes the coordination of movements of different parts of the body, and is particularly aware of the movement of the child's hands and fingers. Researchers reading this chapter would probably want to claim that translators should be trained (as linguistic informants are trained) to use a similar vocabulary so as to produce similar accounts thus 'cleaning up' the description. This would guarantee that the translation would follow the logical structure of normative oral syntax. Interrogating the native signer in sign would not alter the translation problem of providing the reader with normative oral syntax.

The reader will notice also that the native signer adds interpretations that provide specific cultural content to his descriptions, for example, referring to a movement of the hands as 'kind of like the accelerator motion' or 'holding on to a steering wheel'. The iconic nature of the steering wheel idea seems clear. We assume that both describer and reader are socialized to similar kinds of tacit knowledge about their environment that is available to their imagery and activated by actual or recalled movements glossed by the use of specific lexical items. But saying 'his index finger, points towards his ear' presumes that the reader can imagine the relevance of the configuration in the particular context to signify that the child's movements indicate he is 'hearing' something. Recall that we were unable to claim to 'know' and lock in this interpretation of the movements described until we accidentally turned up the volume of the video recorder, which occurred after we had stopped analysing this segment of tape and had gone on to another segment.

A central problem in making the translations was the desire to 'make sense' of what was 'happening' even though each viewing of the tape made the translators feel somewhat anomic and uncertain about the 'real' meaning of what was being displayed on the tape. The apparent uniformity of the two versions of the 'same' video tape display is only possible by selectively choosing particulars that can be justified by reference to oral syntactic general rules that enable the translators to decide to close off further guessing, speculation, uncertainty, bewilderment, and the like. Were we to avoid the use of a descriptive vocabulary or the labels with which we achieve social 'thingness' in our everyday use of oral language, but were to rely instead on a physical description, it would be difficult to link the physical descriptions to the kind of glossing that selectively settles on a particular use of lexical items to achieve socially meaningful descriptions. For example, the description, 'with his index finger, he points back and forth, back and forth, with his right hand, touches his mother, having turned his head from down to up and right . . .' does not readily convey very much information. Yet notice how many perceptual particulars are being attended that cannot be made visible to the reader, but which the viewer recoded as 'touches his mother' and 'turned his head'. Can we presume that the translator is motivated by having settled on a particular substantive characterization that seems appropriate to the setting or by a general rule he guesses might be relevant? Do we assume instead that the translator is merely doing his best to detach himself from a meaning of the scene he wants to intend substantively and is rendering a literal physical description? In that case we would have to negotiate a correspondence between a presumed 'neutral' descriptive vocabulary employed, and a socially 'acceptable' or 'plausible' interpretation of 'what happened' in socially meaningful terms. Several meta-languages, each with an unexplored indexicality, provide a dubious correspondence. We thus would bypass the native signer's language, for we would not know how this section of tape would be described by one native signer to another.

In our work on sign language (Cicourel and Boese, 1972b; Boese, 1971), we indicate how it is possible to 'clean up' the messy versions produced by repeated translations to construct an account that appears to be free of ambiguity-producing particulars or contradictions. Yet each cleaned-up translation, each attribution of meaning can be subjected to an indefinite elaboration that views sign language as a context-sensitive, self-organizing medium of communication generating meanings and accomplishing reference independently of those processes we find in oral language.

A reader trained in linguistics might want to suggest that something like a distinctive feature system is needed. The physical movements of the hands and body could be described by a small number of distinctive features that chunk into more complex labels like 'open', 'closed', 'away', 'towards', 'circular', and the like. Training translators to perform like coders produces the same kind of agreement that linguists (or sociologists using questionnaires) generate when they force their hearing of sounds into a finite number of complex symbols represented by the IPA and the various invented symbols any field researcher finds necessary to develop because of *his* hearing of the sounds. Distinctive features are convenient, elegant, and practical devices for producing a sense of linguistic structure. These interpretations provide a constructed sense of unity and correspondence. I am not saying that we should abandon such constructions for some as-yet-unannounced 'new' and 'objective' procedure. I have none to offer. I am saying that the inherent indexicality and reflexiveness of our constructions of social (linguistic, psychological, political, economic) reality are phenomena worthy of study in their own right. The ethnomethodologist finds the construction of different glosses of central interest, and he views research procedures as members' practices for preserving the mundaneity or meaningfulness of the world (Pollner, 1970). But an examination of these practices reveals the irremedial indexicality of all communication by showing how the indefinite elaboration is resolved to achieve practical outcomes.

Paraphrasing Simon (1969), we can say that the thesis that humans possess a biologically determined competence for language leads to the notion of an inner environment placing limits on how humans process information. Language itself is the most artificial and 'the most human of all human constructions' (Simon, 1969, pp. 51–2). But it does not follow, as Simon would assert, that only the expressible is thinkable, and that if this is true, only the thinkable is expressible. The thinkable is expressible only through indexical expressions. Our reflexive use of the particulars of the setting (the intonation of language use, the social and physical ecology, the biography of the speakers, the social significance of the occasion, etc.) and our kinaesthetic, somaesthetic, perceptual, and linguistic memory, to mention some of the apparently central ingredients, all contribute to the irreparable indexicality of communication. We can refer to these constraints and information processing features, but we find it difficult to describe in detail our ability to make tacit use of them. Everyday language is fascinating because subdomains of its rather awesome flexible structure permit us to construct other artificial languages like logical and mathematical systems or computer programmes that can be set up in correspondence with objects, events, and operations. We can produce elegant machines or linguistic algorithms that enable us to make certain classes of predictions and produce complex activities that humans cannot do or that require very special training and abilities. But our ability to construct machines or develop complex logical systems always presupposes a necessary reliance on the presuppositions of practical or mundane reasoning with its constraints of indexicality and reflexivity which are inherent in the development and in all uses of the sciences of the artificial.

When we try and deal with manual sign languages as used by deaf persons (or for use of oral language by persons who cannot see), the limitations of our speech about signs should be quite apparent. How we go about constructing translations that seek to link speaking-hearing interpretations of the everyday world with deaf manual signers' conceptions of their everyday world, provides us with challenging problems of the processing of information and the creation of expressions representing different levels of glossing. If language is artificial, then oral language conceptions of linguistic universals are equally artificial *vis-à-vis* other possible non-oral languages. If we hope to construct a theory of meaning that enables us to understand how we assign sense to our everyday worlds and establish reference, then we cannot assume that oral language syntax is the basic ingredient of a theory of meaning. The interactional context, as reflexively experienced over an exchange, or as imagined or invented when the scene is displaced or is known through a text, remains the heart of a general theory of meaning.

5 Cross-Modal Communication: The Representational Context of Sociolinguistic Information Processing

Sociolinguistics deals with the study of language acquisition and use in socially organized settings. Our claims to knowledge about sociolinguistic settings presuppose implicit and explicit methods which we develop to decide what is to be called information when we act as observers or when we attribute meaning to materials obtained from respondents or subjects we research. As respondents and researchers our acquisition and use of language depend on the ways in which we are capable of recognizing, receiving, processing, and generating whatever we call informational particulars. Oral and written language index and impose an immediate gloss over our thought and the various sensory modalities we use for processing and communicating information. The representation of information from our thoughts and several modalities by verbal communication stresses context-free expressions, yet everyday exchanges are invariably contingent productions embedded in emergent, contex-sensitive informational environments. Everyday social interaction among hearing subjects is a creative activity which utilizes several communicational modalities.

Much of the creative activity of the everyday social interaction of hearing persons is hidden from us because it is tempered by selective attention, constrained by the sequential production of oral expressions, informed by and dependent on short- and long-term memory and grammatical and conversational systems which organize information normatively. Examining the communicational strategies of the deaf, however, can help clarify and deepen this conception of information processing. The absence of a basic modality like hearing and normal speech forces us to re-examine our understanding of how language reflects our thinking and memory, and how the latter processes alter any figural recognition or feature extraction that can be said to operate on cross-modal sensory inputs. Deafness in a culture that is verbally oriented means limited access to idealized 'native' oral language normative expressions for representing different sources of information. The context of communication becomes the focal point for generating and locating the meaning of everyday exchanges among the deaf.

The plan of this exploratory paper is to present selected materials from studies of hearing children and deaf adults to suggest how different modalities contribute to the production and understanding of everyday communication. The materials I will present are a small part of a larger corpus of data and do not reflect all of the complexities of the framework being developed, nor the subtleties that can be found in video tapes which are currently being analysed. The general thesis of the paper is an old one: researchers and subjects face similar problems in representing their complex informational experiences because of their reliance on, and preoccupation with, verbal modes of representation which do not index the interplay between normative social constructions and emergent settings adequately.

Communication in the classroom

A study conducted with several former doctoral students (Cicourel *et al.*, in press) underlined the importance of the interactional setting in the child's learning of classroom exercises and his performance on standardized tests. The verbal and nonverbal activities of the setting were central for understanding the child's grasp of the teacher's educational goals. A basic issue (Cicourel, in press a) was how the child was able to represent his knowledge of the immediate setting and his retrieval of past experiences in a context of selective attention. In this paper I focus on the common dilemma mentioned above whereby the researcher and the subjects studied rely on verbal representations to index an interactional context whose complexity as an information processing and generating system dramatically exceeds the verbal data base available.

The remarks that follow are based on a video tape of a hearing first-grade classroom lesson conducted by a teacher with five students. The lesson was intended to teach the children how to form subject–verb–object (SVO) sentences using locatives.

An initial problem we face is deciding the kind of stimulus field the children attend and understand, and how the teacher orients herself to the children's responses. In examining the video tape I presume much more than is available from the tape itself because I know something about the classroom independently of the tape. My memory provides background information which is imposed on the film and integrated with my viewing of the tape as I make observational claims which seem to be clear and obvious. Depending on what I think I see or hear and imagine the teacher and children to be doing in the setting captured by the perspectival view of the video camera, I selectively attend information and create judgments in a context that I hope represents what is happening on the video tape in some logical fashion. My description trades on terms I presume will be intelligible and convincing to the readers of the paper.

A brief examination of the dialogue will reveal that the organizing framework for the interaction is more than a sequence of exchanges between teacher and children where the teacher controls the right to speak by inviting responses from individual children. The children seem oriented to their particular circumstances despite the fact that the lesson is designed to be a coordinated venture whereby all children engage in the same task. The lesson begins with the following remark by the teacher:

1. T: All right, let's take our green crayon and make a line at the bottom of our paper.

The teacher's opening remark is not prefaced by a statement outlining the intentions of the lesson. She *does not say*:

'Children, today we will play a little game. The game will show you how to tell someone what you are doing. The game will also tell someone where different things are if they see you making something with a crayon or pencil or clay or sand or other things. The idea of the game is to make up something called "sentences" to tell someone what you are doing. Let me give you some examples of what a sentence is like.'

I could go on and provide less formal talk and examples and perhaps try to explain the purpose of the lesson more fully to the children. I am not sure if my brief attempt to introduce the lesson to a hypothetical audience is any more reasonable than what the teacher actually did with the lesson. I want to raise the issue of what it is that we should assume about the child's ability to receive, recognize, and represent information when we attempt to teach him or her something, particularly when what we seek to teach is (like language) presumed to be known by the child implicitly. The teacher's strategy seems to be one of trying to explicate the nature of the lesson as different stages of it are presented to the child.

The classroom setting needs to be clarified further before proceeding. The teacher and children are seated around a circular table. The teacher's back is close to one wall and she faces the classroom. The camera is directed to the teacher but picks up all of the five children involved in the lesson. The teacher and students have a sheet of paper in front of them and crayons are available. I cannot clearly see the children's papers but can catch occasional glimpses of the teacher's sheet as she uses the crayon. The teacher tries to monitor the other children distributed throughout the classroom while attending the smaller group of children.

As I review the tape over and over again, I find it difficult to describe what I think I 'see' and 'hear'. I think I 'understand' many kinesic-visual (Birdwhistell, 1970; Ekman and Friesen, 1969) and auditory non-verbal activities that are 'happening', but find it difficult to represent them verbally for the reader. As I notice the children communicating to one another with glances, one word statements, pointing gestures, nonverbal auditory outbursts, touching each other, and the like, I assume that various kinds of information are being exchanged but I cannot be explicit about the presumed content. The same would be true for the teacher's actions.

The teacher's opening line says to use the green crayon to make a line at the bottom of the page and her remark seems fairly obvious, but the children did not automatically pick up their crayons and begin drawing the line. They looked at the teacher and at each other's paper (in some cases) before commencing the activity. Although the children did not seem to object to different terms used by the teacher like 'make a line' or 'bottom of your page', the ambiguity of the instruction was not clarified. Should the line be horizontal? Or vertical? And where is the bottom of the page? Mehan's (1971) analysis of this setting found this to be a problematic issue. I assume that the children were monitoring the teacher's movements to resolve ambiguities. The teacher assumes that the children not only possess various 'normal' conceptions about particular lexical items and adult syntax, but that the phonological forms she uses are obvious stimuli for the children. Yet her repeating of instructions and frequent glances at the children's papers suggest doubts about the clarity of her instructions. But the lesson was not the first exposure to an organized task, nor was it the first day of class. We must allude to an unspecified notion of prior 'background' whereby long-term memory permits the children to attend this particular lesson as 'life as usual' despite some unfamiliarity with the specific task presented by the teacher. Everyone seems to be oriented to the setting as if it were unremarkable and the teacher's use of language assumes that everyone is capable of using some unspecified notion of standardized signals and coding rules for processing the information generated by the teacher. The teacher repeats herself as the children carry out the instruction she gave them.

2. T: Take a green crayon and make a line at the bottom.

It is difficult to assess the children's ability to follow the teacher's verbal instruction when it appears that they are utilizing kinesic-visual information as a basic frame for monitoring their own, the other children's and the teacher's actions. The video tape is not clear enough for me to assert that the children's faces reveal frowns which would contradict my claims that the children seem to understand the lesson. The teacher's possible presumption that her actions are clear and do not require additional clarification is slightly compromised by her repeating most of the initial remark.

Ci, sitting directly to the left of the teacher with a good view of the teacher's paper produces the following:

3. Ci: Like this?

With her question Ci looks up to the teacher and seems to be asking for a confirming statement or a glance. The teacher's next remark seems to be directed to the entire group as she glances around the table, but she also may be telling Ci that her green line is fine ('yeah').

4. T: Okay, yeah, all right, now. . . .

The teacher's visual scan of the group seems to be quick and perfunctory. But notice how my interpretation of the scene I can only partially describe for the reader trades on <u>my unspecified common-sense conceptions</u> of what is 'perfunctory' about a 'glance' and various other meanings that I presume are obvious because of my membership in the society, and my ability to go beyond the oral information given. <u>These unspecified common-sense</u> meanings attributed to the activities are <u>difficult to objectify for the reader but are an integral part of the 'data'</u>.

5. Ri: *Now* what are we going to do?

The remark by Ri seems to presume that the first instruction was obvious and executed properly. But we have no way of specifying precisely how obvious and context-free the teacher's prior verbal instructions were for Ri or the extent to which kinesic-visual information was central to his actions.

6. T: Now take your orange crayon and make an orange worm under the green line. We'll pretend that that's grass.

The teacher's instruction can be interpreted as signifying that any discrepancies between her understanding of what is happening and the children's understanding are irrelevant. She assumes that the term 'worm' is clear, thus does not describe what an orange worm should look like, and presumes that the children are aware that the phrase 'that that's grass' refers to the green line. The children do not seem to be responding to this request. The teacher glanced around the table when she gave this last instruction, and she continued to glance at the children as she said the following.

7. T: [Looking at Ci] It's just a little wiggle. Here, let me show you on this one. An orange worm.

The teacher's remarks are accompanied by her producing a 'little wiggle' with an orange crayon on another sheet of paper rather than the one on which she had drawn the green line. This different sheet of paper seems marked by 'this one' and her comments presume that the kinesic-visual information available to the children is now sufficient for them to follow her instructions. She drew the 'worm' as she uttered 'orange worm'. Je, who was sitting to the right of the teacher, then makes the following remark.

8. Je: Hey, can you make it on yours?

This remark presumes that Je observed what the teacher had done and ties in with the teacher's reference to 'this one' in (7). Thus, 'make it on yours' is asking the teacher to make the orange worm on the paper that contains the green line. Je pointed to the sheet with the green line. We can wonder if the other children were bothered by this discrepancy or were normalizing it, but the video tape does not help us explain their silence.

9. T: No, I'm, watch . . . watch . . . you make it on, [Je: over here?] make it [pause] [Ci: (tapping on the teacher with her crayon) under?] listen! I'll only say it once. Make an orange worm under the green line.

Can I now argue that the previous discussion of the dialogue whereby I assume that the teacher acts as if her instructions are obvious is now mis-leading? The teacher's remarks seem to imply that she is replying to Je's 'make it on yours' and Je's pointing ('over here') to the sheet with the green line, when she says 'I'm watch . . . watch . . .' I assume the teacher is telling Je that she doesn't want to demonstrate each instruction on her own paper, but that she wants to watch the children carry out her instructions on their papers. Ci taps the teacher with the crayon while asking 'under' and I assume she is trying to remember if the orange worm is to be under the green line. The teacher seems a bit irritated when she says 'listen!', her elbows are on the table and she raised her two arms as if to quiet Je and Ci who are on her right and left, respectively. The doubts expressed by Ci and Je about the teacher's actions may or may not be tied to the next remark by Do.

10. Do: Like that?

I have no way of showing that the children are attending to the remarks by Ci and Je other than to say that they look up from their papers continually and could have easily seen the discrepancy between the teacher's making the green line on one sheet and the orange worm on a different sheet of paper.

11. T: Beauuutiful! Okay.

The teacher appears to be looking towards Do when she makes this last remark, not at Do's paper, but glancing around the entire room. We could assume that the children can all receive this remark as indicating that their efforts are satisfactory rather than inferring that the children are monitoring the exchange between the teacher and Do such that they realize that it is Do that is being told how appropriate her drawing is. There is difficulty here in deciding what the children are attending and how their glances provide informational particulars which might be presumed and indexed by the verbal materials. Perhaps the children are not paying any attention to such particulars. Yet how I direct the reader's attention to what I think I see as relevant particulars structures the kind of inferences that are made.

12. Ri: I made two orange worms (laughs).

The remark by Ri reveals his understanding of the task at hand but is ignored by the teacher and the other children. Ci is tapping the teacher again here with her crayon and the teacher turns towards her and says:

13. T: We're going to pretend that that green line is the grass, okay? Can you pretend that with me?

It is difficult to speculate on the teacher's motivation for being redundant about her remark pretending the green line is 'grass'. The teacher looks at Ci when she says 'Can you pretend . . .' and I think Ci gives her a nodding acknowledgment and might have said 'yes'. There was too much background noise for me to feel certain. Without the video tape we would have to presume the remarks are directed to the entire group. The next remark by the teacher begins to address the purpose of the lesson; to encourage the children to create standardized S V O sentences using locatives.

14. T: All right. Where is the orange worm Do?

The teacher's 'all right' may be a signal that the important part of the lesson is about to begin, or it might be a way of telling Ci and Je that it is time to settle down and pay attention to the next remark. The teacher looks across the table at Do waiting for an answer. Here we are forced to assume that the teacher and children 'know' that they are expected to recognize the request as a formal demand for a verbal representation of the information. But the request also could be presumed to be curiously redundant given the fact that everyone has been drawing an 'orange worm' for some time. The teacher does not say what is expected in the way of a response.

15. Do: Right there.

Both Do and Di seem to point to their papers as Do says 'right there'. The answer seems perfectly obvious within the context of the lesson and the video perspective available. The teacher is not satisfied with the response but does not indicate reasons for not accepting it.

16. T: Okay, tell me where he is.

The teacher refers to the 'worm' as 'he' as if this designation is clear, but does not explain that she wants a more elaborate response. Mehan (1971), in an earlier and independent analysis of this scene, notes that the teacher does not explain that the child's initial response is not a complete 'answer'. The implied elaboration suggested by the teacher can be made to appear 'obvious' from the point of view of an adult but we are hard pressed to justify any claims that would argue that the child understands the teacher's remark as a request for a more elaborate answer. But the child's response can retrospectively be seen as an elaboration despite not being a complete S V O sentence of the form the teacher wanted to elicit.

17. Do: Under the grass.
18. T: Okay . . .

The child seems to have accepted the teacher's previous request to view the green line as 'grass'. The teacher's 'okay' presumes unstated details are implied and thus allows Do's response to pass as 'correct'.

The sequence examined above presupposes but does not make visible 'interpretive procedures' presumably at work in the production of the dialogue. The children exhibited a 'normal' facility with language that made it possible for them to represent the task at hand, but their truncated utterances traded on several modalities and presumed an ability to remember and integrate the relevance of key terms like 'green', 'orange worm', 'under', and so on. My interpretation of the dialogue, however, reveals a use of unexplicated interpretive procedures. I must continuously trade on what I think are obvious appearances and remarks while calling the reader's attention to objects, expressions or movements. Meanwhile I think I recognize, yet fail to call into question, appearances that could challenge a normative or standardized account of what I think is happening. I continuously use immediate appearances available from the video screen to recall retrospectively other elements which have occurred or details available to me from my memory of the original setting. My attempts to use 'obvious' informational particulars from the video tape as well as descriptive accounts of information I experienced in the setting are not easily represented by standardized verbal constructions. My own difficulties with trying to find verbal expressions to describe the video tape underlines what I assume is central to the child's task: to represent his thoughts and understanding of the setting and the task by the use of verbal constructions intended to displace and clarify his experiences. When Do says 'right there', the displacement is contextually clear, as would be a pointing operation without a verbal accompaniment. The child's use of language is context-sensitive and presupposes the relevance of unstated information and reasoning. The lesson is designed to teach adult conceptions about the formation of context-free sentences. But the lesson presupposes the context-free, context-sensitive distinction it seeks to teach and test.

My description of the context is central to how the reader makes sense of my inferences, and my interpretations must presume information that is not available for examination. When we present the child with a task that is available kinesically and visually and indexed verbally and then request or demand that an adult representation of the solution be presented, we presume that tacit use of other modalities is involved, but our evaluation of the response does not make explicit how selective attention and contextual interference are integral features of the cross-modal integration and representation of information.

Representing manual sign language verbally

The hearing person has difficulty comprehending how manual signs are as 'natural' for the deaf as speaking is for hearing persons. It is difficult for the deaf to understand and use speech but their use of signs poses basic theoretical issues which highlight our understanding of cross-modal communication. Linguistically the problem is compounded by the fact that prior and recent studies underline the lack of correspondence between the word order of oral language syntax and manual sign language as practised among deaf persons whose first language is manual signs (Furth, 1966; Cicourel and Boese, 1972a; Schlesinger, n.d.; Bellugi and Siple, 1971; Stokoe, Casterline and Croneberg, 1965). Every attempt to describe the 'syntax' of manual sign language must face the problem of having to utilize oral categories which are normative to oral language.

Sociologists use the term normative to signify tacit and explicit rules which are prescriptive and proscriptive for some group. The reference to such rules is similar to a linguist's notion of grammatical rules; they are idealized instructions for recognizing or producing some state of affairs which others can implement or accept as 'normal' or 'correct' or 'appropriate'. Grammatical structures in oral languages are powerful but learned rules for representing cognitive activities necessary for attributing and creating order and meaning from everyday experiences. Normative categories are necessary for the assumption that intersubjective communication exists regardless of the differences in meaning, or distortions or assumed or imputed 'errors' which can be delineated by particular observers or participants of some communicational exchange. When linguists engage in semantic analysis, or when students of artificial intelligence construct programmes for parsing sentences or for the semantic analysis of sentences, tacit use is made of various kinds of normative categories in the data base used to describe segments of speech. A similar tacit use is made of normative categories that index semantic information contained in a lexicon or dictionary. The cultural meanings employed by the researcher trade on his intuitive knowledge of some native language.

The role of memory and attention are central for any discussion of cross-modal communication, but it is not clear how we can represent their relationship to normative rule structures. We are unclear as to how thought and attention organize and reorganize what is recognized and stored as information and represented by oral outputs which participants treat as descriptions of the 'same' events they presume to have experienced. The verbal outputs that index a particular setting, and the complex connection between our thinking and possible selected sources of information, are difficult to disentangle because talk indexes itself and our thought processes, while displacing other sources of information simultaneously. The problem is also complicated when different sources of information and thought are indexed by manual signs and other bodily movements, but represented by verbal expressions in correspondence with oral language categories and rules. References to the importance of nonverbal communication among hearing persons do not deal with body movements associated with manual sign language usage. The significance of body movements for researchers has often been conceptualized narrowly by the use of a structural linguistics model and not seen as a problem in cross-modal communication.

The ethnographic context

My first task is to show how a hearing person, asking a deaf subject for the appropriate signs corresponding to oral language lexical items which the researcher organized into sentences, is able to record oral descriptive statements about the deaf person's signs. At a later date the researcher should be able to transcribe his descriptive statements and produce the appropriate signs which a third person can act out or can recognize as identical to the original written sentences. The procedure is straightforward and presumes considerable knowledge which a normal hearing and seeing person utilizes but does not recognize as relevant to the production of everyday communication.

Imagine the following scene: a living room occupied by a deaf woman, her deaf child of approximately three years of age, and a hearing researcher. The researcher writes out sentences on a sheet of paper in English and asks the woman to translate them into signs. Asking the woman to use signs involves making a kind of circular motion with the two hands (palms facing each other) while pointing to the written sentences. These movements were intended to signify that I was asking the woman to translate the sentences into appropriate signs. But the term 'appropriate' is not clear here. I had also written on the sheet of paper that I wanted her to translate the sentences into the kind of signs she used with her deaf friends, hoping she would give me 'natural' signs, or the signs that the deaf use among themselves. The 'natural' (or native) signs do not have a one-to-one correspondence with the meaning and syntax of oral language English, while another version of sign language (call it second language signing) is in correspondence with oral language English syntax and lexical items.

As I wrote each sentence on the sheet of paper the woman ignored my request for native sign order and instead gave me signs that had second language sign ordering. The word order of oral/written English was preserved, and there was a one-to-one correspondence between each English word and a signed or a finger-spelled version of the English word if no sign was appropriate. Before presenting the sentences a few words clarifying communication among the deaf is necessary.

Most deaf persons are trained to read lips, simulate speech and read texts of oral language. The creation of manual sign language has been a centuries-old response among persons born deaf for developing communication with each other. One way the reader can think about this problem is to imagine two deaf persons trying to communicate with oral language. An understanding of their simulated speech depends on how well they can articulate different lip movements with oral language terms. Reading lips is difficult if the person whose lips you are trying to read possesses a different dialect or is a stranger. Because the deaf do not have any auditory feedback from their own lip productions, they can only monitor their own lip movements by examining themselves in a mirror, or by their memory of appropriate articulatory or other activities associated with the pronunciation of oral lexical items.

When a hearing person attempts to comprehend a deaf person's speech he needs as much contextual information as possible to locate the sound patterns. This contextual information (particularly its acoustical features) is only partially available to the deaf person despite the availability of important visual cues. A similar problem exists for the hearing person trying to describe a deaf person's use of sign language. The deaf person may use native or second language signs and in each case embellish his use of signs with paralinguistic information further elaborated by contextual cues which are emergent in the setting but primarily of value to the deaf. When the deaf read lips it is difficult for them to sense that a person is trying to be friendly by his intonation patterns, or that a person's voice reveals irritation by what is being said about someone. These elusive judgments of friendliness are represented by other modalities and influence the significance of the signs and paralinguistic information being received. Communication between deaf persons and hearing persons who do not know sign language is similar to man-machine exchanges; there is a sharp reduction in the forms of information that can be conveyed. Even the various gestures both parties use are linked to different language systems.

I attempted to describe the signs I observed by speaking into the tape recorder and found it difficult to report simple, clear, meaningful movements as generated by the deaf subject. Part of the difficulty can be attributed to my own ineptness in trying to use a descriptive vocabulary that would delineate movements by the two hands, arms, head, and the upper-body area according to specifiable regions of the head, face, upper chest, lower chest, and abdominal region. *I attempted to specify many additional details of the movements I witnessed because they seemed significant at the time, but also because I could not be certain about what was insignificant.*

A serious problem that emerged here had to do with the nature of the signs the present (and later) subject used, differences in what was felt to be the appropriate sign for a given oral lexical item. There were differences in what could be described as 'slang' and 'correct' signs. The female subject gave me signs which were translations of sentences written on a sheet of paper and involved difficulties associated with my deciding on the 'nativeness' of the signs. She gave me the same oral language word order I gave her, but her signs seemed to be informal or casual movements I could only describe as 'fluent'. The significance of this last remark cannot be underestimated because one native signer can detect another native signer with apparent ease, and a native signer can also detect a second language signer who might be a proficient signer. Similar observations can be made about dialect differences among oral language users. If the signs are native, there will be considerable variation in where the hands, arms, shoulders, and head will move, making it difficult for a researcher inexperienced in sign language to produce descriptive statements about the signs. It becomes difficult to pinpoint the exact location of a movement, and especially difficult to specify when a sign begins and when it ends or where another sign begins.

Specifying the exact location of a sign depends on how well two interlocutors know each other's signing. If they are native signers, this becomes difficult for a researcher because the more native the sign, the more variability likely in its execution, and the more native intuition required to locate the sign in the existing or unfolding context of tacit but multiple sources of information available to a native deaf signer. Good second language signers might miss many of the variations and subtleties generated. Hence, it becomes especially difficult for a novice like myself to pinpoint what I think I am observing because different pauses, hesitations, facial expressions, body movements, all seem important, yet I cannot describe all of them. I observe several sources of information simultaneously, but my ability to describe what I think I see is limited by the sequential production of speech I am capable of emitting.

The subject was given the following instructions on 12 January 1971. The interviewing was done in the subject's home. The instructions were written out. 'Shirley, I need your help in how to translate something into signs that you would use with good friends at the Deaf Club in Oxford.' I then presented the following sentence:

1. The bear gives the monkey to the man.

I then gave additional instructions: 'Please do not follow the English as it is taught in school, but try and tell me the signs as you would do it for a friend who *does not* read or write or speak well. Otherwise I will not learn to sign as the deaf do it'. I then gave her the following sentences:

2. The man saw the boy.
3. The man is easy to see.
4. The man is eager to speak.
   (anxious) (he wants to very much)
5. To see the man is easy.
6. The man told the boy to leave.
7. The man persuaded the boy to leave.
   (convinced) (talked him into)
8. The man ordered the boy to leave.

After giving the subject the first sentence ('The bear gives the monkey to the man'), my verbatim remarks to the tape recorder begins as follows:

'*Bear*, is the two hands underneath the armpits like, alright, circular motion, that's bear.
Bear . . . bear, bear, ah bear!
I'm sorry this is bear, bear is the two fists closed and crossed in front of the chest.
Bear, okay, bear . . . okay, *gives*, and the two hands go out, *gives*, the, ah, but look, uh, *monkey*, ah *monkey* is the two hands underneath the arms, the two hands underneath the two armpits.
The *monkey*, *to*, she finger-spelled *t-h-e* and *t-o*, *to-the-man*, and *man* is the fist [right fist] up against the chin.
[The tape is suddenly silent as I wrote out the instructions to myself about how to sign.
Okay, I'm telling her (in writing) try and tell me the signs as you would do it for a friend who uh, does not read or write, or speak well.]
She's signing to herself what I've just written, alright, to see what I what I mean.
Signing to herself.
Because, uh (long pause) otherwise I would not be able to sign as the deaf do, is what I just wrote.
Okay.
So now we start over again, okay, now, the first sentence: The bear gives the monkey to the man.
Okay.
[The first sentence was shown to her again.]
Bear gives the monkey to (finger spells *t-o*) the man.

Okay, alright, uh, now, uh . . . now here's uh another one, let's see, a second sentence I'll put down will be, uh, let's see:
'The man . . . saw the boy.'
She finger spells *t-h-e*, *man*, and then she did the sign for, then she finger spells uh uh *t-h-e*, *the-man-saw*, she put the . . . right index finger to the eye and made it out, *saw* [the finger goes away from the eye, but not down, though slightly at the end, as I now recall.]
and then she finger-spelled *t-h-e*, and makes the sign for *boy* with the right index finger rubbing parallel uh to the chin, not parallel, but yah, uh at right angles to the chin, I should say.
Okay?
[Now she's giving me the correct English normative word order.]'

The above transcription should give the reader some idea of the difficulties of trying to record orally what is being perceived as various sources of information (including a reaction to my own talk) where an attempt is made to be literal in one's description of an unusual activity. The difficulties I encountered are not merely deficiencies in my ability to use English precisely, but the fact that such description of visual experiences has no clear correspondence with oral language usage. An additional problem has to do with the signer's precision in presenting the signs to me. I am assuming that a 'relaxed' informal atmosphere existed in the subject's home setting, but the reader has no way of checking this out. Because of the relaxed atmosphere I assume existed, I further assumed that the signs were not carefully designed to satisfy some idealized version of manual signs (accompanied by pictures) often presented in books or dictionaries. The relaxed nature of the signs means that there were discrepancies between the ideal display of a series of pictures and the practical execution of the actual movements. A machine graphics programme would be expected to present an idealized manual sign system. If a machine could 'read' video tapes of native signing, the pattern recognition problem becomes difficult in the same sense that it was for me or would be for any human. It is difficult for anyone to recognize sound patterns in a foreign language he knows moderately well when used by natives in relaxed, informal settings. But the deaf pose a more difficult problem because we are dealing with a kinesic-visual system that does not readily exhibit the kinds of systematic structures claimed for oral languages.

Language without a clearly identified syntax

The issue of language without a clearly identified syntax is perhaps strange to a reader whose thinking is accustomed to the ordering found in standardized language constructions. Sign language is based on kinesic and visual information which we force into a foreign oral accounting scheme. The oral accounting frame contains its own logical relationships which we cannot suspend even if we are aware of their constraints during usage.

As soon as we try to explain a language based on visual and kinesic properties said to be organized without an oral syntax conception of rules, we are caught in an interesting dilemma.

We need an organizing framework to describe what we think we see or hear. We employ a framework for oral language which is said to have universal structures (Greenberg, 1966), and the system of manual signs does not seem to possess the syntactic structures basic to the idea of a universal linguistic framework. There is no difficulty demonstrating how this non-oral manual sign system works. We can make predictions about activities that will take place, indicate the signs necessary to communicate with deaf children without presupposing the child possesses any oral language structures, and then witness the activities carried out only requiring us to assent by nodding our heads. Hearing persons can obviously engage in nonverbal activities but they invariably resort to oral accounting which must be described within a linguistic or conversational framework. The accounting process is highly idealized when model sentences are employed. Everyday conversational exchanges produce less linguistic idealization during communication. But model sentences and conversational exchanges miss much of the context indexed orally. Descriptions of manual sign language can clarify the centrality of context in cross-modal communication. Earlier I briefly illustrated the problem of producing clear descriptions of manual signs. I now present idealized versions to show how presumed 'obvious' context-free structures can be formed which obscure the informational base.

The different sentences I presented to the deaf subject, and the signed responses I received can be presented in idealized oral language as follows:

1. The bear gives the monkey to the man.
Finger spell *t-h-e*.
Close the two hands into fists and cross them in front of
the chest.   = *bear*
Open the two hands as they are both extended in front of
the chest with the arms parallel to the ground about the
level of the lower chest.   = *give*
Finger spell *t-h-e*.
The two hands, slightly cupped, underneath the armpits,
with the fingers moving back and forth.   = *monkey*
Finger spell *t-o*.
Finger spell *t-h-e*.
The right fist underneath the chin.   = *man*

2. The man saw the boy.
Finger spell *t-h-e*.
Sign for *man* (see above).
Right index finger next to the right eye, slightly closed fist,
with the hand then moving away from the eye directly
down so that the forearm is almost parallel to the ground.   = *saw*
Finger spell *t-h-e*.   (actually *see*)
Right index finger (but with fist closed) touching the
bottom of the chin (but not underneath) and finger
pointing horizontally to the left.   = *boy*

3. The man is easy to see.
Finger spell *t-h-e*.
Sign *man* (see above).
Finger spell *i-s*.
Right fist closed with index finger extended, touching and
slightly tapping the right cheek area.   = *easy*
Finger spell *t-o*.
Sign *see* (see above).

4. The man is eager to speak.
Finger spell *t-h-e*.
Sign for *man*.
[The subject was puzzled by *eager* and I substituted
'*anxious-like*' in its place but this substitution also proved
difficult so I tried '*he wants to very much*' and this seemed
to be meaningful as she proceeded to give me the sign
for *want*.]
The right fist closed against the right side of the chest, moves
down while opening the fist so that the palm is against
the body as it crosses from the right side to the left
(of the person doing the signing) moving down towards
the stomach area on the left side.   = *want*
Finger spell *t-o*.
The right index anger extended (with the rest of the hand
made into a fist) is brought up to the mouth with the index
finger almost touching the mouth and than a slight circular
motion is made with the index finger, and the hand is
dropped to the lower chest region.   = *speak*
(A certain amount of 'movement emphasis' can be
added to *want* to signify *want very much*.)

5. To see the man is easy.
Finger spell *t-o*.
Sign *see*.
Finger spell *t-h-e*.
Sign *man*.
Finger spell *i-s*.
Sign *easy*.

6. The man told the boy to leave.
Finger spell *t-h-e*.
Sign *man*.
Right index finger (hand partially closed) placed close
underneath the chin and moved away from chin area
(away from the body) in a circular motion.   = *told*
Finger spell *t-h-e*.   or *tell*.
Sign *boy*.
Finger spell *t-o*.
Left and right palms close to the chest with the right palm
covering the back of the left hand partially, both hands
moving outward in a sweeping motion, palms up and
forearms extended but elbows bent. [Or, as one informant
told me, the right hand with thumb extended could be used
as *go* in place of *leave*.]   = *leave*

7. The man persuaded the boy to leave.
Finger spell *t-h-e*.
Sign *man*.
[Subject did not understand *persuaded*; I then wrote
talked him into and she signed *talk in-to*.]
Right index finger (hand closed) extended is placed near
the mouth (points to the mouth) and then moved directly
away from the face and body with the forearm ending
up parallel to the ground.   = *talk*
[There are no established signs for pronouns and pronominal
reference (except to finger spell the word). A general
strategy for dealing with pronominal reference is to use a
pointing gesture in a context to signify someone present
and referring to him after he leaves by pointing to the
space or location where he stood or sat. Thus pronominal
reference can be represented by location in a context when
the participants have been talking about someone who was
present earlier or who is known by where he sits or some

characteristic activity. A simple sweeping motion is used
which points to the location or in the general direction of
a nearby room and implies someone not present but
understood as known to the signers.]
Right hand (open but slightly cupped) is put underneath
the left hand, both hands palms down, but the right hand
moves through the underside of the left hand to signify
going *in* something.   = *in*
Finger spell *t-o*.
Finger spell *t-h-e*.
Sign *boy*.
Finger spell *t-o*.
Sign *leave*.
[The sentence signed is also represented in (7a).]

7a. The man talked him into, the boy, to leave.
The final sentence 8 is a variation of 7 and involves
another complication because of the lack of native signs
for the oral language lexical items.

8. The man ordered the boy to leave.
Finger spell *t-h-e*.
Sign *man*.
Extended index finger of the right hand (fist closed,
knuckles on the right side) up against the chin with an
up and down motion and then away from the chin area.
[But this is not a correctly defined sign which would be
unambiguously understood by native or second-language
signers.]   = *ordered*
Finger spell *t-h-e*.
Sign *boy*.
Finger spell *t-o*.
Sign *leave*.

The reader will have noticed that my attempts to render the oral descriptions
of the signs as edited glosses are not always very convincing because the
movements implied are often ambiguous. It is not merely the case that I was
unfamiliar with British sign language at the time the above materials were
obtained, *but that oral descriptions (even with time for extensive editing) of
visual-kinesic information always presupposes unstated assumptions and
meanings that cannot be clearly objectified for someone who has not experienced the setting.* But even experiencing the setting does not guarantee
consensus or complete agreement, only a tacit arrangement to claim that

the 'same' object or event was witnessed. The representation problem is basically a negotiated accomplishment which trades on idealized, context-free rules or norms for creating an important (but nevertheless 'real') illusion of 'similarity', 'sameness' or 'consensus'. These 'illusions' are socially organized cognitive constructions. Their construction can be partially clarified by reference to the previous materials where the terms *speak*, *told*, *tell*, *persuaded*, *talked him into*, *talk into*, *talk*, *talked*, *ordered*, are used. These terms presumably index related activities for which slight variation in the base signs exist but the base movements can be embellished in several ways by the deaf to communicate other connotations. Alternatively, we can see the variations as a function of my inexperience with signs, particularly how signs are to be described. The materials are listed in Table 1.

Table 1

speak 4	Right index finger extended (with the rest of the hand made into a fist) is brought up to the mouth with the index finger almost touching the mouth as a slight circular motion is made with the index finger, and the hand is then dropped to the lower chest region.
told, *tell* 6	Right index finger (hand partially closed) placed close underneath the chin and moved away from the chin area (away from the body) in a circular motion.
persuaded, *talked him into*, *talk into*, *talk* 7	The right index finger (hand closed) extended is placed near the mouth (points to the mouth) and then moved directly away from the face and body with the forearm ending up parallel to the ground.
talked, *ordered* 7a, 8	Extended index finger of the right hand (fist closed, knuckles on the right side) up against the chin with an up and down motion and then away from the chin area. (Ambiguous or incorrect sign.)

My interpretation of what I think I saw produces several variations of what I took the signing to represent as movements. We can attribute this to my noticing different particulars despite an opportunity to edit my descriptions, or we can say that the subject produced natural variations because of the colloquial way a native signer communicates. The edited versions given above in Table 1 are derived from my rambling and verbatim transcription of the tape. As I formalize the descriptions of what I think I witnessed the terms truncate the several sources of information. These sources of information can be called overlapping variations or they can be made to appear as meaningful differences. The right index finger and hand are central to my descriptions and the ambiguity centres around the location of *speak*, *talk* or *tell*. The index finger pointing to the mouth and then away from the mouth in a circular motion indicates the origin of the activity, but the variations I give include an extended area surrounding the chin. There are additional subtleties and ambiguities such as the configuration of the right hand and the role of the left hand, as well as the location of the forearm. The kernel movement of the right index finger pointing first to the mouth area and then away in a circular motion seems clear enough but if the reader tries it, he or she will see that a certain amount of hesitancy is involved, and until you can observe a native signer do it while you try to imitate the movement, you will not feel comfortable with your own efforts. This hesitancy was an integral part of my efforts for several months while trying to learn British sign language. The difficulties I experienced underline the problem of trying to describe unfamiliar activities (that presuppose multiple sources of information) with categories that require considerable elaboration for their comprehension. I found myself trying to use crisp declarative sentences to describe subtleties that I could 'see' and understand but not articulate clearly. This is precisely the phenomena of interest in any study of socio-linguistic activities; the standardized, context-free methods we employ for claiming objectivity in the study of everyday social behaviour can only index information we process from thought and sensory modalities (and their interaction) by a necessary reliance on our memory and a tacit under-standing of what we imagine or feel we experience.

Adequate description is always tied to the practical circumstances of the occasion for reporting or accounting for experiences or observations. My attempts to objectify the classroom setting or the sign language context means subverting my experiences with several sources of information to produce an apparent logical sequence of descriptive statements. I cannot attach a footnote to every statement indicating the subtle kinds of information I intend. Hence my attempts to create 'appropriate' glosses of the descriptions I provide of the signing are similar to the child's truncated expressions when asked by the teacher to 'tell her where the orange worm is'. The child uses a truncated expression that presumes other sources of information are relevant and indeed operative for understanding the significance of the utterance employed. When I attempt to describe the movements of my deaf subject, I create normative categories which I assume are context-free under the assumption that I and others will be able to read or hear my descriptions and reproduce the signs (or carry out some action) initially produced by the deaf subject. The inadequacy of my description is evident from the literal transcription of the tape and from my attempts to reproduce the signs from the transcript. I had to recall my visual experiences of the original setting to communicate my intentions to another signer at a later date, and, as will be seen below, my signing was not entirely successful in producing the written statements I intended when I returned several weeks later and signed most of the sentences to the deaf subject again. Hence all sociolinguistic data are compromised by this representational problem and require explicit theoretical explication and innovative methodological strategies if we are to avoid the dangers of reifying the speech acts we view as basic data.

The issue of how cognitive systems become mapped into linguistic representations is not known, but may be partially clarified by noting the difference in word order between sign languages and oral languages (Cicourel and Boese 1972a; Cicourel, in press a; Schlesinger, n.d.). Some evidence for word order difference can be seen in Table 2. The written sentences were given to the subject on 12 January 1971. On 24 March 1971 I presented the subject with sentences now represented as native sign equivalents. The reader will notice that the first sentence is different from the one presented earlier but retains the same word order and is consistent with the other sentences given in January. I asked the subject to write out the verbal equivalents of the signed sentences I presented to her.

Table 2 **Written representations of native signed sentences by a female subject born deaf**

Signed sentences by researcher	Subject's written representations
1 boy give book man	1 boy give book to man
2 man boy see	2 boy man see
3 easy see man	3 – see man
4 man see eager	4 man see lady
5 man see easy	5 man see girl
6 man told boy leave	6 boy saw man left
7 man persuaded [pushing, pleading motion] please and pray boy go (leave)	7 man – boy left
8 man tell help boy go (leave) (advised)	8 man see help boy left

Except for adding *to* in sentence (1), the deaf subject provided apparent lexical equivalents to my native signs. The word order of (2) and (6) contains a subject-object reversal, while (3) deletes a reference to *easy*. The signs I used for *easy* and *eager* were not clear to my subject, and in (4) and (5) were taken to signify *lady* and *girl*. The sign for *lady* or *girl* can be made on the same right cheek area as *easy* and could have been confused with my unclear signs for *eager* and *easy*. Clumsy signing on my part could account for these discrepancies.

The discrepancies in (7) and (8) point to problems of using standard SVO utterances or model sentences to establish semantic equivalences between two systems of communication. The equivalences ostensibly established in the sentences in Table 2 are misleading because I forced an oral language framework on the research setting at the outset. Hence the way I structure the exchange forced the deaf subject to orient to an oral conception of language. The expressiveness of sign language is distorted by insisting on a correspondence between bounded signs and oral language lexical items. The multiple sources of contextual information essential for native signing are not captured by single frame utterances. The use of words like *persuaded, advised* or *promised* in native signing requires contextual 'build-up' by participants which rely on creating the necessary meanings during the occasion (Cicourel, 1970b). To speak of their equivalents in sign language ignores the difficulties of claiming knowledge about a different system of communication when the conception of language and thought used is conceived initially in terms of context-free oral language grammars.

I presented the sentences initially in written form and asked for sign equivalents that would be used with 'friends' in the hope of obtaining native signing. I received signed sentences in correspondence with oral language syntax (second language signing). The sentences signed in Table 2 attempted to simulate native signing. The subject responded with written equivalents that were 'native-like' and did not reorganize my signs into second language signing. It is like two separate systems that can trade on oral language grammar to represent differently organized semantic domains. Hence a bilingual speaker-signer would be able to keep the semantic domains separated. But the use of similar oral language syntactic representations does not signify equivalent semantic structures or thought processes.

My reaction to the deaf subject's signing reveals how difficult it was for me to represent verbally several types of information which I received simultaneously (including a reaction to my own talk which I perceived as inadequate). The diverse information and parallel processing that occurs is represented by sequential speech productions. In sociolinguistic research we are not clear how speech acts represent the activities of the setting experienced by participants. I cannot say to what extent the deaf subjects' experiences were represented by her verbal expressions. Hence our use of sociolinguistic speech data which are divorced from occasions of use makes it difficult to understand to what extent the talk represents the activities of the setting and the experience of the participants.

The discrepancies between the signing I performed and the written forms produced by the deaf subject cannot be resolved by a simple reference to my ignorance of British native sign language. The problem is complicated by the subject's conception of what I am likely to 'know' and is similar to the visual illusions created by Kolers and Pomerantz (1971). The issue is not the 'objective' facts of how contours are perceived or the features that must be extracted to achieve recognition of a sign or object known to the experimenter. The problem involves the ways in which we respond to and represent information. The subject presumably assumes that I 'think' as a hearing person, but she must also respond to my signing. I cannot monitor the adequacy of my signing but must rely on what the subject writes down even while 'knowing' that this is an insoluble dilemma. Hence our reliance on and use of different modalities, especially our thinking, continually alters the context-free basis we use to 'objectify' a setting. How 'native' must we be to feel 'confident' about signing with persons, born deaf, who are native signers? How are we to represent the information selectively attended? The discrepancies of Table 2 suggest how difficult it is to understand languages that rely on different representational structures. My attempts to learn and study sign language simultaneously reveal the difficulties of such study while exhibiting features of a substantive nature. The subject tried to create coherence by supplying terms that would presumably be intelligible to me. Her signing is equivocal because of the test conditions, but normally we would try to establish contrast sets to pinpoint discrepancies and eliminate ambiguities. Our research procedures are designed to create idealized rule structures. I followed this strategy only in part to underline the negotiated sense in which we create claims of semantic equivalence or contrast.

I hope it is clear that forming a data base by translating manual signs into verbal strings which are grammatically correct is not an easy task. It is even more difficult to translate verbal categories which have presumed clear normative significance for hearing persons into manual signs whose significance for the deaf has a generative cognitive coherence that is tied to the circumstances of the experienced interactional setting. This is especially difficult when it is recognized that no formal syntactic rules have been identified for reformulating intentions which emerge in the context of communication. In our enthusiasm for discovering the grammar of manual sign language we must be cautious in proposing rule structures for signs which presuppose social meanings marked by verbal normative categories in formal ways. Every attempt to claim rule structures in sign language that are similar to oral language syntax requires the use of oral language syntax as a way of formulating the problem. The formalization imposes a structure with built-in meanings which is not easily described, much less defended, in settings where signs are context-sensitive.

The idea of a data base is very misleading because operations on a data base usually imply that the subjects and researcher or experimenter use similar or identical coding rules and signals of the languages involved. When we are dealing with hearing-seeing subjects and experimenters, the issue of how much native competence is presupposed is not addressed but traded on implicitly. When using oral language categories that can have various normative meanings attached to them, *and* manual signs whose meanings are usually tied to the settings in which they are created and/or used, we cannot take the sign-oral category correspondence for granted because we cannot be certain that we know how native signers translate oral language categories into signs and vice-versa.

Theoretical implications

Students of language have always recognized that the verbal constructions of the child or adult do not adequately index the kinds of information available from several sources. The importance of nonverbal information has been stressed repeatedly, but the displacement of everyday meanings expressed by different modalities is usually studied by examining normative or rule-governed verbal utterances as the central carrier of information. The study of nonverbal materials employs a verbal model. I have presumed the familiar idea that we express information in several ways simultaneously. I have explored this familiar theme by suggesting two possible strategies; the representational context of oral and sign language usage. Our reliance on sequential verbal materials and our implicit use of tacit social or cultural sources of information mask or truncate the complex information processing that seems to be effortless exercises for hearing-speaking subjects. The study of social interaction presupposes that participants possess some broad capabilities which I shall gloss as interactional competence. Interactional competence refers to the ability to recognize, receive, process, and generate communicational procedures (which are at the same time informational resources) while simultaneously integrating and elaborating our thinking and reaction to these activities in the act of production or comprehension. The data base or memory simultaneously become informational resources and communicational strategies or procedures (Winograd, 1971; Becker, 1970; Shank, 1971). Sociolinguistic studies recognize but seldom study our ability to attend simultaneously to multiple sources of information which can be processed selectively. Instead our research focuses on data that follow the constraints of our speech organs and idealized cultural rules for generating sequential utterances. The normative ways in which we produce utterances and elicit information, and our formalized conceptions of language structure and its acquisition obscure the complex organization of information processing in everyday settings despite our reliance on everyday exchanges as the source of our data and elicitation strategies.

Representation of experience and interpretative procedures

In Western societies the hearing child between the ages of four and six faces a major problem in moving from his initial reliance on kinesic and nonverbal auditory communication and his acquisition of an oral language which is largely context-restricted, to his gradual partial or extensive mapping of these activities into a standardized oral and orthographic system which stresses context-free constructions. Standardized oral or orthographic systems are intended to displace and index visual, oral and auditory non-verbal, kinesic, proprioceptive and tactile informational particulars. These standardized verbal systems are creatively learned extensions of developmentally acquired abilities. We are not very clear about what is innate about language acquisition or the resultant childhood social structures which are produced, but adults find sense in and accommodate to the child's activities by supplying adult conceptions of meaning. During this period between four and six years of age, the child's cognitive ability to displace objects and events, and their temporal qualities, is limited by the organization of his memory and by his command of context-free communicational devices. Recalled previous experiences seem to be divorced from their real-time adult significance and are often indiscriminately articulated within the conditions of the immediate setting. Perhaps the child has equated several images of prior experiences because of the present context, but for the adult these experiences would be marked as independent and unrelated events.

Children between the ages of four and six do not always produce clearly bounded context-free sentences which conform to a subject-verb-object (SVO) construction when interacting with other children or their parents, but as several studies (Brown, 1970; Menyuk, 1969; Chomsky, 1969; Mc-Neill, 1970; Slobin, 1971; Bloom, 1970) have noted, the sentences can be seen as approximating an adult SVO structure around six to eight years of age. It is difficult, however, to pinpoint the child's heavy reliance on several modalities for communicating intentions and understanding the intentions of others. An important adult criterion of educational success is to observe the child's increasingly more sophisticated use of oral language for displacing information. The use of apparently sophisticated (adult-like) oral expressions does not tell us the extent to which the child understands his own usage *vis-à-vis* adult conceptions of such expressions, nor are we clear about the child's awareness of how the use of oral expressions truncates other modalities when seeking to communicate and understand immediate, past, or future activities.

The study of cross-modal communication and semantic information processing presumes knowledge about the roles of memory and attention (James, 1890; Neisser, 1967; Norman, 1969); for example, how many things we can attend at once. But studies of memory and attention do not always address the ways in which interpretations of the stimulus field and the reflexive thinking of the subject presuppose ideal social conceptions of socially 'appropriate' informational particulars. The organism's ability to execute many disconnected conceptual processes simultaneously hinges on the difficulty of the tasks involved, the number of events it can attend and follow, the ability to retain and retrieve information (Miller, 1956), and the way experiences are socially organized. Access to storage depends on the ways in which information is experienced and organized by the organism's normative accounting procedures. Real-time is a normatively organized accounting device for recognizing and receiving information. The socially defined temporal properties of an event or object depend on our ability to switch our perception from one event or object to another. Our selective attention and retention create different kinds of temporal orderings and thus a coherent organization of experience despite independent observation or evidence by other observers that would claim otherwise.

Sociolinguistic studies must go beyond the use of model sentences and conversational exchanges, because these data bases obscure how different channels of information are selected or rejected. These channels of information are basic ingredients of all interaction settings. The study of how conversational exchanges are accomplished in everyday life assumes that we design our talk so that selection of different pieces or strings of utterances occurs in ways which are presumed to facilitate the conversation. But few students of conversational exchanges view the speaker or hearer's cognitive structures as central processes. A link is needed between ideal normative selection procedures (covering greetings, turns, chaining, nesting, closings of conversations, topicalizing, insulting, distrusting) and the cognitive organization of processing selective cross-modal information. Conversational meaning and rules are not obvious social facts, but contingent productions. The developmental acquisitions of these conversational constraints by children is not clear, but their glossing and displacement of different modalities cannot be ignored if we are to understand sociolinguistic communication.

The ethnography (or ethnographic context) of speaking (Gumperz and Hymes, 1964; Gumperz, 1971) implies that the social setting is an integral part of semantic information processing, and that ideal-normative conversational rules (Sacks, 1970; Schegloff, 1969) exist whereby participants trade on implicit socialization experiences for deciding when and how the selection and generation of different lexical items or strings will occur. The selection of particular strings, accompanied by 'appropriate' pauses presupposes considerable knowledge about how to convey social appearances, utterances and intonational impressions in socially defined and emergent settings.

The picture presented thus far for hearing children may be clarified further if we return to the use of deaf manual sign language. The idea of real-time, intonational subtleties which signal irony, annoyance, pleasure, are not 'natural' acquisitions for the deaf child, but are assumed to be developmentally ordered for the hearing child. The selective retention of information and interference from other channels of communication for the deaf is not as clear as our current speculations about hearing adults seem to be. The deaf child must struggle to learn phrase structure rules and transformations which hearing children presumably learn 'naturally' or ' intuitively'.

The manual signalling systems used by deaf children and adults have localized standardization *vis-à-vis* each other, but achieve context-free status when in correspondence with oral language systems that have standardized grammatical rules. How the deaf, using native sign language not in correspondence with oral language syntax, displace other modalities including their memory and emergent thought is not known. But our attempts to represent sign language orally creates problems which we also face as hearing persons when we rely on oral representations to index several modalities and our emergent and past experiences and thought.

Studies of natural language seldom reveal how model sentences and conversational exchanges connect with other modalities. Our general strategy in the study of model sentences and conversational exchanges is to take output as given and then construct rule structures that may be said to underlie the output. The cognitive activities that presumably order and organize selective memory and selective attention are not examined.

Routine everyday exchanges are cross-modal, self-embedding, self-modifying, and emergent in the act of their production. The outputs of social interaction are cross-modal informational particulars which also serve as 'programmes' or instructions for all participants including the speaker or signer of manual sign langauge. Cognitive structures seem to possess a self-organizing quality, while simultaneously generating rule-governed strings and utterance fragments, visual, kinesic, tactile, and nonverbal auditory information. These processes occur within a socially defined setting that is being reinterpreted continuously. Sociolinguistic studies must ask how memory influences the selection of informational particulars at any point in the conversation. How do conversational utterances become constrained by the existence of information from several sources which emerge simultaneously? Semantic information processing requires a more general cognitive organization that goes beyond linguistic and psychological structures to explain the conditions faced by deaf native signers who find oral language syntactic rules 'strange'. I have called these socially relevant cognitive properties 'interpretive procedures' (cf. Cicourel, 1970a and b for a more elaborate statement and various references). The interpretive procedures are an extension of cognitive structures and facilitate cross-modal communication and understanding. The child must acquire a facility with the following properties to achieve adult interactional competence.

1. Reflexive thinking about informational particulars selectively available from multiple sources in an emergent context (including the speaker or signer's own activities in the setting) provide participants with a basis for creating continuous instructions for programming their activities in socially acceptable ways.

2. Despite cultural differences and different spatial arrangements in the setting, participants must behave as if they share the same social setting and are receiving and processing the same information. Various appearances and utterances (signs) must be treated as 'obvious' despite the possibility that the participants are aware that differences exist and are being communicated in subtle ways.

3. In addition to assuming tacitly that they are oriented to the 'same' environment of objects and thoughts despite cultural differences and the use of a particular dialect or standardized (oral or sign) language, the participants must also be familiar with normative constraints about who can speak first, or next, what topics are considered socially relevant and acceptable, how to terminate an exchange, when someone's talk (or signs) is being insulting, distrustful or 'odd', and the like (Sacks, 1970; Schegloff, 1969). We do not have comparable data on the deaf here. We do not know if the deaf are constrained by sequential ordering or chaining rules, because several signers can allow their signing to overlap continuously and several types of information can be communicated simultaneously which fall under the general notion of kinesic-visual communication.

4. Participants expect each other to possess 'normal form' repertoires of possible appearances, behaviours and utterances (signs) which can be expressed or 'understood' when emergent in contextually organized settings. Participants also assume that each will normalize discrepancies to sustain the social interaction. Thus 'strange' appearances or thoughts about the setting can be handled routinely as 'life as usual' because of selective attention or by the negotiated employment of a common and standardized system of signals and coding rules that are presumed to be reciprocally available to all participants.

5. The previous points imply that the participants must be able to go beyond

the information given to recognize appearances, behaviours, utterances or gestures as meaningful activities, while filling in appropriate information where relevant by linking present informational resources to prior sources and future possibilities.

6. The ability to go beyond the information given and thus retrospectively and prospectively link immediate information to past and possible future objects, events, or thoughts is central for the articulation of idealized normative (signs) rules (like conversational rules or linguistic rules as applied to model sentences) with contingent social settings. Linking stored information about rules and general background to immediate settings highlights the idea of interactional competence.

7. Participants must be capable of articulating immediate settings with idealized rules and general informational particulars of a substantive nature under the assumption that this is a routine feature of the interactional setting, yet simultaneously may or may not recognize that much of what transpires may not be accountable in standardized or colloquial expressions. What is not accountable may be viewed as comprehensible or remarkable, and yet because there is no necessary explicit marking for something attached to the setting we may fail to acknowledge its essential presence in everyday exchanges.

The above elements of interpretive procedures seem to be minimally relevant for the kind of interactional competence necessary for the production of everyday social structures. They provide a link between sociolinguistic activities and cognitive processes.

Embedded or nested signs or conversational sequences presume parallel information processing. With interference such embedding can be altered drastically. Hence in multi-party conversations the 'cocktail party' problem (Cherry, 1953; Norman, 1969), whereby different channels carrying information are selected or rejected, becomes a central issue in assessing the impact of particular channels and how short and long-term memory create the circumstances for embedded sequences or the cooperative construction of signs or utterances. When a subject creates a written text the problem of selective attention and competing channels becomes one of available stored information that serves as data and rule systems for satisfying a variety of considerations like appropriate syntactic organization, possible audiences, masking thoughts, emphasizing certain points and the like. *A central issue is the extent to which the subject has been exposed to different kinds of information and rule systems.* For hearing (and deaf) children the representation of thoughts and intentions, or their understanding of something, is especially difficult.

Our interpretation of a child's classroom activities provides materials that highlight the kind of displacement and social reasoning attributed to the child when we try to articulate the child's performance with the teacher's claimed understanding of the outcome. Attempts to represent manual signs by verbal descriptions underline the problem of integrating cross-modal information particulars and calls our attention to the dilemma of trying to understand cognitive processes independently of communicational modalities. The problems are further complicated by the explicit use of context-free descriptions which presuppose tacit context-sensitive information.

The native competence of deaf manual signers is central to the present discussion because persons born deaf have great difficulty ever becoming native speakers or writers of oral languages. Hence, cross-modal communication involves the difficult problem of translation and equivalence of information from different modalities and the fact that the normative categories used in each language are not in correspondence despite the assumption that the psychological and social realities experienced involve standardizing the 'same' environment.

When I gave my English deaf subject model sentences for translation into sign language, I received signs that contained the same word order despite her problems of finding the appropriate signs for the verbal lexical items. The deaf subject was responding to my stimulus sentences under the assumption that the syntactic rules of oral English were the appropriate data base. The difficulties of finding the appropriate sign translations obscures the lack of correspondence between the possible semantic systems being utilized and also obscures the more central problem of how cognitive systems are mapped into linguistic representations.

Teachers of hearing and deaf children make context-free attributions of competence by the evaluation of performance in context-restricted classroom settings. In each case (referring to hearing or deaf children) the teacher makes judgments about the child's competence by examining the child's ability to represent himself or herself *vis-à-vis* adult performance and competence. Thus a teacher may say that a hearing child has difficulty distinguishing between particular sound patterns and associating them with idealized phonemic representations. A teacher of the deaf with some knowledge of manual sign language may say that a deaf child has written a particular sentence in a way that is not grammatical for oral English because anecdotel evidence suggests that the deaf often produce signs to represent experiences in the order of their emotional significance for the subject. In the classroom setting the (deaf and hearing) child must contend with a system of representation that is different from the ways in which they learn to process received or recognized information. *The child's interactional competence is continually being modified by the ways in which he or she learns or is taught to represent himself or herself in family settings, peer group interaction, and in the school.*

The ability of the teacher or researcher to infer this competence is influenced by the adult's use of standardized SVO or model sentences to teach and elicit information, as well as to evaluate the child's performance. In the case of deaf children an unexplicated adult oral model is imposed or lurking implicitly in the background even when we claim to be studying 'natural' stages of sign language development.

References

AUSTIN, J. L. (1961), *Philosophical Papers*, Clarendon Press.

BACH, E., and HARMS, R. T. (eds.) (1968), *Universals in Linguistic Theory*, Holt, Rinehart & Winston.

BAR-HILLEL, Y. (1954), Indexical expressions', *Mind*, vol. 63, pp. 359–79.

BECKER, H. S. (1963), *The Outsiders*, Free Press.

BECKER, J. D. (1970), *An Information-Processing Model of Intermediate-Level Cognition*, Stanford Artificial Intelligence Project, memo A1/119.

BELLUGI, U., and SIPLE, P. (1971), 'Remembering with and without words', *Current Problems in Psycholinguistics*, International Colloquium of CNRS, December.

BENDIX, E. H. (1966), *Componential Analysis of General Vocabulary: The Semantic Structure of a Set of Verbs in English, Hindi, and Japanese*, Indiana University Press, and *Intern. J. of Amer. Linguistics*, vol. 32: 2, part 2.

BERNSTEIN, B. (1958), 'Some sociological determinants of perception', *Brit. J. Sociol.*, vol. 9.

BERNSTEIN, B. (1959), 'A public language: some sociological implications of a linguistic form', *Brit. J. Sociol.*, vol. 10.

BERNSTEIN, B. (1960), 'Language and social class', *Brit. J. Sociol.*, vol. 11.

BERNSTEIN, B. (1962), 'Linguistic codes, hesitation phenomena and intelligence', *Language and Speech*, vol. 5, Jan.–March.

BIERSTEDT, R. (1957), *The Social Order*, McGraw-Hill.

BIRDWHISTELL, E. L. (1970), *Kinesics and Context*, University of Pennsylvania Press.

BLAU, P. M. (1964), *Exchange and Power in Social Life*, Wiley.

BLOOM, L. (1970), *Language Development: Form and Function in Emerging Grammars*, MIT Press.

BLUM, J. P., and GUMPERZ, J. (1971), 'Some social determinants of verbal behavior', in Gumperz, J., and Hymes, D. (eds.), *Directions in Sociolinguistics*, Holt, Rinehart & Winston.

BOESE, ROBERT, J. (1971), *Native Sign Language and the Problem of Meaning*, unpublished Ph.D. dissertation, University of California, Santa Barbara.

BRAINE, M. D. S. (1963), 'The ontogeny of English phrase structure: the first phase', *Language*, vol. 39, pp. 1–13.

BROOM, L., and SELZNICK, P. (1963 edn), *Sociology: A Text with Adapted Readings*, Harper & Row.

BROWN, R. (1962), 'Models of attitude change', in Brown *et al.*, *New Directions in Psychology*, Holt, Rinehart & Winston, pp. 1–85.

BROWN, R. (1965), *Social Psychology*, Free Press.

BROWN, R. (1970), *Psycholinguistics*, Free Press.

BROWN, R., and BELLUGI, U. (1964), 'Three processes in the child's acquisition of syntax', in Lenneberg, E. (ed.), *New Directions in the Study of Language*, MIT Press.

BROWN, R., and FRASER, C. (1963), 'The acquisition of syntax', in C. N. Cofer and B. S. Musgrave (eds.), *Verbal Behavior and Learning*, McGraw-Hill, pp. 158–97.

BRUNER, J. S. (1957), 'Going beyond the information given', in *Contemporary Approaches to Cognition*, Symposium held at the University of Colorado, Harvard University Press.

BRUNER, J. S., GOODNOW, J. J., and AUSTIN, G. A. (1956), *A Study of Thinking*, Wiley.

CALEGERO, G. (1947), *Estetica, Semantica, Istorica*, as cited in T. De Mauro, *Ludwig Wittgenstein: His Place in the Development of Semantics*, Reidel, D., Holland, 1967.

CAMPBELL, D., (1966), 'Ostensive instances and entitativity in language learning', unpublished manuscript.

CAVELL, S. (1969), *Must We Mean What We Say*, Scribners.

CECCATO, S. (1960), 'Operational linguistics and translations', in *Linguistic and Programming for Mechanical Translation*, as cited in T. De Mauro, *Ludwig Wittgenstein*, 1967.

CHERRY, E. C. (1953), 'Some experiments on the recognition of speech, with one and with two ears', *J. acoustical Soc. Amer.*, vol. 25, pp. 975–9.

CHOMSKY, C. (1969), *The Acquisition of Syntax in Children from 5 to 10*, MIT Press.

CHOMSKY, N. (1965), *Aspects of a Theory of Syntax*, MIT Press.

CHOMSKY, N. (n.d.), *Form and Meaning in Natural Language*, Amsterdam.

CHOMSKY, N., and HALLE, M. (1965), 'Some controversial questions in phonological theory', *J. Linguistics*, vol. 1, pp. 97–138.

CHURCHILL, L. (1966), 'On everyday quantitative practices', unpublished paper presented at the annual meeting of the American Sociological Association.

CICOUREL, A. V. (1964), *Method and Measurement in Sociology*, Free Press.

CICOUREL, A. V. (1967), 'Kinship, marriage, and divorce in comparative family law', *Law Soc. Review*. vol. 1.

CICOUREL, A. V. (1968), *The Social Organization of Juvenile Justice*, Wiley.

CICOUREL, A. V. (1970a), 'The acquisition of social structure: toward a developmental sociology of language and meaning', in J. Douglas (ed.), *Understanding Everyday Life*, Aldine. Reprinted from *Rassegna di Sociologia*, vol. 9, 1968.

CICOUREL, A. V. (1970b), 'Generative semantics and the structure of social interaction', *International Days of Sociolinguistics*, Luigi Sturzo Institute, Rome.

CICOUREL, A. V. (In press, a), 'Some basic theoretical issues in the assessment of the child's performance in testing and classroom settings', in A. V. Cicourel et al., *Language Socialization and Use in Testing and Classroom Settings*, Seminar Press.

CICOUREL, A. V. (in press, b), *Interviews as situated accounts: Comparative Methodological Issues in a Study of Argentine Fertility*, Wiley, Interscience.

CICOUREL, A. V., and BOESE, R. (1972a), 'Sign language acquisition and the teaching of deaf children', in D. Hymes, C. Cazden and V. John (eds.), *The Functions of Language: an Anthropological and Psychological Approach*, Teachers College Press, New York.

CICOUREL, A. V., and BOESE, R. (1972b), 'The acquisition of manual sign language and generative semantics', *Semiotica* vol.3, pp. 225–56.

CICOUREL, A. V., JENNINGS, K., JENNINGS, S., LEITER, K., MACKAY, R., MEHAN, H., and ROTH, D. (in press), *Language Socialization and Use in Teaching and Classroom Settings*, Seminar Press.

COLBY, K. M., TESLER, L., and ENEA, H. (1969), *Experiments with a Search Algorithm on the Data Base of a Human Belief Structure*, Stanford Artificial Intelligence Project.

CONKLIN, H. (1955), 'Hanunoo colour categories', *Southwestern J. Anthrop.*, vol. 11, pp. 339–44.

CONKLIN, H. (1959), 'Linguistic play in its cultural context', *Language*, vol. 35, pp. 631–6.

DAVIS, K. (1948), *Human Society*, Macmillan

DE GROOT, A. D. (1965), *Thought and Choice in Chess*, Mouton, The Hague.

DE GROOT, A. D. (1966), 'Perception and memory versus thought: some old ideas and recent findings', in B. Kleinmuntz (ed.), *Problem Solving*, Wiley, pp. 19–50.

DE MAURO, T. (1967), *Ludwig Wittgenstein: His Place in the Development of Semantics*, Reidel, D., Holland.

EKMAN, F., and FRIESEN, V. (1969), 'The repertoire of nonverbal behavior: categories, origins, usage and coding', *Semiotica*, vol. 1, pp. 49–93.

FESTINGER, L. (1957), *A Theory of Cognitive Dissonance*, Row, Peterson.

FILLMORE, C. J. (1968), 'The case for case', in Bach, E., and Harms, R. T. (eds.), *Universals in Linguistic Theory*, Holt, Rinehart & Winston.

FODOR, J. A., and KATZ, J. J. (eds.) (1964), *The Structure of Language*, Prentice-Hall.

FRAKE, C. O. (1961), 'The diagnosis of disease among the Subanun of Mindanao', *Amer. Anthrop.*, vol. 63, reprinted in D. Hymes (ed.) (1964), *Language in Culture and Society*, Harper & Row, pp. 193–206.

FRAKE, C. O. (1962), 'The ethnographic study of cognitive systems', in Gladwin, T., and Sturtevant, W. C. (eds.), *Anthropology and Human Behavior*, Anthropological Society of Washington, pp. 72–85.

FRAKE, C. O. (1964), 'How to ask for a drink in Subanun', in J. Gumperz and D. Hymes (eds.), 'The ethnography of communication', *Amer. Anthrop.*, vol. 66, no. 6, part 2, pp. 127–32.

FURTH, H. (1966), *Thinking Without Language*, Macmillan Co.

GARFINKEL, H. (1956), 'Some sociological concepts and methods for psychiatrists', *Psychiatric Research Reports*, vol. 6, pp. 181–95.

GARFINKEL, H. (1964), 'Studies of the routine grounds of everyday activities', *Social Problems*, vol. 11, pp. 220–50.

GARFINKEL, H. (1966), Dittoed transcriptions of lectures.

GARFINKEL, H. (1967), *Studies in Ethnomethodology*, Prentice-Hall.

GARFINKEL, H., and SACKS, H. (1969), 'On formal structures of practical actions', in McKinney, J. C., and Tiryakian, E. (eds.), *Theoretical Sociology-Perspectives and Developments*, Appleton-Century-Crofts.

GEOGHEGAN, W. H. (1968), *Information Processing Systems in Culture*, Language Behavior Research Laboratory, Working Paper no. 6, University of California, Berkeley.

GIBBS, J. (1966), 'The sociology of law and normative phenomena', *Amer. Soc. Rev.*, vol. 31, pp. 315–25.

GOFFMAN, E. (1959), *The Presentation of Self in Everyday Life*, Doubleday, Penguin, 1971.

GOFFMAN, E. (1971), *Relations in Public*, Basic Books.

GOODE, J. G. (1960), 'Norm commitment and conformity to role-status obligations', *Amer. J. Sociol.*, vol. 66.

GOODENOUGH, W. (1956), 'Componential analysis and the study of meaning', *Language*, vol. 32, pp. 195–216.

GOODENOUGH, W. (1964), 'Cultural anthropology and linguistics', reprinted in D. Hymes (ed.), *Language in Culture and Society*, Harper & Row, pp. 36–9.

GREENBERG, J. H. (ed.) (1966), *Universals of Language*, MIT Press, 2nd edn.

GREENBERGER, M. (ed.) (1962), *Computers and the World of the Future*, MIT Press.

GUMPERZ, J. J. (1966), 'Linguistic repertoires, grammars and second language instruction', in *Report of the Sixteenth Round Table Meeting on Linguistics and Language Teaching*, Georgetown University, monograph no. 18, pp. 81–8.

GUMPERZ, J. J. (1971), *Language in Social Groups*, Stanford University Press.

GUMPERZ, J. J., and HYMES, D. (eds.), (1964), 'The ethnography of communication', *Amer. Anthrop.*, vol. 66, part 2.

HABER, R. N. (ed.) (1968), *Contemporary Theory and Research in Visual Perception*, Holt, Rinehart & Winston.

HABER, R. N. (ed.) (1969), *Information-Processing Approaches to Visual Perception*, Holt, Rinehart & Winston.

HABER, R. N. (1970), 'How we remember what we see', *Scientific American*, pp. 104–12.

HALL, E. T. (1959), *The Silent Language*, Doubleday.

HALL, E. T. (1966), *The Hidden Dimension*, Doubleday.

HARE, A. P. (1964), 'Interpersonal relations in the small group', in Faris, R. E. L. (ed.), *Handbook of Modern Sociology*, Rand McNally.

HART, H. L. A. (1961), *The Concept of Law*, Oxford University Press.

HEBB, D. O. (1968), 'Concerning imagery', *Psych. Rev.*, vol. 75, pp. 466–77.

HIX, H. (1954), 'Kotarbinski's praxiology', *Phil. and Phenomen. Res.*, pp. 238–43.

HOCKETT, C. F. (1959), 'Animal languages as human languages', in Spuhler, J. N. (ed.), *The Evolution of Man's Capacity for Culture*, Wayne State University Press.

HOCKETT, C. F., and ASCHER, R. (1964), 'The human revolution', *Current Anthrop.*, vol. 5, pp. 135–47.

HOMANS, G. C. (1961), *Social Behavior*, Harcourt, Brace & World.

HYMES, D. (1962), 'The ethnography of speaking', in T. Gladwin and W. C. Sturtevant (eds.), *Anthropology and Human Behavior*, Anthropological Society of Washington, pp. 72–85.

HYMES, D. (1970), 'Linguistic theory and functions of speech', *International Days of Sociolinguistics*, Luigi Sturzo Institute, Rome.

JAMES, W. (1890), *The Principles of Psychology*, Holt, Rinehart & Winston.

JENNINGS, S. (1969), Report of Continuing Research on Linguistic Comprehension, duplicated.

KAPLAN, A. (1964), *The Conduct of Inquiry*, Chandler.

KATZ, J. J. (1966), *The Philosophy of Language*, Harper & Row.

KATZ, J. J., and FODOR, J. A. (1963), 'The structure of semantic theory', *Language*, vol. 39, pp. 170–210.

KATZ, J. J., and POSTAL, P. M. (1964), *An Integrated Theory of Linguistic Descriptions*, MIT Press.

KOLERS, P., and POMERANTZ, J. R. (1971), 'Figural change in apparent motion', *J. exper. Psychol.*, vol. 87, pp. 99–108.

KOTARBINSKI, T. (1962), 'Praxiological sentences and how they are proved', in Nagel, E., Suppes, P. and Tarski, A. (eds.), *Logic, Methodology and Philosophy of Science*, Stanford University Press, pp. 211–23.

KUHN, T. S. (1962), *The Structure of Scientific Revolutions*, University of Chicago Press.

LAKOFF, G. (1968a), 'Instrumental adverbs and the concept of deep structure', *Foundations of Language*, vol. 4, pp. 4–29.

LAKOFF, G. (1968b), *Counterparts, or the Problem of Reference in Transformational Grammar*, Linguistic Society of America.

LEMERT, E. M. (1951), *Social Pathology*, McGraw-Hill.

LENNEBERG, E. H. (ed.) (1964), *New Directions in the Study of Language*, MIT Press.

LENNEBERG, E. H. (1967), *The Biological Foundations of Language*, Wiley.

LENNEBERG, E. H. (1969), 'On explaining language', *Science*, vol. 164, pp. 635–43.

LINTON, R. (1936), *The Study of Man*, Appleton-Century-Crofts.

LOUNSBURY, F. (1956), 'Semantic analysis of the Pawnee kinship usage', *Language*, vol. 32, pp. 158–94.

LYONS, J. and WALES, R. J. (eds.), (1966), *Psycholinguistic Papers*. Edinburgh University Press.

MCCAWLEY, J. D. (1968a), 'The role of semantics in a grammar', in E. Bach and R. T. Harms (eds.), *Universals in Linguistic Theory*, Holt, Rinehart & Winston, pp. 124–69.

MCCAWLEY, T. (1968b), 'Concerning the base component of a transformational grammar', *Foundations of Language*, vol. 4, pp. 243–69.

MCNEILL, D. (1966a), 'Developmental psycholinguistics', in F. Smith and G. A. Miller (eds.), *The Genesis of Language: A Psycholinguistic Approach*, MIT Press.

MCNEILL, D. (1966b), 'The creation of language by children', in J. Lyons and R. J. Wales (eds.), *Psycholinguistic Papers*, Edinburgh University Press, pp. 99–115.

MCNEILL, D. (1970), 'The development of language', in P. H. Mussen (ed.), *Carmichael's Manual of Child Psychology*, Wiley, pp. 1061–1161.

MEAD, G. H. (1934), *Mind, Self and Society*, University of Chicago Press.

MEAD, G. H. (1938), *The Philosophy of the Act*, University of Chicago Press.

MEHAN, H. B., Jr (1971), *Accomplishing Understanding in Educational Settings*, Ph.D. dissertation, University of California, Santa Barbara.

MENYUK, P. (1969), *Sentences Children Use*, MIT Press.

MESSINGER, S. L., SAMPSON, H., and TOWNE, R. D. (1962), 'Life as theatre: some notes on the dramaturgic approach to social reality', *Sociometry*, vol. 25.

MILLER, G. A. (1956), 'The magical number seven, plus or minus two: some limits on our capacity for processing information,' *Psychol. Rev.*, vol. 63, pp. 81–96.

MILLER, G. A., GALANTER, E., and PRIBRAM, K. (1960), *Plans and the Structure of Behavior*, Holt, Rinehart & Winston.

MINSKY, M. (1968), *Semantic Information Processing*, MIT Press.

MORRIS, R. T. (1956), 'Typology of norms', *Amer. Sociol. Rev.*, vol. 7, pp. 610–13.

NEISSER, U. (1967), *Cognitive Psychology*, Appleton-Century-Crofts.

NEWMAN, D. J. (1956), 'Pleading guilty for consideration: a study of bargain justice', *J. Criminal Law, Criminology and Police Science*, vol. 46, pp. 780–90.

NORMAN, D. A. (1969), *Memory and Attention*, Wiley.

PARSONS, T. (1951), *The Social System*, Free Press.

PARSONS, T., and SHILS, E. A. (eds.) (1951), *Toward a General Theory of Action*, Harvard University Press.

PIKE, K. L. (1954), *Language in Relation to a Unified Theory of the Structure of Human Behavior*, Summer Institute of Linguistics, Glendale.

POLANYI, M. (1958), *Personal Knowledge: Towards a Post-Critical Philosophy*, University of Chicago Press.

POLLNER, M. (1970), *On the Foundations of Mundane Reasoning*, unpublished Ph.D. dissertation, University of California, Santa Barbara.

QUILLIAN, R. (1968), 'Semantic memory', in Minsky, M. (ed.), *Semantic Information Processing*, MIT Press, pp. 227–70.

RAWLS, J. (1955), 'Two concepts of rules', *Phil. Rev.*, vol. 64, pp. 3–32.

REITMAN, W. R. (1965), *Cognition and Thought*, Wiley.

ROSENTHAL, R. (1966), *Experimenters Effects in Behavioral Research*, Appleton-Century-Crofts.

ROSS, J. R. (forthcoming), 'On declarative sentences', in R. Jacobs and P. Rosenbaum (eds.), *Readings in English Transformational Grammar*, Ginn-Blaisdell.

SACKS, H. (1966a), *The Search for Help: No one to Turn To*, unpublished doctoral dissertation, University of California, Berkeley.

SACKS, H. (1966b), Unpublished lecture notes, University of California, Berkeley.

SACKS, H. (1967), Unpublished Lectures, University of California.

SACKS, H. (1970), Unpublished Lectures, University of California.

SARBIN, T. R. (1953), 'Role theory', in Lindzey, G. (ed.), *Handbook of Social Psychology*, Addison-Wesley.

SCHEGLOFF, E. A. (1969), 'Sequencing in conversational openings', *Amer. Anthrop.*, vol. 70, pp. 1075–95.

SCHLESINGER, I. M. (n.d.), *The Grammar of Sign Language: Some Implications for the Theory of Language*, duplicated.

SCHUTZ, A. (1953), 'Common-sense and scientific interpretation of human action', *Phil. phenomenol. Res.*, vol. 14, pp. 1–38.

SCHUTZ, A. (1955), 'Symbol, reality and society', in L. Bryson, L. Finkelstein, H. Hoagland and R. M. MacIver (eds.), *Symbols and Society*, Harper, pp. 135–203.

SCHUTZ, A. (1962), *Collected Papers I: The Problem of Social Reality*, M. Natanson (ed.), Nijhoff, The Hague.

SCHUTZ, A. (1964), *Collected Papers II: Studies in Social Theory*, A. Broderson (ed.), Nijhoff, The Hague.

SHANK, R. (1971), *Intention, Memory and Computer Understanding*, Stanford Artificial Intelligence Project, Memo A YM-140.

SHIBUTANI, T. (1961), *Society and Personality*, Prentice-Hall.

SIMON, H. (1969), *The Sciences of the Artificial*, MIT Press.

SIMON, H., and BARENFELD, M. (1969), 'Information-processing analysis of perceptual processes in problem solving', *Psychol. Rev.*, vol. 76, pp. 473–83.

SLOBIN, D. (1971), *Psycholinguistics*, Freeman.

SMITH, F., and MILLER, G. A. (eds.) (1966), *The Genesis of Language: A Psycholinguistic Approach*, MIT Press.

STONE, G. P. (1962), 'Appearance and self', in A. Rose (ed.), *Human Behavior and Social Process*, Houghton Mifflin.

STOKOE, W. C., CASTERLINE, D. C., and CRONEBERG, C. G. (1965), *A Dictionary of American Sign Language on Linguistic Principles*, Gallandet College Press, Washington D.C.

SUDNOW, D. (1965), 'Normal crimes: sociological features of the penal code in a Public Defender Office', *Social Problems*, vol. 12.

TURNER, R. H. (1962), 'Role-taking: process versus conformity', in A. Rose (ed.), *Human Behavior and Social Process*, Houghton Mifflin.

VENDLER, Z. (1967), *Linguistics in Philosophy*, Cornell University Press.

WARD, R. E. *et al.* (1964), *Studying Politics Abroad*, Little, Brown.

WEINREICH, U. (1966), 'Explorations in semantic theory', in T. A. Sebeok (ed.), *Current Trends in Linguistics, III*, The Hague: Mouton, pp. 395–477.

WILLIAMS, R. M. (1960), *American Society*, (rev. edn), Knopf.

WINOGRAD, T. (1971), *Procedures as a Representation for Data in a Computer Program for Understanding Natural Language*, MIT Artificial Intelligence Laboratory, Project MAC TR-84.

WITTGENSTEIN, L. (1953), *Philosophical Investigations*, Blackwell, Oxford; and trans. by G. E. M. Anscombe, Macmillan, New York.

ZIMMERMAN, D. H., and POLLNER, M. (1970), 'The everyday world as a phenomenon', in H. Pepinsky (ed.), *People and Information*, Pergamon.

Acknowledgments

I am grateful to the following publishers for permission to reprint the materials contained in this volume:

Chapter 1 appeared in *Studies in Social Interaction*, edited by David Sudnow, The Free Press, 1972.

Chapter 2 appeared originally in *Rassegna Italiana di Sociologia*, vol. 9, 1968, and then later in *Understanding Everyday Life*, edited by Jack D. Douglas, Aldine, 1970.

Chapter 3 first appeared in *International Days of Sociolinguistics*, Luigi Sturzo Institute, Rome, 1970.

Chapter 4 was published in *Current Trends in Linguistics*, vol. 12, edited by T. A. Sebeok, A. S. Abramson, D. Hymes, H. Rubenstein, E. E. Stankiewicz, and B. Spolsky, Mouton, The Hague, 1972.

Chapter 5 was published in the 23rd Georgetown Round Table proceedings, Monograph 25, *Georgetown University Monograph Series on Languages and Linguistics*, 1972.

In preparing Chapters 2 and 3 I received support from the Faculty Research Committee at the University of California, Santa Barbara, and the Social Science Research Council. I am grateful to Kenneth and Sybillyn Jennings for their helpful criticism and suggestions while preparing Chapter 3. Chapter 4 draws upon research sponsored by The Division of Education of the Ford Foundation for the Study of Communicative Competence in Children and Classroom Performance. I am grateful to Hugh Mehan, Sybillyn Jennings, and Thomas Peterson for their extensive and very helpful remarks. Chapter 5 reflects preliminary research completed during the author's tenure as a National Science Foundation Senior Postdoctoral Fellow at the University of London Institute of Education. I am grateful to Shirley Collins and Percy Corfmat for their help with British sign language. I am pleased to acknowledge a number of helpful suggestions made by Robin Battison that were incorporated into the manuscript.

Author Index

Subject Index